Mme. Vickers

notre-dame of paris

notre-dame of paris

by Allan Temko

 Time Reading Program Special Edition

TIME INCORPORATED / NEW YORK

TIME INC. BOOK DIVISION

EDITOR *Norman P. Ross*
COPY DIRECTOR *William Jay Gold*
ART DIRECTOR *Edward A. Hamilton*
CHIEF OF RESEARCH *Beatrice T. Dobie*
EDITOR, TIME READING PROGRAM *Max Gissen*
DESIGNER *Norma Levarie*
RESEARCHER *Seena G. Harris*

PUBLISHER *Jerome S. Hardy*
GENERAL MANAGER *John A. Watters*

TIME MAGAZINE

EDITOR *Roy Alexander*
MANAGING EDITOR *Otto Fuerbringer*
PUBLISHER *Bernhard M. Auer*

COVER ILLUSTRATION *Jerome Snyder*

Contents

Genealogical and chronological charts are provided on pp. 312 et seq.

Illustrations

Following page 310

Editors' Preface

It has been said, and rightly, that no period in history has been more maligned than the years from 400 to 1400 A.D., loosely known as the Middle Ages. For all the light that scholars have shed on them, the ugly adjective "dark" clings to this era like a birthmark. If the word was ever valid, it was no longer so after the Sixth Century; there was much more to these years than serfdom and siege, sickness and starvation. A little more than half a century has passed since Henry Adams, in his book *Mont-Saint-Michel and Chartres,* saw the uniqueness of the Middle Ages, not in their courts or castles or battles, but in their cathedrals.

Though no imitator of Adams, Allan Temko is in the Adams tradition—as the distinguished American critic, Lewis Mumford, observes in his Introduction to this special edition of Temko's *Notre-Dame of Paris.* Temko's book is, strictly speaking, merely the life story of the famous church. But in telling that story it provides a brilliant insight into medieval times; from the day it first appeared in 1952, it has been recognized as one of those books in which scholarship and exuberance—so often natural enemies—form a special partnership.

Allan Temko does not have the usual credentials of the American scholar. He got his B.A. from Columbia College in 1947 and thereupon went west to start his career unglamorously as a copy boy for the San Francisco *Chronicle.* That lasted until the summer of 1948 when Temko took off for Europe to attend school under the G.I. Bill. He "studied"—the quotation marks are his—at Grenoble and Paris and returned to the United States to do graduate work at the University of California at Berkeley, where he now teaches.

For all this restlessness, Temko was never drifting. Ever since he first picked up *Mont-Saint-Michel and Chartres,* the sweep of Adams' approach had been an inspiration. Now he too began poring over the façades and windows, the vaults and spires of western Europe's great cathedrals as another scholar might read ancient documents. Finally, after years of studying books and buildings, he was ready to begin his *Notre-Dame of Paris.*

In the course of the book, Temko rarely lets the reader's attention stray from the site where the cathedral stands, for this was the stage on which the greatest part of the Gothic drama was played. At one time, the primitive people of Paris worshiped pagan gods at this spot; it was not until the Third Century that the Pope sent to the Ile de France its first bishop, Denis, whom the inhabitants duly tortured and beheaded. But inexorably Christianity took hold until all of Gallic society was in its possession. In the year 582, Gregory of Tours recorded that a powerful count, a longtime enemy of the throne, flung himself at the mercy of Queen Fredegund as she was attending Mass. That was the first written evidence of a cathedral on the Ile de France.

The great patron saint of the Parisians in those days was Stephen, the first martyr to die for Christ. But by 775, after more than two centuries of spiritual struggle, the Virgin Mary took St. Stephen's place, and when the 12th Century bishop, Maurice de Sully, started his ambitious enlargement of the cathedral, it was to Mary ("Our Lady," *Notre Dame* in French) that he dedicated his efforts. Off in the distance, kings and princes clashed and Christians marched against Islam, and all this Temko records. But he never loses sight of his central theme. The genius of the age and the sweat of its people were poured into the cathedral until it became the climactic achievement of medieval Paris.

Temko has an impressive mastery of architectural detail, and taken by itself his narrative of the building and renovating of the cathedral is a sound history of Gothic architecture. Christianity had already spread a white robe of Romanesque churches across Europe, but not until the triumph of the Gothic did medieval man have an architecture befitting the loftiness of his faith. The ribbed vault reached out to heaven, and the graceful buttresses permitted the structure to stretch itself almost beyond its own limits; it was no accident that they were called "flying." As for the façade, Temko exclaims, "What verve in execution!" And he notes how the great modern French architect, Le Corbusier, taking a ruler and compass to a photograph, revealed the façade's immaculate geometry.

"Outlined in ink," Temko writes, "the great square contained in the façade emerges vividly; a great circle, to which the sides of the square form tangents, emphasizes the wall's geometric purity. . . . The radius of the circle—roughly sixty-nine feet—provides the module for the composition. Arcs drawn to the same radius from any number of critical points will fall strikingly across the various compartments of the wall and will indicate, among other things, how the module determined the height of the towers."

Temko's passionate admiration for the art and craftsmanship of the Middle Ages includes, too, the era's bridges, workshops, mills and public hospitals. "Medieval accounting," he says, "did not keep separate books for utility and art. . . . Virtually everything man touched for practical use from the eleventh to the fifteenth centuries became lovely, which is a test of a civilization. There was almost no medieval bad taste." When the medieval skills degenerated in later years, the "Neo-Classic Age men could not imagine how the marvelous straphinges of the northern and southern portals [of Notre-Dame] had been devised. It was as if Daedalus had made them, but Daedalus had flown away." Over the years, the great cathedral suffered every kind of mutilation short of actual destruction— tasteless gilding and ornamentation, sacking by a mob, decades of neglect and ruin when the kings of France refused funds for repairs. Yet the cathedral "stood erect only by the integrity of its medieval workmanship."

The integrity went far beyond the builder's art. Henry Adams saw in his cathedrals the same "organic unity" that ran throughout medieval intellectual life, culminating for Adams in the *Summa Theologica* of St. Thomas Aquinas. Temko sees something similar in Notre-Dame—the expression of a social and spiritual endeavor that embraced an extraordinary range of professions and classes. Of early medieval man, Temko says, "His religion was the only impulse that urged him to build, for in general his will was to destroy." What is remarkable is that the impulse touched lord and laborer, artist and bishop alike—a blending of groups that perhaps no other age has equaled. "Notre-Dame was built by a superb common effort in which the entire community took part, the manual laborer as well as the master artist, the serf and villein as well as the merchant and prince. The Cathedral was not isolated, as was the inhuman pyramid of Cheops. It was the organic heart of Paris, and from it flowed hope, confidence, joy, and exaltation, in which the working people had a full share."

The Middle Ages were, of course, a time of paradox. Society was stratified yet synthesized, cruel yet devout, plodding yet inspired, selfish yet capable of the most extravagant self-sacrifice. Lords had almost total power over their people, but kings bathed the feet of the poor and ailing, for however wealth and power were divided on earth, no one doubted that everyone had his chance at heaven. And this, Temko says, is the message that the builders of the cathedral sent out to all the world.

"They had attained the pinnacle of their Christian ideal, which was enough. At the summit of the façade the Church Militant is the Church Triumphant, and the sky, as the architect wished, is subject to Notre-Dame. Heaven drifts between the towers, governed by rock, mastered by idealism. The high air is fixed, fluid, alive. And here is the Cathedral's gift. . . . Christian architecture, in all the churches of the Renaissance, the Neo-Classic Age, and the Baroque could do no more."

Temko's love affair with the medieval ideal leads him to regard its passing not as progress but as one of the great tragedies of history. He admits the barbarities of the age, yet he is persuasive when he pleads that in a larger sense it had a superior compassion, the great saving grace of the compassion of the Virgin. "Notre-Dame is her Cathedral. It is suffused with her vitality and love. It is her personal shrine as the Parthenon was Athena's. Its restless confidence is the Virgin's restless confidence for humanity. In the great moment of the Middle Ages, Mary lifted and civilized the entire Western World. In an era of continual male brutality, her emblem, the rose, became the sign of the less brutal woman; and as long as the West responded fervently to her, she made it lovely. A new stage of beauty, she proved in the Romanesque, the Transition, and the Gothic, lies always beyond the stage of beauty just achieved, idealism beyond idealism, god beyond goddess; a strange proof, perhaps for life beyond life. And so the Cathedral is never in repose but is perfectly equilibrated. When most calm, it lifts, and lifts again, in a further serenity. Balance equals tension. Beauty equals power. The Virgin is at work."

—THE EDITORS OF TIME

℞ Introduction

This is more than a book about an important work of architecture: it is a study of a people, a culture, an historic region, and a vivid, formative moment in human history. With good reason Allan Temko has called this book a biography; for an ancient building has many of the attributes of personality; and to follow its conception and gestation, its growth and training and discipline, its trials, its mutilations, its restorations, is to achieve a better understanding of the creative process in all its manifestations.

The personality of the Cathedral of Notre-Dame has taken shape through many periods, and still bears their imprint. Its character was first visibly formed during the radical transformations of adolescence, when the naïve integrity of Romanesque building was modified by the straining vigor of a new style—never quite free from the threat of a self-destruction—symbolized by the ogive, the flying buttress, the pointed arch. Later, Notre-Dame went through the grave trials of maturity, when it bore physical impoverishment and social erosion, sometimes threatened with radical surgery, or again subject to ruffianly assaults, which cost it some of its most precious works of sculpture. And by now, as so often happens with the aged, it has outlived its old friends and neighbors, the buildings that once crowded close and by contrast exalted it: so the cathedral stands today isolated in space but even more isolated in spirit from the life that clatters around it in all its aimless lunatic dynamism: still proud and still inviolable, however exposed.

Buildings are fortunate, not merely because they may outlive many frailer human lifetimes, but because they retain, even at the point of decay, a fuller reminder of their great presence at the moment of arriving at maturity. In its old age, Notre-Dame brings into our day its own expressive countenance: severe but benign. And if we listen well to what this building says, we shall understand not merely the difference between our own overmechanized culture and that of the medieval period but also those underlying forces that make for continuity, and give each of us, just because we are human, an opportunity to find some missing part of our being in this ancient structure. If a building is a person, then a great building is a great person; and to have conversation with this cathedral, with Mr. Temko as intermediary and interpreter, is to add to the dimensions of one's own life.

This architectural biography carries on and renews a tradition that has partly been allowed to lapse through the excessive application of what one might call "high fidelity" scholarship. This brand of investigation is particularly fashionable in the United States today; its chief mark is that its scientific passion for minute analysis allows disjointed parts and fragments, provided they are open to exact observation through documents or physical relics, to distract attention from the whole that gives them significance. Mr. Temko is young enough to have been thoroughly trained in these methods, and can use them for what they are worth: but he does not make the error of mistaking exactitude for significance. He has rather used his discipline in the service of a sounder tradition, with richer cultural affiliations and more rational purposes. His exemplars are John Ruskin's *The Stones of Venice* and, of course, Henry Adams' *Mont-Saint-Michel and Chartres*.

In mentioning this book in the same breath as its great forerunners, I am not so foolish as to anticipate the judgment of history on an untested contemporary work—though neither would I timidly withhold my belief, expressed before it was first published, that this is a book of unusual imaginative power and historical penetration. But it is instructive to view Adams' book and Temko's together, not only for the differences they reveal between two phases of scholarship but even more for the differences they point up between two marvelous monuments, Notre-Dame of Paris and Chartres.

Temko's treatment of Notre-Dame offers a bold contrast to that of Adams; and as far as the architecture itself goes, this more even-handed and thorough approach is not to the later historian's discredit. In laying the cultural foundations for Notre-Dame, Temko is, however, almost as exhaustive as Adams: he digs below the surface of medieval Paris till he reaches both geological and historic bedrock; and he has, in addition, the advantage over Adams that another rich half century of medieval scholarship has provided. Even more than Adams, Temko sees this great work in its popular setting, as an expression of the urban democracy of the Ile de France region, and particularly of Paris herself. Today, he points out, the building still stands high in popular favor, though the intellectuals have deserted it in favor of Chartres. On an Easter morning, as I myself lately witnessed, the broad plaza before the Cathedral is filled to overflowing with crowds that can no longer be accommodated within the packed interior. So, too, in following the building through the ups and downs of its existence, Temko emphasizes a lesson that the present generation needs to master: the lesson of organic form and purpose—of continuity through change, of continuous adaptation without self-betrayal or surrender.

What must be stressed about Notre-Dame itself is that this building represents an aspect of the Middle Ages that until our time was too often overlooked or misinterpreted: a side that harmonizes with the Cartesian bent of the French mind, established long before Descartes, which made the French master masons the chief exponents of both the daring technical experiments and the liberated architectural forms that were long afterward to be misnamed "Gothic." For the dominant note of Notre-Dame is its rationalism and formal logic. This building, above all its great front face, is a manifestation of classic order: the strong impression it makes—though at a distance from which no medieval eye ever beheld it—is that derived from its formal symmetry, its repetition, balance, conscious control.

By the same token this cathedral shows little of that brilliant improvisation and accidental irregularity that marks the second spire of Chartres: indeed, apart from the gargoyles, Notre-Dame is almost the last place to look for the supposed romanticism and mysticism of the Middle Ages. Here even the emphasis on height, which on the whole denotes a truly medieval character in sacred buildings, as in the Cathedral of Coutances, is lacking: there is an even balance between verticality and horizontality. Only within the nave do the eye-lifting vertical lines prevail; and one must skirt the building on the river side to capture the esthetic effect, at once acrobatic and grotesque, most people seek in Gothic buildings.

Now the point is that medieval architecture, like medieval life, embraced both sets of qualities: dogma and unrestrained fantasy, tight formal logic, always returning to its premises, and bold experimentalism venturing into realms from which it might not return: tearing down solid walls for the sake of more light, or leaping higher than ever before into the air for the sheer exhilaration of the leap itself, exalted by the thought of heaven. The reader who follows Allan Temko's exposition intelligently will no longer be the victim of those false pictures of the medieval period that still linger even in academic circles, the residue of the 18th Century's anticlericalism and 19th Century's smug belief in its own ineffable progress. Temko does not idealize medieval culture: far from it. But he does something better: he *realizes* it. And the picture he presents of the Paris that saw the building of the Cathedral is one of the best short introductions I know to help one enjoy what is left of medieval Paris today.

In one respect, happily, Allan Temko has taken a leaf directly from Adams' book, though this is just the leaf that a more superficial scholar today would be most likely to drop, with a disdainful gesture, into the academic trashbasket. Temko seeks to understand this sacred edifice in terms not only of the general culture of the period and its historical setting, but of the religious cult that helped to produce it, the cult of the Virgin Mary. To explain Notre-Dame in all its magnitudes, he takes the Virgin as seriously as the builders of the Cathedral took her: for him as for Adams, she is a Goddess who commands, an Eternal Mother who protects, and also a woman who must be pleased.

This is the right state of mind for understanding this mode of building. Such subjectivity, when conscious of its own intentions, comes far closer to a rigorously objective approach than a seemingly more detached and dry method that would seek to explain the work of art solely in terms of technical traditions and innovations, of purely formal affiliations with similar work in other places, and of the cost of labor, the sources of raw materials, and the supply of capital. The fact that with all his use of source material Temko dares to take these subjective liberties and present his observations with such intellectual freedom, indeed with such positive gusto and verve, is what makes this book far more than a merely competent scholarly treatise.

A final word about the author himself. Though this first book of a young scholar—he was only 31 when it was first published—deals with an historic subject, it was written by a spirit entirely at home in the contemporary world. So it is no surprise that instead of following up his first success in this field with a similar work, or at least a further contribution to the period he had explored so exhaustively, he has devoted himself rather to modern architecture and urbanism. Today Temko seems on the way to becoming one of the most challenging interpreters of architecture in its broadest sense that this country has produced since Montgomery Schuyler laid the foundations for American architectural criticism in the 1890s.

During the last few years Temko, who has been teaching at the University of California in Berkeley, has become a positive influence in the San Francisco Bay region, where his stringent critical appraisals in the San Francisco *Chronicle* have already brought about more than one architectural improvement, from the removal of a blatant sign on the roof of a business building, to the radical redesign of a proposed bridge across the Bay. So, in carrying forward the tradition of Ruskin, Schuyler and Adams, Allan Temko, by his very success in the present work, should give encouragement to other young scholars, once they are done with their academic teething rings, to look for something better than new supplies of rubber and plastic for their daily food. He has demonstrated that one does not have to choose between veracity and vitality, any more than one must choose between the historic and contemporary, since the great historic moments remain contemporary, and what is sound in contemporary work will, in less than half a century, become historic.

By now I have said enough to indicate the scope and promise of this book and its author. Whether the reader is interested in history or architecture, in biography or in religion—or simply in human development generally—he will find, I believe, that this book has something to give him.

—LEWIS MUMFORD

ACKNOWLEDGMENTS

The author wishes to express his thanks to Mr. Erwin Panofsky and to the Princeton University Press for permission to reprint the translations from Mr. Panofsky's *Abbot Suger on the Abbey Church of St.-Denis* which appear on pages 73, 81–82, and 237; to Librairie Armand Colin for authorization to translate the passage on page 247 from Henri Focillon's *Art d'Occident*, as well as the passages on page 296 from *L'Art Religieux du XIIIe Siècle en France* by Emile Mâle; to H. Laurens, Editeur, for the use of figures B, C, and D, taken from Marcel Aubert's *Notre-Dame de Paris, Sa Place dans l'Architecture du XIIe au XIVe Siècle;* to A. Morancé, Editeur, for figures A and E, from M. Aubert's *Notre-Dame de Paris, Architecture et Sculpture;* to Alfred Kröner Verlag for figure 3, from *Die kirchliche Baukunst des Abendlandes* by Dehio and Bezold; and, especially, to Mme. Marie-Zéline Faure-Sadoul, for the house at Gravigny, where much of this book was written.

A.T.

for Becky and Susannah

the
idea
of
a cathedral

And Solomon stood before the altar of the Lord in the presence of all the congregation of Israel, and spread forth his hands toward heaven:

And he said, Lord God of Israel, there is no God like Thee, in heaven above or on earth beneath . . .

But will God indeed dwell on the earth? behold, the heaven and heaven of heavens cannot contain Thee; how much less this house that I have builded?

—From Solomon's prayer at the dedication of the Temple
I KINGS 8: 22-27

THE IDEA OF A CATHEDRAL

tHERE ARE as many ways to approach Notre-Dame as there are streets in Paris or roads in France. But perhaps the best is along the quays of the Left Bank on a summer morning, following the river, catching glimpses of the Cathedral through the trees. From a distance the great double towers alone are visible, guarding Paris with their brotherly strength. The strength was expected, but what was unforeseen is their pure white radiance. The towers are a startling white in the vivid Parisian air. They are as new, as bold, as young and optimistic as seven hundred years ago, when the last stones were fitted in the cornices before the year 1250.

Quite suddenly the towers vanish in the green chestnuts and oaks, and the charming stage scenery of Paris intervenes, like a blithe Dufy. Paris, the world's Paris: the crowded bookstalls, the intellectual posture of the promeneurs; the barges smacking upriver, the Louvre across the Pont des Arts, the elegant triangle of the island in the Seine, the Pont Neuf, the roofs of the Cité; and again the white towers of Notre-Dame, perhaps with tricolors flying, and the blue sky of France as a background. Finally, at the Place Saint-Michel, the entire western façade of the Cathedral comes into sight, like an enormous postcard, and so familiar that the tourist puts down his Kodak at once.

The traveler feels that if he knows anything in Europe he knows this church. At first it seems no more strange to an American, say, than the Washington Monument. There stands Notre-Dame, seven and eight centuries old, exactly as it appears in technicolor travelogues! The church is a model of calm and majesty, a serene emblem of civilization. All is recognizable: the three great sculptured portals, the Gallery of Kings, the perfect rose window and lovely open colonnade above it, and, surmounting the whole, the lordly towers which were sighted far down the Seine. Yet as the visitor crosses the Petit Pont to the island and arrives at the cathedral plaza—the "parvis" whose name derives from the Medieval French *paradis*—as he stands on the parvis and stares upward at the proportions of this western wall, he wonders if he knows the church at all.

The Cathedral is alive! Alive as the summer sunlight, alive as the river flowing past, as the green trees, alive as nature! The Cathedral moves, breathes, aspires to Heaven with a human impulse. And so young in line and feeling that the prepossessing skyscrapers back home seem antiquated and even shabby in comparison. Young! It takes an Alice to walk through this looking-glass. The Cathedral is younger than today's newspaper and stands a better chance than the newspaper of being considered interesting tomorrow. For, whatever its other qualities, Notre-Dame is never boring; and this is one test of a masterpiece.

Not every church is so. Across the Seine, on a much lovelier square of the Left Bank, is the neo-classical mass of Saint-Sulpice, larger in nearly all its dimensions and built five centuries after the Cathedral. At Saint-Sulpice, Americans feel instantly at home. They would not be surprised to turn a corner in Chicago and find it standing in the Loop. But Saint-Sulpice is as interesting as the central office of a metropolitan bank, and as spiritual. Some time between Louis VII, who reigned when Notre-Dame was begun in 1163, and Louis XV, whose taste was so perfectly expressed in Saint-Sulpice, terminated in 1745, Europe grew less beautiful; and it is worth comparing these two famous churches to remark the difference. Notre-Dame, smaller and older, is easily the more impressive in scale, the more modern in conception, the more idealistic in tone, the more vivacious in detail.

The façade of the Cathedral triumphs, in spite of an isolation for which it was never intended. Today it stands as an ornament for the baroque city of the Second Empire, cut off from the daily life of the people by its vast plaza and circle of abstract parks. But on a square this size—forty times larger than the parvis of the Middle Age—a charging mob could be shot to pieces before it advanced twenty yards. This is precisely what Baron Haussmann had in mind when he planned it. The Baron was keenly aware that in the eighteen years from 1830 to 1848 Paris was barricaded no less than two dozen times by its insurgent working class. Each time they rose up, like their fathers in 1789, the furious poor attacked the Cathedral with a savage instinct. Once or twice they penetrated the interior, sacked the furnishings, and planted the tricolor on the towers. Haussmann wished to place Notre-Dame forever beyond their reach. He did not succeed. During the Commune of 1871 the tidal force of history again surged ferociously across the parvis. The church was again invaded and set on fire, and the archbishop was executed by a squad of grimy irregulars. What the Baron did succeed in doing was to harm the scale and utterly change the mood of the Cathedral's place in the center of Paris.

Strange, this need to protect a work of art which had once received the most exquisite devotion of the working people. The story of their disenchantment is one of the tragedies of Western civilization, since, when they lost the Cathedral, they found nothing to replace it. The working class of modern France, like its bourgeoisie, lives in an artistic vacuum. For comparison, in the single century from 1170 to 1270 the medieval French built some eighty cathedrals and five hundred large churches of the cathedral class. The Cathedral of Paris, geographically and chronologically, was at the heart of this movement.

Notre-Dame was built by a superb common effort in which the entire community took part, the manual laborer as well as the master artist, the serf and villein as well as the merchant and prince. From their collective energy and enthusiasm the Cathedral emerged as the crowning structure of the walled city of the Middle Age. Paris then crowded about the church with inexpressible love. Hundreds of simple dwellings clustered beneath its walls, hiding the base of the monument; and from their midst the shape of the cross jutted in an astonishing display of mass and power. The size and scale of Notre-Dame, which not even the fortified palace of the king could challenge, were an absolute indication of its unique place in the lives of the people. The Cathedral was not isolated, as was the inhuman pyramid of Cheops. It was the organic heart of Paris, and from it flowed hope, confidence, joy, and exaltation, in which the working people had a full share.

By modern definition, the medieval community was of course a slave society. Scholarship such as Coulton's has made it impossible to romanticize feudalism. The serf, in spite of theoretical obligations owed him by his lord, was usually exploited in practice. Nor did a day pass when bones were not smashed on the wheel or eyes blinded in prisons. But this is not the entire story. A paradox distinguished the Middle Age from the Money Age which succeeded it, and which is not yet ended. The paradox lay in the medieval Church, which was one Church and all Churches, so that, when it split open in the Reformation, it hatched a thousand creeds and ideologies, none of which has shown itself nearly capable of holding together human life in the West.

Christianity, now fragmented and vanishing, with very little practical relation to industrial society, then affected the total range of human existence. The fields could not be tilled, nor trade conducted, nor wars fought, nor ships navigated—even the dead could not be buried—without its indispensable benediction. Kings, including such great warrior kings as Philip Augustus, learned this to their sorrow when angry popes placed their realms under interdict. All belonged to the Church, and the Church belonged to all. Its gods and demigods watched over every human action, provided for every human contingency, inspired every human creation. Feudal politics, the feudal economy, and feudal art became inseparable from the magical rule of the priests.

It is important to realize what this magic meant in practical results. The magic worked, as penicillin works today, although the ordinary man had as little real knowledge of its secrets. He knew its main principle, which is all that mattered. Medieval Christianity carried with it the ideal of the New Testament, with its promise of reward in Heaven or penalty in Hell; and however far reality may have wandered from it, the ideal was never lost. On the contrary, it frequently emerged in splendor, thrusting above medieval society in the profile of a church. When, in the construction of a cathedral, the loose feudal economy for a moment grew cohesive and society collectively endeavored to be worthy of its Christian abstractions, medieval France could match its achievements against those of any state, including the Athens of Pericles.

Like Athens, it was far from perfect. Some of its inventive geniuses

—Abélard is the first victim to come to mind—were condemned for impiety and corruption of youth. Yet no social architecture has surpassed the cathedrals. They are light-years away from the useless pyramids, to which dogmatists try to compare them. They are also a considerable distance from the skyscrapers. The illiterate workmen on the towering steel cage of *Christ in Concrete* had no share at all in the ideals of their enterprise; their ancestors, who may have tumbled as tragically from the lofty framework of Notre-Dame, at least had a part in their church. After they built their Cathedral, there was a place—and it was not a negligible place—for them within.

And so, for a true understanding of the Cathedral, it must be seen in its Gothic context, in the framework of an age of beauty and brutality for which no generalization is possible, to which no single aphorism applies. To call the best medieval moment a unity is to misrepresent and underestimate it. Yet the entire Middle Age was colored by a rich popular sense of the beautiful. It is safe to say that even the beggars on the parvis, to whom such writers as Henry Adams have thrown alms across the centuries, were moved by the loveliness of Notre-Dame. So were the harlots, from whom Adams shied away; the merchants, whose busy trade he attempted to ignore; the knights and gowned ladies he uncritically admired. So too were the ascetic saints. No man was more outraged by sumptuous medieval architecture than Bernard of Clairvaux; no man was more sensitive to its attraction. "O vanity of vanities, yet no more vain than insane!" he cried out in the name of the starving about the year 1125. "The Church clothes her stones in gold and leaves her sons naked." Nevertheless Bernard knew how to describe Romanesque sculpture with a scornful vividness that reveals an awful struggle with its beauty. He was a pillar of the Church Puritan, which until the sixteenth century would remain part of the Church Catholic.

Bernard's terrifying picture of the age of construction is a distortion. He exaggerated, as saints will. The image of the ill-clad slave is haunting, but, in fact, a dramatic improvement in living conditions took place at the moment the cathedrals rose. Serfdom declined, famine grew rare, and, thanks to a developing textile industry, men were better clothed. Population increased. After a long period of weakness the Capetian Dynasty was able to form a strong central government with its capital at Paris and to consolidate most of the territory of modern France in a national state. New cities were founded by enlightened royal policy; old cities fought with success to rid themselves of crippling feudal obligations. Anarchy was vanishing from the countryside. The horde of vicious minor princes was disciplined and half exterminated by the Crown. The Crusades drained off many of the rest. Innumerable abuses were corrected; law was codified; the Church itself was reformed and liberalized. Under more peaceful conditions than had been seen for centuries, agriculture flourished, trade expanded, travel grew simplified and relatively safe. Thousands of homes, granaries, mills, bridges, schools —every type of useful civic structure—were built. There seems to have been wide enthusiasm for bathing and personal cleanliness. Medicine, mathematics, and so many other sciences were rediscovered that several historians have called the period a renaissance.

Paris was a perfect symbol of the improving times. The capital abandoned its timid, insular confinement and breasted out in faubourgs on either bank of the Seine. Population doubled and redoubled until, about the year 1200, it approached one hundred thousand. For the first time since Gallo-Roman days the streets were paved. The cemetery was enclosed. The Grand Pont and the Petit Pont were rebuilt in stone. The hospital of the Hôtel-Dieu was enlarged and renovated. The Schools, to which students flocked from all of Europe, were at last combined in a university. The three-hundred-year-old Carolingian Cathedral was torn down and replaced by Notre-Dame.

Not only architecture but all the arts climbed with the improved standard of life. They also broadened for a mass audience. Literature in the popular tongue, a popular theater, and a popular taste for music emerged simultaneously.

Yet architecture, which in a cathedral or abbey could, and did, serve as a home for all the other arts, reflects as nothing else the aesthetic climate of a nation. It is the key to the health of a society. A prideful society, like the France of Louis XIV, the "Sun King," cannot help building badly; and not only history, but the present cost of repairs for the Palace of Versailles, has found it out. The Middle Age, whose churches have withstood whole eras of misunderstanding and mistreatment, built with infinitely more thoroughness, sincerity, and accomplishment.

Medieval architecture began rising on the swell of the Romanesque as early as the tenth century. A great church, Saint-Germain-des-Prés, was consecrated in Paris shortly after the year 1000. But the Romanesque enjoyed its most impressive triumphs outside the Paris area, which throughout the eleventh century was torn by feudal chaos. It was in Normandy and on the Loire, in tough Auvergne, in Burgundy and Languedoc, that the Romanesque produced its best churches.

Gradually, however, as heroic original art invariably does, the Romanesque began to give way to an impulse it found too eloquent to refuse. From about the time that a French army took Jerusalem in 1099, a new structural member—the ribbed vault—overturned the whole French theory of construction. Where, precisely, the ogival rib was invented is still something of a mystery. Archaeologists have searched as far as Armenia and in the hot Spain of the Saracens for its beginnings. What is most fascinating about the ogive, however, is not its slow passage across Europe but its instantaneous success as soon as it was discovered by the French. Some traveling architect noticed the ogive serving as a reinforcement for ordinary groin or barrel vaults in Normandy or in Norman England and carried the device to Paris, where it was given a treatment as revolutionary, as audacious, and eventually as universal as steel-cage construction. Paris in the twelfth century was closer than is generally imagined to the Chicago of the nineteenth.

The new architecture, using the ribbed vault exclusively, spread through the royal domain of France with a speed no artistic movement has ever equaled. Properly, the Ile de France never developed a "school" of the Romanesque, as did Poitou and Burgundy. Its long-delayed Romanesque was the Gothic Transition, and this may be dated from one of the major events of art history: the rebuilding of the Parisian Abbey of Saint-Denis after the year 1130, or just at the time that King Louis le Gros drove his enemies from the gates of the capital and established a regime of peace. From Saint-Denis —the royal basilica—the Transition traveled outward on the web of roads to every part of the whole kingdom. In a single generation the Cathedral of Sens, the Cathedrals of Noyon, Senlis, and Laon, the western façade of the Cathedral of Chartres, and, quite literally, hundreds of smaller monuments, were rebuilt in what might be called the Ogival Revolution. "Gothic"—the barbarous misnomer applied by the Renaissance—was a name invented long after the fact. The ribbed vault—the ogive—is the single fundamental of the Gothic; and the stylistic pointed arch, which developed naturally with it, is incidental in importance. It was the ogive alone—later aided by the flying buttress—that enabled men to build more flexibly, more imaginatively, and on a scale unprecedented in European life.

Notre-Dame of Paris stands at the center of this outbreak of creation. It is the last great monument of the Transition and the first great monument of what may be truly called the Gothic. The Cathedral is no less than fifty per cent taller than any of its ogival contemporaries. Its vaults—nearly a hundred and ten feet above the pavements—compare with those of the thirteenth-century cathedrals, like Bourges and Reims, which were to profit so from its audacity.

A study of Notre-Dame provides a virtual education in Gothic art. From the laying of the first stone in 1163 to the completion of the last flying buttress after 1300, the Cathedral spans the age of construction like a stone bridge of time. Its dates are ideal for a history of art. The choir—the earliest portion of the church—was built from 1163 to 1182 and belongs to the Transition. The nave, largely completed before 1200, is part of a maturing Gothic not yet in full control of its structural power. The western façade, erected in a solid fifty years from 1200 to 1250, stands, with the nave of Amiens, as the model of Gothic perfection. The late thirteenth-century transept roses display the *rayonnant* Gothic, which, for all its glory, had already entered a decline. The Cathedral is a mirror of a total art. It also reflects, with an objectivity that is almost terrifying, the brilliant upsurge of the Capet Dynasty, its classic moment of power under Saint Louis, and its eventual disintegration and decay.

Notre-Dame, more than the Louvre, incalculably more than Versailles, is France. Every distance from Paris to the borders of the nation is measured from the parvis of the Cathedral and not, significantly, from the Opéra or the Arc de Triomphe, or even from the second most important monument in the city, the Tour Eiffel, the earliest tower of steel. Every road in France centers inwardly on the Cathedral. One may start walking to Notre-Dame on the green roads of Normandy or in sun-driven Provence.

France, Paris, Notre-Dame: all are old now. All are losing their associations with the past at a speed conservatives find frightening. Yet it is hard to imagine that they will ever lose their quite particular ancient beauties. French history has no more impressive witnesses than the Cathedral and the island on which it stands. Once the Ile-de-la-Cité was nearly ten yards lower, just above water level, and subject to flash floods. In prehistoric times it was perhaps a third of its present area. The island has never been properly excavated, but if archaeologists were permitted to dig systematically, they would find the story of France accumulated in layers as strikingly defined as geologic strata. The eastern end of the island has been a repository of idealisms since men first built a tabernacle there of branches and reeds. From the floor of the Seine upward, there must be scores of buried pre-Christian shrines: first the fragile Gallic sanctuaries of wood, and then a whole series of Roman temples in stone. Finally, high on the accumulated mound, so close to the surface that they seem incredibly recent, is a collection of Christian edifices, resting directly beneath and around Notre-Dame. Under the parvis and the façade are the foundations of a Merovingian basilica of the Dark Age, known to have existed as early as 582, and under the patronage of Saint Stephen. Beneath the nave, transept, and choir stood the Carolingian Cathedral, dating from 857, and perhaps several earlier churches, dedicated to the Virgin.

Mary—Notre Dame—Our Lady of Paris! The Cathedral is consecrated utterly to the supreme Christian goddess. A host of heavenly powers attend her—Saint Stephen, Saint Marcel, Saint Denis, Saint John the Baptist, Saint Anne, and Saint Geneviève; but none has an importance in this church approaching that of the Virgin. She appears in each of the three main portals, and two are given almost exclusively to her. Far overhead, poised on the balustrade, she is seen once more, flanked by angels, benignly protecting her city and her people. The rose behind her, and it was a huge wheel of gold in the Middle Age, is Mary again, for she herself was *"super rosam rosida"*—"the rose of roses": she exercised the most lovely of feminine prerogatives and took the flower for her sign. The Virgin also appears in two portals on the northern side of the church; again at the high altar; again in a famous fourteenth-century statue at the *croisée* of the transept; and in a multitude of smaller images in stone and glass.

It is still too early to enter the Cathedral. Instead, it may be illuminating to cross back to the Left Bank and study it from the Quai de Montebello. From a slanting perspective the expanse of Notre-Dame seems endless. Hundreds of vertical elements leap to support the tall walls. The spectacular flight of the flying buttresses is never ended, but soars and returns, soars and returns, leaping, leaping, leaping along the enormous circle of the apse. Across the southern transept spreads a rose window which may seem more impressive than the rose of the western façade. Both roses are Mary's. Both must be studied and restudied, measured, dated, and analyzed before a final judgment is possible.

If any judgment is to be made! The Cathedral does not care. It has been admired and will be admired until atomic Domesday. It has been hated and is detested still. It has been victimized by ideologies that have nothing to do with the Virgin or the Middle Age and made to serve as an argument. And although in a long series of revolutions the priests have been chased from the sanctuary, it is still used for the exclusive purposes of the Roman Catholic Church. It is endlessly polished and repaired by professional archaeologists, although any farmer could tell them that the rain washes best. It is the smoky industrial suburbs of Paris that need cleaning, not Notre-Dame.

The Cathedral should be seen only as the incarnation of an idealism, and no more. It is the concentrated ideal beauty of a lost community, like the temples of Athens or the cave drawings at Lascaux, and as innocent as they of any modern conception. The ideal was losing favor by 1500; it was irretrievably lost before another century had passed. In that time the Council of Trent had occurred and the Huguenots had stormed into Notre-Dame. The Protestants were expelled almost immediately, but the Catholic clergy that returned differed from the clergy that had left. They too, like the Huguenots, wished to transform the interior of the church. They replaced the rich medieval stained-glass windows with white glass to admit more light. They mutilated the central portal so that the canopied litters of the Bourbon kings could pass unencumbered beneath. They parsimoniously refused to repair the church—as one would repair even a barn—until it stood erect only by the integrity of its medieval workmanship.

Fashions in cathedrals change. When the Renaissance arrived, Ronsard spoke of the Middle Age as *"le vilain Monstre Ignorance."* The men of the Enlightenment used terms harsher still. Then, slowly enough, the intellectuals rediscovered medieval beauty. They saw it as Romance. Erroneous as this may have been, there are worse ways of looking at Notre-Dame. A century ago the only architecture worth its romantic salt to avant-garde thinkers was the Gothic, and the most exciting church in all the world was the Cathedral of Paris. Victor Hugo climbed into the towers and shouted among the bells. Heine strolled through the transept, saw that he was in an immense hollow cross, and wept. Aesthetic Victorians, fortified by Walter Scott, sailed the Channel to deliver Pre-Raphaelite homage at the altar of Our Lady of Paris. Americans came by the thousands, during the Henry James period, to stare earnestly at the façade and price the Méryon engravings.

Today only the tourists return with the same enthusiasm. The intellectuals left Paris for Chartres—like the poet Charles Péguy, who made the journey on foot—about the turn of the century, and have not returned since. Yet even Chartres, with its wealth of statuary and glass and its magnificent old spire, is losing favor. When medieval art is mentioned, rather than the northern cathedrals, strange assonant southern names crop up. Moissac and Souillac, and Conques in the Rouergue. The Romanesque has come into its own, and with reason. But although the Cathedral of Paris is no longer the intellectuals' church, it is still the one and only Notre-Dame for the ordinary person.

Perhaps this is for the best. The Cathedral, in any case, does not care. It gives not so much as a shrug for the busloads of Americans, of Swedes and excitable Spaniards, of Germans, Turks, and resolute Dutch, who make it the shrine of their tourists' pilgrimage. It simply lifts upward before them, calm and majestic, more than two hundred feet to the summits of the towers. Then suddenly it thrusts higher, like a temple in the East. There is an acceleration toward Heaven. The church seems to mount in the air and fly forward. And as the wall leaps higher, higher, impossibly higher, Notre-Dame reveals its secret. It possesses the essential variety of life itself—

and at the same time the serene power of a peak in the Andes! The lavish, squandered variety, carved into the stone, joins with the total design to soothe, delight, enchant, and ravish, rather than disturb.

All this may be understood. Notre-Dame may be studied until the stone population of the walls are better friends than the busy twentieth-century French crossing the parvis will ever be. But to recapture the passion and love—the faith—of the age that created these angels and demons, these queens and kneeling kings, to see in entirety the men and women who constructed this church, is quite another matter.

As each step is taken toward the Middle Age, it retreats with a bright gesture, like an exit in a miracle play. To understand, it is necessary to beat backward across the centuries, beyond the misused and unhappy Industrial Revolution, beyond the deceptive Baroque Enlightenment and the cruel Renaissance, across the chasm of a lost religion to the communal Middle Age, however imperfect it may have been, when men as at few moments in history enjoyed their joint capacity to create.

And then—with the Middle Age rising squarely in the façade of the Cathedral—still farther backward! Turn to the small park beside the Seine where Charlemagne, an aged Christian emperor, rides forward before the church on his bronze war horse. If it is still early morning, and there is a mist on the river, the task will be easier. Into the mist then! Backward across the mist of ages, before Charlemagne, before Clovis, Constantine, and Caesar, before Vercingetorix—to the green beginnings of time, for the sources of the Cathedral!

ORigins

Thou art the life of souls, the life of lives, having life in Thyself; and changest not, life of my soul.

SAINT AUGUSTINE

Chapter One

FOUNDATION STONES

ONCE, BEFORE Noah was dreamed of, the sea covered all. The Ile de France was a salt lake, hundreds of fathoms deep, in which not even the tip of the Eiffel Tower would have been awash. The Atlantic poured over the wide basin of the Seine and flowed to the foothills of the Vosges and the Jura, not far from the Rhine. And since Britain was not yet an island, hunters could cross on foot from Dover to Calais, chasing abstract reindeer whose horns were simple curves.

The sea ebbed, and men found a fertile and wooded country where the water had been. It was an ideal seat for a civilization. Great forests, which were not to disappear until after the Middle Age, stretched for miles along the Seine. The weather was mild. There was grazing land, there was game in the woods, and the system of quiet rivers—the Seine, the Marne, the Oise, the Eure—made it relatively easy to travel from place to place. Beyond this, the country was lovely. Wild crocuses sprouted in the meadows; finches sang in the forest; and beneath the earth, although the early men did not know how to cut it, the sea had deposited deep bands of fossil rock —tough granite and heavy limestone, which one day would be carved into cathedrals.

And so the first Parisians settled in the Ile de France, bringing with them their gods and their arts, for the two were inseparable. On a bend in the Seine they found an island naturally suited for defense, with a low hill on its eastern point; and since the summits of hills were sacred, they built a temple of branches and leaves at the crest and installed their gods on the Ile-de-la-Cité. Paris then could not have looked anything like Paris today, but the gods bear some resemblance.

Men adored a stone, a spring, a green tree. They sacrificed to the sun and the moon and to the brighter stars. They dedicated altars to beasts and reptiles and various birds—to the hawk, the serpent, the hound, and the bear. They worshiped a powerful wind which sometimes swept over the uncultivated fields. There was a god in the white waterfall, in the solemn lakes, in every well, in caverns, or where paths met, and on hilltops. The gods were numerous, fierce, jealous, and as complicated or uncomplicated as the humans who enshrined them; but among the gods was a mother deity, a neolithic madonna who occasionally held a child in her arms, and both mother and son have had a certain following in France to this day.

These gods, or their near descendants, were waiting when the Romans came. Caesar himself was struck by the savage piety of the Gauls and the dogmatic pride with which they defended their immortals. But, being a Roman, Caesar could describe these rural idols only in Roman terms, much as a Christian in Japan today tries to imagine the Virgin prefigured in the stone image of Kwannon. The Gallic gods, to Caesar, were Mercury, Mars, Jove, and Apollo, and —for want of a better name—Minerva, applied to the mother divinity, who probably embodied the attributes of a score of Roman goddesses—Ceres and Proserpine, and perhaps even the chaste Diana, among them. In course of time she received the Latin name Matrona.

The native gods outlasted the Romans and the fine Vitruvian city the conquerors constructed on the south bank of the Seine. Once, in what is now the Latin Quarter, stood a Roman theater, an aqueduct, an arena, splendid residences, and an imperial palace of which nothing remains but the ruins of the Thermae that are part of the Cluny Museum. Along the banks of the Seine, on the present site of the Quai de la Tournelle and on the southern shore of the island, was the busy port of the *nautae,* who were not at all simple sailors, but rather early shipping capitalists whose river trade made them the wealthiest mercantile group in Lutetia, as the Gallo-Roman city was called. It was these *nautae* who replaced a wooden Gallic shrine on the Ile with a stone temple dedicated to the old gods and the new.

There can be little doubt which set of gods the conquered Gauls preferred. In 1711 workmen digging beneath the choir of Notre-Dame unearthed four carven altars which came from this vanished temple of the *nautae,* and are now at the Cluny Museum. One stone not only bears an inscription to that effect (*Nautae Parisiaci publice posuerunt*), but, more important, also carries the name of the Emperor Tiberius, who reigned during the lifetime of Christ. Here, then, is the earliest date that may be associated with the Cathedral, and it may be that of the Crucifixion itself! So much the better. It shows what was going on at the other end of the world while the Redeemer was dying in Palestine.

Roman gods, the official gods, occupy more than half the faces of these altars, and they are conventional enough: a rather unimpressive Jupiter, a Mercury, Vulcan with his mallet, and Castor and Pollux leading their horses. None is very exciting. But the Gallic gods! Even when they share a stone with their dull Roman neighbors the Gallic gods are breathtaking.

The largest altar, which stands about four feet high, belongs to four gods. On two sides are Jupiter and Vulcan, for whom the sculptor clearly felt no great enthusiasm; they are altogether ordinary figures. But on the third face of the altar is another world: the green living world of the Gallic Druids, who, according to Caesar, were the theocratic rulers of the tribes he vanquished. Here is a brawny, half-naked woodsman, standing in the midst of foliage with a small hatchet in his hand. Apparently he is stripping a bush of its leafy branches, an unimportant enough task for a Paul Bunyan, but the determination of this god's face, the set of his chin and eyes, reveal that his work is serious indeed. Perhaps the green branches he is stripping are the sacred mistletoe of the Druids, perhaps not; botanists, who have never seen such a shrub, disagree. Yet the strong presence of nature in this bas-relief is unmistakable. The tree is growing and green, the god is alive and powerful, and the natural religious force of the sculpture flows as freely as the Seine in winter. The god is Esus, and experts say that he was a "strong-man" god: a divinity for workers or sailors who required muscles for their toil, an ancient relative of Hercules, and a predecessor of the giant Gargantua, who fifteen centuries from now—for these are the first years of the Christian Era—will carry off the tremendous bells of Notre-Dame. One day, too, a colossus of Saint Christopher will stand in the nave of the Cathedral, and remain there as a Christian titan for four hundred years.

Esus was a much less friendly giant. Human sacrifices were employed to appease his huge forester's anger. Criminals, or chance victims of the community if no criminals were available, were tacked to oak trees in his honor, or perhaps burned in the great cages of wicker that Caesar writes about. But Esus, terrible as he is, might seem comparatively tame, merely a crude woodland bully, if archaeologists could guess the solemnities with which the Gauls worshiped the beasts on the fourth face of the altar—the Bull and the Three Cranes: Taurus Trigeranus.

At first glance the bull seems anything but sinister. He too is portrayed in the center of a forest and stands half-hidden by the boughs of willow trees. He is a short, rather chunky little bull, with a certain coyness of expression that would go straight to the heart of Walt Disney. Yet all the skill of the Gallo-Roman sculptor has been lavished upon him; the clear look of the eyes, the furrows in the handsome brow, the broad strength of the muzzle, are carved with a grace and a sureness that not even the Esus received. Over the bull's back is draped a cloth that may have been a sacrificial robe, and near the robe stand two small wading birds, with a third crane on top of his head. The scene is singularly tranquil. Common robins may be singing in the willows. But there is a strange uneasiness about this sturdy little bull and his three magical birds, a brooding secret in this clearing which is forever lost, like the strange battle smiles of the warriors on the frieze of the Parthenon. M. Stéphane Czarnowski demonstrates that perhaps the bull is a cousin of the mythical beast who swam to Crete with Europa, but anyone's guesswork is as valid as his. The aficionado may have as much fun as he likes speculating about this father of all toros. Concerning the cranes, M. Czarnowski is much more precise. He writes that in Celtic mythology they were considered birds of wisdom, announcers of the seasons, and guides of travelers. They were also, he adds, messengers of divine vengeance, vengeance which in this case could mean being stuck to oaks with javelins.

One more altar in the Salle des Thermes requires examination. This is a flat stone, scarcely eighteen inches high, and on one of its four sides is the curious face of Cernunnos, still another Gallic immortal. Almost nothing is known about him except his looks, which is quite enough. Cernunnos is an elderly monster with a rough beard and eyes that burn unforgettably from deep within the stone. Springing from above his ears are twin horns with a heavy ring suspended from the arc of each.

These Gallic gods died stubbornly. The Roman gods, however, fell easily, long before the empire; and Edward Gibbon took half his lifetime to connect the political with the religious collapse. From Asia Minor the resistless Christians marched over Europe on foot, sailed the Mediterranean, crossed in caravans to Carthage; and soon, sometime during the prelacy of Pope Fabian (236-251), the Church felt strong enough to succor its embattled pioneer communities, such as the heroic colony of Saint Irenaeus at Lyon, and formally to evangelize Gaul. It was a great undertaking, and hazardous for the times, but never before or since have missionaries enjoyed such results. According to tradition, seven bishops were dispatched from Rome, and they quickly spread a delicate but unbreakable network of primitive Christianity over most of the territory of modern France. The name of Christ the King was whispered, sung in secret, and thundered in the open at last. Saturnin, or Sernin, carried the Gospel to Toulouse, Trophime to the luxurious resort at Arles, Paul to the seaport of Narbonne: the three great episcopal cities of the Midi. In the cruder north, Martial set up headquarters at Limoges, Stremien built a church at Clermont, and Gatien preached at Tours, which was already a crossways of roads. And to the farthest outpost came the most important of all, if only because he was to become the patron of kings, Denis, Bishop of Paris, the first prelate of the Ile de France.

The third century, like the twentieth, was an age for martyrs. Only two of the seven bishops, however, perished as they preached the Church of Christ in Gaul: Saturnin of Toulouse, who was lashed to the tail of a bull and driven down the steps of the Capitol; and Denis of Paris, who was beheaded.

Of Denis not much more is known than his martyrdom. The earliest surviving document to mention him, the *Historia Francorum* of Gregory of Tours, followed his death by more than four hundred years. Gregory, writing after 575, declared merely that "the blessed Dionysius, Bishop of Paris, after suffering various torments for the name of Christ, died under the sword." Since Denis and his fellow evangelists were sent to Gaul by Pope Fabian sometime before the Pope's death in 251, it may be assumed that the Patron of France arrived in Paris about 240 and that he was executed during the persecutions of the Emperor Decius between 249 and 251.

Happily the legend is more generous than scholarly facts. Over the centuries the monks of Saint-Denis, in particular Abbot Hilduin, who composed a life of the saint about 835, invented a complete biography for their patron. The Denis revered by the Middle Age was believed to have come to Gaul not in the third but in the first century. Far from being an obscure citizen of the Western Empire with the Latin name Dionysius, he was a renowned theologian of the East, Dionysos the Areopagite, from the Athenian suburb of Ares, himself legendary, who had been converted to Christianity by no less a personage than Saint Paul.

When this Denis, who was first Bishop of Athens, later was sent to Gaul, he was accompanied by Rusticus, a priest, and by the deacon Eleutherius. With their aid Denis founded a clandestine Christian community in pagan Lutetia. Its first church was a crypt in the Parisian catacombs, located in the Roman quarries on the Left Bank, which still may be visited. The second church was the home of a private citizen, within the limits of the city, but again on the Left Bank rather than the Ile. This part of the legend cannot be much different from the actual facts.

After the Church was established at Paris, the legend continues, Denis evangelized Meaux and Rouen. At the same time twenty of his disciples, among them Saint Lucien of Beauvais, Saint Crépin of Soissons, and Saint Valerien of Reims, founded communities elsewhere in northern France. This progress continued mightily until Denis, Rusticus, and Eleutherius were arrested by the Roman authorities. They were ordered to deny their faith. When they refused they were cast into dungeons.

Although Denis was by now ninety years old he was subjected to torture. He was flogged by twelve soldiers and loaded with chains. A collar of stone crushed him to the ground beneath its weight. He was roasted on a grill, but as the flames rose about him he preached the Lord, saying: "Thy Word is enflamed, and Thy servant cherishes It." Then he was exposed to wild beasts who had been kept for days without food; the Sign of the Cross calmed them instantly when they ran upon him. Whereupon Denis was thrown into a furnace, "but he felt no pain." Finally he was attached to a cross, tormented for hours, and returned to prison with his two companions and many other believers. And when Denis celebrated Mass in the jail and gave them Holy Communion, Christ appeared, surrounded by an immense brilliance. The Savior took the Host and administered it to the saint, telling him: "Receive my flesh; a great reward awaits thee."

The next day Denis, Rusticus, and Eleutherius were led to a statue of Mercury, at the crest of Montmartre. After they refused to sacrifice to the pagan divinity they were beheaded. Two blows were necessary in the case of Denis, since the first cut off only his cranium. The second severed his neck, but as soon as the head touched the earth it was picked up by its former possessor. The body marched away, the head in its hands, and the lips chanting psalms in the saint's strong voice, to the accompaniment of angels. The body walked thus for five miles, until it came to the village of Catolacum, the saint's chosen resting place. There, when the persecution subsided, a simple monument was raised above the grave of Denis and those of his two fellow martyrs, whose bodies had been recovered from the Romans by a pious Christian lady.

Archaeologists, in their analysis of the legend, assert that the decapitation took place not on Montmartre but almost certainly in Catolacum itself, where the cult of Saint Denis was celebrated as early as the fifth century, whereas the Montmartre episode was not invented until the eighth. Today Catolacum—the modern town of Saint-Denis—is one of the most wretched manufacturing suburbs of Paris; and the working people hardly look up as they pass his basilica on their way to a Communist meeting or to a cinema. But the medieval church of Saint-Denis, the great local architectural rival of Notre-Dame, still stands; and it must be visited many times if the Cathedral a few kilometers away is ever to be understood.

Other saints followed Denis. More than half the men and women in France bear their names today. They formed a battalion of giants, larger than life, greater than the great gods of Gaul, and they triumphed. The God they preached was One God and All Gods, and they themselves were gods of a sort. They were makers of miracles, healers of the sick, defenders of the weak, preachers by the wayside, like the Redeemer before them. Far away in Africa, about the year 400, Saint Augustine told the world about the new God of Gods.

What are Thou then, my God? what but the Lord God? For who is Lord but the Lord? or who is God save our God? Most highest, most good, most potent, most omnipotent; most merciful, yet most just; most hidden, yet most present; most beautiful, yet most strong; stable, yet incomprehensible; unchangeable, yet all-changing; never new, never old; all-renewing . . . ever working, ever at rest; still gathering, yet nothing lacking; supporting, filling, and overspreading; creating, nourishing, and maturing; seeking, yet having all things.
. . . Oh! that I might repose in Thee!

The Romans, their polite gods exhausted, found this argument unanswerable; the Gauls stubbornly retreated to their dark woodland shrines, where Saint Martin of Tours carried the battle to them. This hero, who was more or less contemporary with Saint Augustine, incarnated the growing strength of Christianity, which of course was now the religion of the emperors. Martin was, in a sense, the first Christian bigot in France. He was a remarkable personality, split down the center by an incompatible mixture of force and mildness. He was a creature of brutal exterior environment and gentle inner faith. A soldier and the son of a soldier, he had been born at a military post in Hungary, on the violent Danubian frontier, where the huge shapes of hostile gods loomed always behind the undisciplined enemy tribes. Like any general, Martin collected his hatreds, and he bound them together in the single target of the Devil. But the Prince of Darkness was a wily opponent, full of tricks and deceits. Martin was compelled to struggle against him night as well as day. In his hermit's cell near the Loire, which would have done credit to the barren Thebaid, he suffered alarming visions of Satan, who appeared in a number of disguises which would have delighted Anatole France. Invariably the Devil chose the blue French evening to enchant him as blond Venus.

Martin fought such provocation angrily. The saint invaded oak groves and cut down the sacred trees. He smashed images. It is no accident that his fête is November eleventh, which apparently was the date of pagan autumnal sacrifices. Martin simply stepped in and conquered a living religion as green and vigorous and with roots as deep as the consecrated oaks. Miraculous wells became baptismal fonts, and where a Druid tree had been he built a church with its wood.

Martin was elected Bishop of Tours in 371, when he was about fifty-five years old, and churches grew like mushrooms on the soil of France under his patronage. Tours, of course, led the way, with a rich basilica and monasteries, but Paris followed closely. Sometime before his death in 397, the saint came down to Paris from Amiens on the road which is still called the rue Saint-Martin. He had just concluded a campaign in the superstitious north, venturing as far as the Rhine, where he battled uncompromisingly with Thor. His disciple, Sulpicius Severus, has left a vivid portrait of the old man returning from his wars, dressed in a camel-hair shirt and long black robe, his uncut hair streaming over his shoulders, his bony feet nude. He was mounted on a humble donkey, a surprising creature who leaped away in long bounds, with the saint on his back, when irate heathens counterattacked. The Parisians thronged from the city to greet Martin, and among them was a leper covered with hideous sores. Without hesitation the saint jumped from his ass and kissed the man on his cankered lips. The leper was healed instantly, and the next day, his skin cleansed of any stain, presented himself in church to offer thanks to the Lord.

Where was this church in which the leper prayed? No scholar has ever found out. Marcel Poëte, the greatest of Paris's many historians, thought it might have been located on the island, which had been walled after the first raid of the Franks and Alamans in 276, a century before, and which was again the heart of the city. Perhaps it was one of several churches which were surely standing on the Left Bank, as were the subterranean chambers in which Christians had congregated since the times of Saint Denis. By the fourth century, thanks to Constantine, the Church had taken a place in the open air; and a cathedral church, the formal seat of the bishop, already may have been designated.

There is some evidence that if such a cathedral church existed at the turn of the fifth century it was situated on the emplacement of Notre-Dame, or at any rate somewhere near the Seine. For, about 400, a young priest named Marcellus—Saint Marcel—fetched water from the nearby river for the sacramental washing of his Bishop's hands. When the Bishop, Saint Prudentius, examined the water, however, he found it mysteriously changed to wine. Astonished, he poured the liquid into a chalice, from which all the Christians of the city received Holy Communion; no matter how many tasted from the cup it remained full.

Marcel, like Martin, was a renowned thaumaturge, of whom not much is known except his miracles. He is said to have been born in Lutetia, of common parents, and became distinguished for his gifts while young. An evil blacksmith asked the boy to take a piece of red-hot iron in his hand, to tell its weight. Marcel obliged, remarking: "It's warm enough, but it weighs only nine pounds." When the metal cooled it was put on a scale, and the saint's estimate turned out correct.

Marcel's most spectacular feat took place after he succeeded Prudentius as bishop in 417. Seven centuries later, when Notre-Dame was constructed, the miracle was so highly valued that it was depicted in two of the six portals. According to the *Golden Legend*, a noble lady, notorious for her vices, died and was buried in the Left Bank cemetery, near which a village had been established that is still known as the faubourg Saint-Marcel:

But here is what happened to the body, which is impossible to relate without secret horror and profound compassion for the deceased: a horrible serpent came to devour the corpse, making its home in the tomb, and eating her remains for nourishment. The inhabitants of the place fled terrified from their homes. The Blessed Marcel understood that it was necessary for him to vanquish the monster; and he therefore assembled all the people of the city; and then, leaving them a certain distance behind, went forth alone to the scene of combat. When the serpent, coming from a wood, returned toward the sepulcher, Marcel confronted it, praying. From that moment, the monster seemed to beg for grace, bowing its head and wagging its tail. Then it followed the saintly Bishop for nearly three miles, in plain view of the people, who uttered thanks to Marcel, and heaped invective upon his enemy. Then Saint Marcel spoke to it commandingly: "From this day, go live in the desert, or dive back in the sea!" And no trace has been seen of it since.

Marcel died in 436 and was immediately sainted by acclamation. His bones were placed beside the episcopal altar, where they remained, in cathedral after cathedral, until Notre-Dame was sacked during the French Revolution.

By the first half of the fifth century, if not earlier, the Cathedral and most of the other churches of Lutetia were concentrated within the walled Cité, for reasons of security. Rome had collapsed with a frightening sigh. The entire barbarian world was on the move, seeking a place in the empire. Behind the Goths and the Visigoths came Attila and his Huns, who were diverted from Paris by the prayers of Saint Geneviève (c.420-512), but devastated much of northern Gaul nevertheless. The Huns eventually moved onward, but with them had come the Franks, emerging from the cold plains of Germany with gods whom the now Romanless Gauls had half forgotten.

The Church wavered, bent before the savagery, and finally held. Before they themselves knew it, the Frankish kings were not only Christians but soldiers of the Lord. Under Christ's banner they triumphed over pagans in Lorraine and heretics in the Pyrenees, until all France was theirs, and they fought on against one another. A curious mixture of pagan and Christian energy was released as France writhed beneath these superstitious despots, a phenomenon that was to be repeated infinitely more beautifully after the conversion of the Normans in the tenth century. Abbeys and basilicas shot up everywhere. Clovis was baptized by Saint Rémi at Reims in 496, in a weird ceremony that attracted, so says the legend, the Holy Ghost to appear in the shape of a dove to anoint the king. Twelve years later, in 508, Clovis is found on the summit of the hill on the Left Bank, amid the ruins of the Roman city, dedicating an abbey to the Holy Apostles Peter and Paul. Urged by devout Queen Clothilda, he hurled his battle-ax as far as he could, and thus fixed the size of the new church he had endowed for the monastery. Later the abbey was placed under the patronage of Saint Geneviève, whose miraculous tomb it possessed, and who gave her name to the entire hill.

Clovis's son Childebert founded a second Parisian monastery, which, if anything, was more resplendent. In 542 he returned from a successful war with the heretical Visigoths in Spain, carrying with him loot from their Arian churches, including relics of the martyr Vincent and a great, jeweled crucifix. With this treasure he established the monastery of Saint Vincent and the Holy Cross, which ultimately became known as Saint-Germain-des-Prés, in the fields of the Left Bank. The little church of Saint-Julien-le-Pauvre was also founded at this time, a tiny forerunner of the charming twelfth-century Saint-Julien which still stands near the southern shore of the Seine.

On the Right Bank, too, several churches were surely constructed by this time, among them a priory to commemorate Martin's meeting with the leper. It grew into another spacious monastery, whose land is now occupied by the Museum of Arts and Métiers, and where the exquisite but desecrated medieval church of Saint-Martin-des-Champs remains as a poignant souvenir of the ancient Christian warrior and his kiss.

And in the village of Catolacum, a few miles downriver, a chapel had been built above the once ignominious grave of the Apostle of Gaul. In time it would become the most wealthy and powerful monastery of Capetian France, the Abbey Royal of Saint-Denis.

The first cathedral on the island would seem to date at least from this outburst of construction in the sixth century, but conceivably it was situated there much earlier. It was doubtless standing on the Ile during the time of still another famous bishop of Paris, Saint Germain, who died in 576 when, as Notre-Dame would later face the medieval château of the Capets, it already confronted the palace of the barbarous Frankish kings.

Chapter Two

THE CATHEDRAL OF SAINT STEPHEN, PROTOMARTYR

ONE SUNDAY morning in December—the year is 582—a horseman galloped northward to Paris. The country was a forest, through which the Roman road passed in a broad, straight, powerful line, like a strong river. Here and there was a clearing, with a patch of cultivated land, a rampart, a chapel, a few huts, and then the forest would begin again, as thick and menacing as before. The rider himself was as dark and threatening as the forest. His cropped right ear showed that he was a runaway serf, but the elegance of his clothing and the easy power of his movements revealed that he had risen to high position since his days of slavery. In truth, he was not a villain of Sir Walter Scott but a historical figure: Leudaste, the deposed Count of Tours, and an enemy of the Crown. His visit to Paris this day in 582 was recorded and provides the first written evidence for the existence of the Cathedral.

As he approached the capital the forest thinned, and Leudaste entered farming country. The land was rich, so fertile that it plowed open like a heavy mineral, but it had been wasted by war. Not a tenth of the arable soil was being used. All else was abandoned and melancholy with ruins. At intervals Leudaste would see the skeleton of a villa or a temple. Only the road was intact, and it too needed repair.

At the village now called Arcueil, Leudaste rode parallel to the heroic round arches of the Roman aqueduct which had once carried perfect water ten miles north to Paris. The arches held staunchly, as one or two of them do today, but the waterway, the massive sluice in which a man could stand erect with his arms stretched wide, was filled with rubble and slime. The Parisians, already medieval, had forgotten how to use Roman machinery and had learned to drink from the Seine.

After the aqueduct, whose arcades continued for miles beside the road, the next landmark for Leudaste was in Paris itself: the gilded roof of the Abbey Church of Saints Peter and Paul, which Clovis had founded some seventy-five years earlier on the Montagne-Sainte-Geneviève. Today the Panthéon, crowning the Left Bank with its heavy dome, stands on approximately the same spot. Leudaste mounted the slope and passed the monastery near the crest of its hill. From the summit he looked out on a green panorama of the Ile de France; and directly below, crowded against the wide bend of the river, was the Paris of the Dark Age.

It would be difficult, without the obvious geography of the Seine, to recognize the modern baroque capital from this battered ancestor. Barbarian Paris—the Paris which somehow remained a city after the collapse of Roman Gaul—was a violent country town of ten or at the most fifteen thousand souls. Today it has vanished as completely as its superb contemporaries in Asia which have been covered with sand. Except for the ruined Thermae, the debris of other monuments, and the shape of streets in the oldest quarters, there are only rare documents, such as the *Historia Francorum* of Gregory of Tours, to bring the city alive. Gregory's chronicle, unsophisticated as it is, reads like the list of terrors in the *Odyssey:* Sisyphus exhausted and dismayed at the base of his impossible hill, without the force to roll the heavy stone of civilization upward.

Rome had perished, but if Leudaste took the trouble to look about he was surely impressed by the forlorn grandeur of the past. How much of Lutetia was still standing at this time is a matter of doubt; probably more survived than is generally believed, but in such poor condition that it was unusable. Rising above the remains of patrician residences were the ruined theater, the arena, the white temples and triumphal arches. The monuments had been serving as quarries for three hundred years, ever since the Parisians stripped them of stone to wall the island. In course of time they would disappear altogether. Throughout the Dark Age the beautifully tailored Roman materials were employed for every sort of building project, for barns and sarcophagi, for fortresses and abbeys.

At the foot of the hill Leudaste came to the spot now occupied by the elegant late-Gothic church of Saint-Séverin and by the fascinating neighborhood that Elliot Paul has sentimentalized. On these ancient streets and alleys, pressed against the southern bank of the river, medieval Paris had taken form. The rectangular Roman street pattern was as smashed as Humpty Dumpty and would never be put back together again, not even by Baron Haussmann. Life was crowded and intense, and so illogical as to be maddening. It was also perilous. Men walked the streets armed with swords and wicked daggers called scramasaxes, which left an irregular wound.

The fast-talking, excitable, polyglot population of this quarter has changed little in fourteen centuries. On the rue Galande and the rue de la Huchette, sitting by the rich-smelling casks in the wineshops, the Parisians argued in uncivil Latin, which was the first equivalent of argot. They spoke in a dozen accents and occasionally in pure foreign languages; sometimes, even then, they screamed with the gargling cry of the African. Most of them, of course, were descendants of the ancient population, Gauls with Roman blood, who each day lost some claim to their former gentility, although they still dressed in fine woolen robes when they could afford them. There were also the Frankish soldiers of King Chilperic, wearing hides and furs and jeweled buckles—bullying blond giants who reacted to any provocation, like so many Siegfrieds, with a predictable Teuton display of force. There were supple merchants from the Middle East— Syrians, Jews, Egyptians, Greeks, whose wares included spices and embroidered textiles, perfumes, gems, and aphrodisiacs. One of these tradesmen became Bishop of Paris: in 591, the Syrian Eusebius purchased the episcopal throne and filled the Chapter with fellow Easterners before being chased from the Cathedral by the indignant congregation.

Except to antiquarians, Leudaste has been lost in this vivid crowd which surges through the *Historia Francorum*. But on this Sunday fourteen hundred years ago the outlaw dramatically threw himself upon the mercy of Queen Fredegund while she was attending Mass in the Cathedral, and Gregory of Tours' account of the episode contains the first documentary evidence of the church on the Ile-de-la-Cité. Before 582 the texts are silent concerning its location, and Gregory himself tells little more than its site.

Fortunately the foundations of the lost Cathedral were discovered beneath the parvis during the last century—wide brands of masonry which extended some forty yards westward of the present façade of Notre-Dame (Fig. 1). These outlines have again been buried, but they may be studied in the excellent drawings of Albert Lenoir's *Statistique Monumentale de Paris*. The drawings not only give the basilica's general dimensions and dispositions, but also reveal the quality of its materials and such relevant details as the substructure of a porch, which evidently supported a bell tower.

The briefest glance would have shown that this was no classical temple. Taken as structure alone, it was plain to the point of barrenness. But even in December, when the Paris sky is dark, this church sparkled with many lights. The Merovingian architect gave extreme attention to the surface texture of his building. He took a variety of brilliant objects—tile, brick, glass, stucco, and colored stone, the best materials he could find to capture and reflect the sun—and embedded them directly in the masonry, not in chance patterns but in organized designs which would display light more effectively. He encrusted the walls with swastikas and spirals, six-petaled roses, triangles and hexagons of flashing brilliance; and capped the whole with a roof of bright copper alloy.

Such surface splendor, Louis Bréhier has explained, is the first principle of barbarian art: showy decoration, at the expense of monumental sincerity. A jewel box? Yes, the Romans would have said, a box indeed, a childish mass of stones! Compared with the Maison Carrée, for example, the Merovingian church would seem clumsy and, what is worse in a religious edifice, coarse. The Maison Carrée, it is true, profits from the hot Provençal sunlight and lifts upward with an easy southern grace and a Mediterranean sense of relief and shadow, but even on a dull October afternoon, with the mistral blowing, the grace, the light display of strength, the effortless harmony of the proportions, are unmistakable. The sixth-century basilica could not have seemed so on the most pleasant day of the Parisian summer. It crouched heavily at the sacred tip of the island, like a rough northern beast. It had exterior power, and fury perhaps, but in a strict sense it was savage and hung bangles from its nostrils with childish pleasure.

But the Romans could not have understood this church. By the sixth century Vitruvius was as dead as Vergil, and the Merovingian

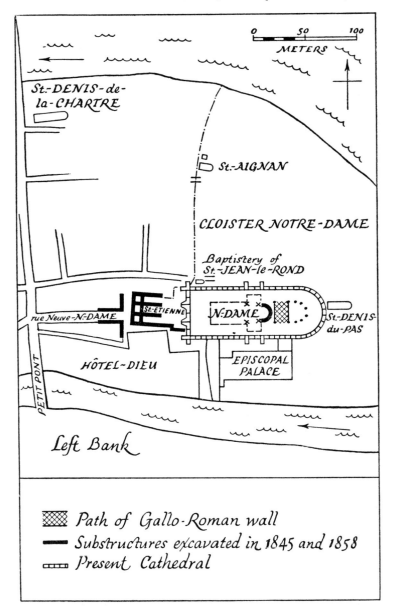

0 50 100
METERS

St.-DENIS-de-la-CHARTRE

St.-AIGNAN

CLOISTER NOTRE-DAME

Baptistery of St.-JEAN-le-ROND

rue Neuve-N.-DAME   St.-ÉTIENNE   N.-DAME   St.-DENIS-du-PAS

PETIT PONT

HÔTEL-DIEU   EPISCOPAL PALACE

Left Bank

▨▨▨ Path of Gallo-Roman wall
▬▬ Substructures excavated in 1845 and 1858
▭▭▭ Present Cathedral

Fig. 1.   THE CATHEDRAL AREA

was content to let him lie. To debate the problems of a volume in space, or of a line in perspective, appeared as useless to the barbarian as it was incomprehensible. For what was lacking in the sixth century, more than the classical ability to build, was the will to construct in the classical manner. A new aesthetic chemistry was loose in France.

The discovery of this new sense of beauty in the Dark Age must be counted one of the triumphs of modern archaeology. Previously scholars had dismissed the period as an era of continuous degeneration, unable to copy Rome and equally powerless to create for itself. Nothing could be less true. The sixth-century artists in France were far from being great original masters, but what ideas they did import came from the East and not from Rome. A real understanding of the Merovingian basilica can come only from a tour of Asia Minor, and in search of its secrets such voyagers as Jean Hubert have pushed off to Egypt and Palestine, and come upon sumptuous churches in the Syrian desert and colossal mosques in Turkey. In the year 582, it may be recalled, Sancta Sophia was new, and the Byzantine glory of the world. A serious exploration, however, can only pause at the Dardanelles. It should continue to the Euphrates and then to the hills of Armenia, and farther, beyond the Caucasus, to what was once a frozen barbarian steppe, where there are still amazing painted churches on the monotonous plain.

Was the contemporary Cathedral of Paris in their class? It is altogether possible. Admitted that without its superficial ornament the Cathedral would have seemed excessively plain, so sober structurally as to appear inert, and lacking the visible tension and equilibrium which make for successful art—granted all this, the walls may have had a certain rugged attraction. If strength alone counted, they were superb. In places they were nearly two yards thick, and for foundations they had the immovable remains of the Gallo-Roman city. But as no book of history can, Lenoir's drawings of these walls reveal what the fall of Rome meant in terms of techniques. The lowest sections were composed of dressed rectangular stone of the old Roman construction. Higher, in the barbarian work, the masonry grew irregular and ceased to travel in delineated rows; the stone, hammered to shape rather than cut, had the look of chaos.

For all the massiveness of its construction, the church was not large. It was about one hundred and sixty feet long, roughly a third the length of the present Cathedral; its width of seventy-two feet was half that of Notre-Dame. If it were sitting on the parvis today, it would appear dwarfed by its enormous successor. A guess would place its elevation at sixty feet to the summit of its bell tower, or nearly to the western rose of Notre-Dame.

This tower, one of the earliest in France, is intriguing. As a motive in Christian architecture, the tower has easily been the most popular in the West, challenged only by the dome. Together with other towers rising at this time, the Paris *clocher* would take a permanent hold on the Gallic imagination. The idea of a tower is of course at least as old as the ancient fiasco at Babel, but the French acquired it from a more recent East, where churches were equipped with minarets and Mass was announced by a powerful voice, like a pronunciamento of Heaven. In France, on the other hand, there was a bell at Tours before the barbarian conquest, and it may not have been the first. Sometimes the clocher stood free, like a campanile. More often, as at Paris, it was likely to be held aloft by the massive piles of a porch, a sort of *atrium* preceding the nave, where the poor gathered for shelter and pilgrims stopped to pray to special saints. Mosaics and paintings probably adorned the central portal, and the pillars and doorway were provided with sculpture. This carving was necessarily abstract, since effigies—that is, identifiable human or animal figures —would have smacked of idolatry.

It goes without saying that the Church had not yet won the final battle against paganism. The old gods of Gaul were tenacious and fought on in guerrilla action. In the secrecy of the forest the impieties of the vanished order were stubbornly celebrated, sometimes in the name of the new God Christ. From backward areas such as the Druid Ardennes came dreadful rumors of human sacrifice, offered to Jesus by country priests. The church at Le Puy was inscribed with the name of an Auvergnat god as heathen as Esus the Woodsman. Crosses replaced the dolmens, and chapels stood on the sacred pinnacles of rock, but the people trembled when a shadow passed overhead and the thunder spoke. Resistance to change was of course most intense in the country, and it is revealing to discover that *paysan* and *paien,* peasant and pagan, derive from an identical root. Even in Paris the Hill of Montmartre retained the most venerable associations despite a Christian priory at its summit. For Montmartre never meant Mount of Martyrs, in honor of Saint Denis and his companions, as is sometimes supposed, but Mons Mercore, Mount of Mercury, where the Traveler ruled for centuries as god of the Hill.

If the recent wars of Saint Martin prevented the Church from approving stone images, paintings and mosaics were paradoxically quite acceptable. They were approved as illustrations of the liturgy, and a divine host of Old Testament prophets, the apostles, various angels and saints, and possibly the Savior too—either as a bearded Syrian or an imberbe Good Shepherd—looked down at the faithful as they entered the shrine of the Blessed Saint Stephen. For this Cathedral of Paris was not dedicated to the Virgin but to the Protomartyr, who was stoned by the Libertines.

II

O Lord, let Thy works praise Thee,
That we may love Thee!
And let us love Thee,
That Thy works may praise Thee!

The prayer is simple, as Saint Augustine intended, as direct and unaffected as the structure of the church, but, like the Church, founded on rock and built to last for ages. The basilica of Saint Stephen was radiant with the presence of this Lord, this Maker of all Works, who filled its interior with salvation. For if God seemed absent from the violent streets, He compensated the Dark Age with a pure concentration of divinity within His temple. Men ran trembling and exhausted into His church, prostrated themselves before the altars, and sought the calm of Heaven. The basilica—like the best Renaissance churches—was wider than it was high; that in itself has usually been a comfort to the harassed. Width is the great calming proportion. The groping vaults of the Gothic—restless, intellectual, theologic, inordinately ambitious—demanded a supreme confidence from the community that built them, a sureness the Dark Age could not possibly possess. The Gothic, if fault were to be found with it, was too literate, too rational in its endless search for the irrational. But this is to cavil. The sixth century, which could barely read, is exempt from such criticism, and stands as far below the

Gothic triumph as its poet Fortunatus stands below Dante. The sixth century knew nothing, except the vague disappearance of the past and the certain peril of the future. And its Church, because it could not do otherwise, made its God more accessible than most gods have been.

In plan, the basilica was a model of simplicity. It was a great oblong hall divided into a central nave and two side aisles, terminating in a transept and, probably, a semicircular apse. In elevation the church was hardly more complex. Twin lines of pillars swept the eye down the nave. These columns, to judge from other Merovingian structures, supported either a flat architrave or an arcade of round arches. Very likely, too, there was an open gallery above each aisle. Overhead, resting on the tops of the walls, were the functional beams of the roof, cut from the thick oaks of France and visible for all to see.

Such was the conservative plan of the church. It instantly revealed the calm proportions of the whole and provided a perfect tray for the rich dish of adornment that the Merovingians placed on the altar of the Lord. Never has decoration been more concentrated. The Dark Age abhorred the vacuum of an empty surface. Walls, floors, ceilings, were alive with color. Hundreds of lamps and candles intensified the effect. There was light everywhere. It filled the hollows of the nave with a luminous splendor and played on the enameled roofs. The frescoes were as iridescent as a Persian vase, and on the magnificent floor the mosaics unlooped their designs like pools of a reddish-black ocean storming in the candlelight.

When chroniclers of the Dark Age spoke of such basilicas they were free with adjectives. *"Splendens, rutilans, nitens,"* they wrote; *"micans, radians, coruscans":* splendid, brilliant, shining, glittering, dazzling, radiant! Perhaps they did not here exaggerate, as they did in so much else. The Merovingian churches were colored with energy and imagination that approached fury. In this the entire community must have been grateful to the Franks, who, more than any other group in the realm, save perhaps the Syrian merchants, insisted on these golden interiors. The Franks may have known almost nothing of construction and might have been hard-pressed to build a livable house, not to mention a cathedral, but their jewelry—the brooches, pins, and pendants, the sword hilts and scabbards, which are now the treasure of museums—reveals an infallible taste for decoration.

Art historians debate where, precisely, the Franks developed this savage love for color, this greed for show, but it would seem that they had adored gems and precious metals since they first gathered in a tribe and lived in tents on the Asian steppes. Other nomads carried the same taste down across Turkestan into Asia Minor, where the civilizations of Persia and Byzantium brought it to exceptional beauty; and a visit to the Cabinet des Médailles of the Bibliothèque Nationale, where the Sassanid Cup of Khosru and the Frankish Gourdon Chalice stand in adjoining vitrines, shows how that taste remained fairly static in the West while it moved to glory in the East, but remained essentially the same taste nevertheless.

Yet Gaul had known the Orient for centuries and never before had exploded this decorative magic. Rome and its white temples may have been the great barrier, but the Romans appreciated Asiatic color and frequently used it—in the Roman way, to be sure—in their more lively buildings. The explosion, the Dark Age would have said, was less a political than a religious one. Christianity had charged France like a Leyden jar, until it sparkled at every foreign contact. Fortunatus, in a poem on "The Church of Paris," explained it this way: "If the magnificence of the Temple of Solomon is justly praised, our church, whose art is equally splendid, is more beautiful because of faith: the walls of the Temple of Jerusalem were covered with precious metals, but these walls tinctured with the blood of Christ shine more brilliantly."

The mosaic floor of the basilica, for example, consisted of no less than three designs, one probably for the nave and the others for the side aisles. Fragments of these mosaics have been unearthed, and the one at the Carnavalet Museum gives a partial impression of the sea of colored marble which flowed throughout the church and spilled in the aisles like an Asian waterfall. Unlike some pagan floor mosaics, they contained no representational images of the Divine, no portraits of saints or apostles, for the Dark Age would not tread upon the faces of the holy. On the contrary, they were pure abstraction. The key to their effect was an almost excessive use of white as a background: the sixth-century craftsman sought the effect of gems and ebony dropped in a field of snow. The white, with exquisite purity, curled like surf against the black shores of great revolving patterns, and disappeared only to reappear in the turbulent centers of the mosaic as a foil for deep reds and burning yellows; white against black, then black against red, and red against white, with wild yellows floating between, tracing ingenious crosses of Christ the length of the nave.

And the mosaics were rivaled by the glass. The French, who had learned glassmaking from the Romans, were so skilled in the art by this time that the ignorant believed such intensities could be obtained only from molten jewels. Gregory of Tours tells of a sacrilegious thief who stole colored glass from the church of Isseure and melted it in a crucible to obtain its precious contents. Similar stories have been told of the best medieval glass, which is an indication of the ability of the Merovingian artist. Although it is possible that the glass was set in lead or wood, the windows of the basilica more likely were not true windows at all, but thin slabs of perforated stone. In each hole of the slabs was a vivid morsel of red, warm green, or hot white crystal, to judge from the favorite colors of Merovingian cloisonné. The glass was not painted with images, nor was representationalism its purpose. What was wanted was a non-objective effect, more abstract than any abstraction, with not a hint of a recognizable form. Think of a velvet sprinkled with garnets and emeralds —and there you have it.

The light of these windows played magically on the basilica's marble columns. At the Cluny Museum, two of these heroic pillars are on display: jet black, nearly a yard in diameter (80 centimeters), and four yards tall. Surmounting one pillar is a Corinthian capital, in white marble, of the best imperial style. Since fragments of other pillars and capitals were found in the same excavation, it is assumed that these were part of an entire set, probably acquired from a pagan temple, which bordered each side of the nave.

Above these stately black colonnades, if the basilica was similar to other Merovingian churches, a heavenly host of prophets and apostles, bishops, confessors, and martyrs towered in purple frescoes. At the rear of the vessel the golden light of Paradise shone from the mosaics of the apse. Gold and other precious metals were fused with the marble altar. And beneath this treasure was a prize more valuable than all the rest: the humble stones stained by the blood of Saint Stephen, first to perish for Jesus Christ.

The Protomartyr was the great god of the Merovingians. It

would be three hundred years before the Virgin, to whom shrines were just beginning to be consecrated in France, would supplant him as the major Patron of Paris. In the sixth century, however, she could not challenge Stephen, whose story was the favorite lesson of the Dark Age. To a society which each day saw the guiltless dead in the street, the brief passage from Acts became a religion in itself: the cult of the martyr. Every child knew that Stephen had been one of the first seven deacons elected by the Christians of Jerusalem to assist the apostles, and how Stephen, "full of faith and power, did great wonders and miracles among the people." When "stiffnecked" Jews disputed with him, "they were not able to resist the wisdom and the spirit by which he spake." Consequently they accused him of blasphemy, and he was brought before a hostile Council, where his face seemed "as it had been the face of an angel." Stephen's indignant reply to his accusers (Acts 7:2-54) only increased their fury. They "stopped their ears, and ran upon him with one accord, and cast him from the city, and stoned him."

But as he died Stephen called upon God, saying, "Lord Jesus, receive my spirit"; and then he forgave the stoners, crying in a loud voice, "Lord, lay not this sin to their charge. And when he had said this, he fell asleep." Such innocent suffering, with its priceless reward, was the single hope of an age whose victims were burned alive, strangled, mutilated, hung up by their hands, flogged, stabbed, poisoned, beheaded.

Inseparable from the lesson was the Mass. The nature of this service is known from another poem by Fortunatus, describing a ceremony at which Saint Germain himself officiated. In their majestic white robes the priests began their choral processions to the sanctuary. A corps of young deacons marched ahead with crosses and censers and sacred relics; then Bishop Germain, "a second Aaron," wearing his golden episcopal crown; then the singing priests, chanting the Glory of God, of Christ the King, of Stephen the Holy Martyr, raising their voices to the painted rafters, filling the nave with the black passionate music the Dark Age adored.

Chapter Three

THE SECOND CATHEDRAL: THE TRIUMPH

OF THE VIRGIN

A T THE END of the sixth century the full night of the Dark Age was upon France. In 584 King Chilperic was murdered in a lightless courtyard, and his widow, the cruel Fredegund, was immediately suspected of the crime; she frantically sought refuge in the Cathedral of Paris, the one place of safety she could find. Clotaire II followed Chilperic, and the civil war between cousins and brothers continued. The country was devastated while the descendants of Clovis wassailed with hornfuls of honey and absinthe at their military feasts.

In this perpetual midnight man reverted to an almost neolithic savagery and lost the bulk of his civilized arts. He huddled before the encroaching forest and scratched the earth with wooden implements. Because he could scarcely write he left no coherent record of his suffering and tragedy; but his crude expressions in stone speak clearly enough. In architecture he came to forget every useful lesson of the ancient world, so that, even if he had wished to construct truly, he could not. He had forgotten how to vault buildings in stone, and he had half forgotten how to carve. He had a certain feeling for decorative splendor, and a strength that was not in the least the strength of refinement, and nothing more. His religion was the only impulse that urged him to build, for in general his will was to destroy. His cities, like his architecture, declined; his politics, and every other social talent, vanished. A useful community project like the Pont du Gard would have overwhelmed him.

France became a rural anarchy, tormented by passing warriors. Yet some arts endured, and it is not odd that funerary sculpture was among the foremost. Tombs of important citizens, such as that of

Saint Agilbert, a Bishop of Paris who died about 680, reveal the artistic mood of the period as nothing else; indeed, little else survives. Agilbert's tomb, in the burial crypt of the Convent of Jouarre, of which his sister was abbess, carries a remarkable bas-relief of the Last Judgment. The carvings are battered, but a moving scene of Merovingian exaltation emerges from them nevertheless. The Savior is seated on a boldly fashioned throne, surrounded by the Elect; the Damned, who add terrible vivacity to the Last Judgments of the later Middle Age, are absent. In the Dark Age salvation rather than damnation was essential to the Church; and here the Elect, almost naked in loincloths and scarfs, stand in a calm, close-eyed trance, raising their arms to Heaven.

Amidst continuous violence only the Church was permanent, and the people of Paris never ceased to enlarge and embellish their Cathedral. By the first half of the seventh century, possibly before the end of the sixth, they erected two sister basilicas beside Saint Stephen's. The new churches were properly *con-cathedrals,* since they were under the immediate direction of the bishop; but the episcopal throne, the *cathedra* itself, remained in Saint-Etienne, near the stones of Stephen's martyrdom. One of the new basilicas was placed under the patronage of Saint Germain, a tremendous figure in local theology; the other was dedicated to the Holy Virgin.

This, about the year 600, is thought to have been the earliest shrine consecrated to Mary in Paris; yet the mother goddess had long been revered in France. Like her sisters who were adored in Etruria centuries before Christ and who would one day become the madonnas of the Italian Renaissance, she had been incorporated in the expanding symbolism of Christianity as it traveled westward from Asia. When it was that this universal goddess was first called Mary by the people of Gaul, no one can exactly say. There is evidence that the cult of the Virgin was practiced as early as the second century by the persecuted community of Saint Irenaeus at Lyon. The year 500 would seem a more suitable date, however, since churches began to be dedicated to her about that time, at Clermont, Poitiers, and elsewhere. Yet, in almost every region of France, clay, stone, or wooden figures of mothers have been found, shaped by a tradition which was strong five times five hundred years before then.

In the East, on the other hand, she was already an empress in 500.

Crowned with the imperial crown of Byzantium and robed more regally than any queen on earth, she ruled the Eastern Empire with a warm oriental flush of mystery. She was the patron saint of Constantinople and ruled the Byzantine world under a number of titles, the chief of which was Theotokos, Mother of God, accorded her by the Council of Ephesus in 431. But Christian worship of Mary goes much further back than the formalities at Ephesus: the magnificent Virgin and Child of the Santa Priscilla in Rome dates from the second century and the subterranean art of the Persecutions. By the fifth century the Virgin's image in itself had become miraculous, and after the Council of Ephesus it burst forth in gold on the walls of hundreds of basilicas. The Mother of God reigned in majesty in churches from Ravenna to Jerusalem, high above the master altar in the golden half-dome of the sanctuary.

The Virgin's image was carried to the extremities of the Mediterranean world at the mastheads of the Byzantine navy. It was under her auspices, for example, that the fleet of Heraclius left Carthage in 610 to depose Phocas at Constantinople. Similar voyages, at a time when a good breeze carried a vessel across the Mediterranean in ten days, to accept Gibbon's figure, brought Mary to France; and in the year 610 she almost certainly had her own church in Paris.

The next two hundred and fifty years conceal a titanic battle between Mary and Stephen for supremacy in the Cathedral. She fought with subtlety, charm, and grace, and her gains are barely perceptible in the old documents. Slowly her altar began to attract the multitude, and her miracles commenced to surpass those of the Protomartyr. Saint Germain was left behind, a very poor third, as the two giants contended. Wonderful tales were circulated of the Virgin's bounty and pity, her inexhaustible patience and strength. Her priests related that when the skeptical Apostle Thomas, who as usual had been absent while great events were occurring, denied her Resurrection and Assumption, he received her glittering girdle from Heaven as an answer to his doubts. This sash found its way into the Treasure of the Church of Paris, and gradually, before such arguments, Saint Stephen gave ground. In 775 a document actually placed Mary first among the Patrons of Paris, Stephen second, and Germain third.

For the moment, however, Stephen remained in command. His church was larger than Mary's, and local tradition gave him strong support. At Chartres, where the mother divinity has always ruled, Mary arrived from the East to a city that was exclusively hers, but Paris had belonged to Esus the Woodsman and the virile Taurus, and there the Virgin encountered vigorous male opposition. Her temple in Paris was at first probably a private chapel, or *cellula,* of the Bishop, and located near the episcopal palace for his special use, as elsewhere in France. It may have been no larger than the Merovingian crypt of Saint-Laurent of Grenoble, whose interior measures twenty-five by thirty-five feet at its widest points, a small room indeed.

Without doubt this tiny church of the Virgin was expanded and enriched during the seventh and eighth centuries; in the year 700 Queen Hermentrude presented it with a set of silver dishes, a crucifix of gold, and an illuminated missal worth twice as much as the other gifts combined. Perhaps the church was rebuilt several times. It exists only as a reappearing name in the ancient cartularies, a mysterious growing force in an age when Christianity itself was growing and strengthening, rising on a swell of human faith, and capable of miracles and convincing explanations. Architecturally, nothing can be said of Mary's primitive basilica. It was probably a smaller version of Stephen's, and in the beginning much less elaborate. At the time of Charlemagne's touchingly inadequate "renaissance," when after two centuries of anarchy there was an official attempt to revive arts and letters, the Basilica of Notre-Dame must have appeared as a brilliant younger sister to her venerable brother Saint-Etienne, for the two-hundred-and-fifty-year-old Cathedral was as stately and imposing as the Emperor.

The people of Paris probably saw Charlemagne only when he periodically passed through their town on his way to the wars, although, on occasion, he lingered to make gifts to their Church. Charles himself could scarcely read, and it is certain that his plans to restore classical culture affected them little. For one thing, the political center of gravity and the intellectual atmosphere of the court, such as it was, had shifted from the valley of the Seine to the Rhineland. The leading monasteries of France, such as Saint-Martin of Tours and Saint-Denis, and a few noble castles may have profited from the visits of foreign professors such as Alcuin, who came from

Britain, but the common folk knew little of these academic developments. There was local peace; there was the illusion of a strong government, although no one was more aware than the ordinary Parisian of how far from being centralized it actually was; and the people were more or less left alone to their daily toil on the lands of the Church or secular lords, to their amusements such as the hunt and the dance, and to the solace of their religion.

Life in Paris about 829, when the prelates of France held a Great Council in the Cathedral of Saint-Etienne, might have been pleasant enough. Compared with pre-Carolingian days, it must have seemed paradisaic. Marcel Poëte describes the town as prosperous, although still largely situated on the walled island, and surrounded by woods and cultivated fields. The air was clean, sanitation was better than is generally thought to have been possible, and the atmosphere was not at all urban but rural and close to nature.

In this early ninth-century setting of simplicity and strong faith the priests ruled with an absolute hand. The place of the Church in the everyday life of the people was enormous, and would have seemed so not only to the twentieth century but also to the Catholic twelfth. It dominated politics and the economy with equal vigor, controlling the business life of the community by its capital and governing by theocratic right. The Bishop was supreme. Assisted by a corps of priests and monks, he was the real lord of the city. *"Un être sacré,"* Poëte calls him, a sacred being who as often as not was sainted by popular suffrage as soon as he died. As the tie between Paris and the Crown loosened under the Rhenish Carolingians, his power increased progressively until he was a great secular noble as well as spiritual dictator. And the Pope in Rome was as distant as the Emperor at Aix-la-Chapelle.

True, there was a Count of Paris, who lived in the Merovingian fortress on the island, but his authority was negligible within the limits of the town. He administered only secular territories without the walls, over which he quarreled constantly with the Bishop—and usually lost. Inside the city the Bishop could not be challenged. The invisible weapon of excommunication was always by his side, and he could call down a miracle from Heaven if need be. The poor and ill were dependent upon him. Traders could not operate against his wish. He maintained the ramparts, armed the militia, and dispensed justice.

At the eastern end of the island it would be difficult to recognize the formidable group of churches, Chapter houses, cloisters, and Bishop's palace, at the time of the Council of 829, as the same religious establishment seen by Leudaste in 582. The Cathedral of Saint-Etienne, of course, would appear largely unchanged, except that its roof may have received a new coating of gilt, but its dependencies had greatly expanded. To the left of the Cathedral stood the circular Baptistère of Saint-Jean-le-Rond, dedicated, like every baptistery in France, to Saint John the Baptist; and near the baptistery would be found the main cloister and residences of the Cathedral Chapter. Behind Saint-Etienne—that is, on the emplacement of the present Cathedral—were the subordinate basilicas of Saint-Germain and Notre-Dame. The Virgin's church, which may still have possessed a special relationship with the Bishop, was probably located nearest the Seine, on whose bank rose the episcopal palace. This fortified château had been incorporated with the Gallo-Roman rampart, and was now a secular as well as temporal stronghold. Finally, completing the circle of the Cathedral, was the Hôtel-Dieu, founded by Saint Landry, Bishop of Paris, who died in 656, and consecrated to Saint Christopher, who prevented sudden death.

From either bank of the Seine the island must have appeared picturesque, a word that both French and American tourists employ today. Between its lordly extremes—the episcopal community on the east and the castle of the Count on the west—lay a cluster of humble dwellings, which held most of the city's population. To try to recapture the feeling of this lost ninth-century Paris, one must visit the ancient Cité at Carcassonne and stare at its twisting streets. The whole was surrounded by a wall, entered only by the two bridges, which were defended on either bank by a châtelet, ready for any emergency.

The most dire emergency was soon at hand. The Carolingian Empire was dissolving in the quicksands which had been its foundation, and after the briefest of respites the call to arms was again sounded. Down from Scandinavia swept the Norse pirates, clad in wild armor, worshiping the misty gods of the fjords, sailing hundreds of miles in boats shaped like ferocious birds. These savages, like a thousand Beowulfs, invaded the peaceful valley of the Seine, bellowing war songs, looting, burning, slaughtering. Again and again they carried the battle into the heart of the Ile de France, mounting the river in their long boats to sack Rouen and Mantes and destroy the church at Chartres. The French, defeated in the field, repeatedly bought their liberty with ransom, which only made the Normans think of returning to the rich country upstream.

Paris was a fort. The relics of Saint Germain and Saint Geneviève were brought from the abbeys for safekeeping within the walls. Then, in the coldest winter weather, the Normans were under the walls! They had set fire to the bridges and were scaling the ramparts. Rather than be put to the sword, the Parisians surrendered. Their defense had scarcely presented an obstacle to these hardy Normans, who now in the Christmas season—December 28, 856—were dictating terms on the island. And their terms were severe.

The Parisians elected to save three churches, all the Normans permitted them, in exchange for an immense sum of gold and silver —"*multa solidorum,*" says the chronicle. Their choice was interesting: the Cathedral of Saint-Etienne, which they evidently valued more highly than the Basilica of Notre-Dame; and the abbey churches of Saint-Denis and Saint-Germain-des-Prés. Every other church in and near the city, the Virgin's among them, was looted and burned. The town itself was pillaged, and the fortified palaces of the Count and the Bishop wrecked, for the Normans even then had a reputation for thoroughness.

The Parisians had only their religion to fall back on. And as they looked at the scorched walls of Saint-Etienne, standing alone where once there had been half a dozen basilicas and chapels, they may have reconsidered their parochialisms. Stephen, hitherto unconquerable, had been vanquished by the pagans. Perhaps the Parisians thought they had been neglecting stronger gods, perhaps not. In any case, they examined the remains of Mary's church, standing directly behind Stephen's, and, collecting what resources were left to them, with a determined municipal effort decided to erect a new cathedral in her honor. The Virgin, after three centuries in Paris, had triumphed in the midst of disaster.

The Normans returned to Paris in 861, and again in 865, to delay construction of Mary's Cathedral, but each time they were induced to leave by force of arms or force of money, probably by both. The city, says a poem of the period by Abbo, a monk of Saint-Germain-des-Prés, was now consecrated to the Virgin alone: *"Urbs in honore micat celsae sacrata Mariae";* and her Bishop, an extraordinary figure named Gozlin, was not only ruler of the inhabitants but also their military commander-in-chief. His lieutenant was the Count of Paris, Eudes Capet—remember the family name. Eudes fought like a lion and was much admired, but his power and influence did not approach that of the Bishop. Gozlin (the name has come down through the French and British aristocracies as Jocelin) was both a noble and a warrior, a statesman, diplomat, and scholar, as well as a very able prelate. Under his direct supervision and Mary's divine guidance, the Parisians were building fortifications as well as a church; and when the Normans arrived for the ultimate battle in November 885, the second Cathedral had been completed and Paris was at last equipped to repel the pagan assault.

An army of forty thousand Normans is said by Abbo to have appeared before Paris, and even if it was only half that size, it must have equaled the number of defenders. Goaded by their fierce and sarcastic women, the blond giants mounted attack after attack against the ramparts, their shields painted black and yellow, their conical helmets gleaming, their arms and faces bare, as they appear in Abbo's poem. Each time they were driven back, the dead pouring forth blood and the wounded howling. Once, when they opened a breach in a tower, the Normans stood momentarily face to face with a small group of French, Count Eudes in the center with sword in hand; but inexplicably the pagans hesitated when they could have stormed in and won. Then fire and darts showered down from overhead, and the opportunity was lost forever.

The siege dragged on for four years. Plague erupted from the carnage in the Cité, but the island held under the bombardment of the Norman engines. In their fury the invaders slaughtered the helpless. They murdered prisoners and sliced their bodies to pieces beneath the walls. At this sight, writes Abbo, Bishop Gozlin burst into tears and cried out to Mary: "Beloved Mother of the Redeemer, of the Salvation of the World, Star of the Sea more brilliant than all the stars of Heaven, hear my prayer with kindness. If it pleases Thee that I continue to celebrate the Mass, please ordain that this impious and ferocious, this hard, cruel, and atrocious enemy, who massacres captives, be himself snared in the nets of death!"

This appeal, called out from the ramparts by the weeping Bishop, tells more of ninth-century Christianity than all the Church histories. That it was heeded goes without saying. The Virgin replied immediately. She directed a flying shaft at a Norman, struck him mortally, and left him, ignominious, on the ground with his mouth open. No people could lose with such an ally. Gozlin himself was killed leading his troops a few months later, but his successor, Anscheric, brought the war to a victorious conclusion, and in 889 the city was free from fear for the first time in half a century.

Anscheric put only the finishing touches on the second Cathedral. Probably he did no more than terminate the program of decoration and enlarge the cloister. After the defeat in 856 the Parisians had worked quickly, and from the facts available it seems that the main body of the church was completed in ten or twelve years. The speed of construction, considering that the Normans were continually present, may indicate that the preceding basilica of the Virgin was not completely destroyed when the pagans burned it; it is possible that the walls remained intact. In any case, the project was enough advanced in 868 for Mary's church to receive the episcopal throne from Stephen's, and with it the translation of sacred relics. For when Saint-Etienne lost the seat of the Bishop, it also relinquished its most precious instruments of salvation, including a Nail from the True Cross, which Charlemagne had received from the Patriarch of Jerusalem and piously presented to the Church of Paris.

Gradually the importance of Saint-Etienne diminished. It became known rather affectionately in documents as the *"vetus ecclesia Sancti Stephani"*—the "old" Cathedral, and fell into disrepair. Henceforth almost every gift mentioned in the Cartulary was for the new Cathedral of Notre-Dame.

Whether this church was more beautiful than Saint-Etienne in its heyday, the most skilled archaeologist would hesitate to say. Probably not. The Parisians, if anything, were less able constructors in the ninth century than in the sixth. They were still content with vaults of wood, and their masonry remained a hashed *opus mixtum*. The Carolingian renaissance perhaps had started people thinking again on a monumental scale, but after the Merovingian nadir they scarcely could have relearned such techniques as existed at the break-up of the Western Empire. In ravaged Paris, particularly, traditions were conservative and dull; and as architecture the first Notre-Dame was certainly less interesting than Saint-Etienne, as Aix-la-Chapelle is less interesting than Ravenna.

Evidence for this assumption, of course, is rare. Not a stone, tile, morsel of glass, can be surely attached to the Carolingian Cathedral. Its massive foundations, which formerly existed beneath the choir and nave of Notre-Dame, have disappeared. But this much is sure: the Carolingian Cathedral stood on the same central axis as the present Notre-Dame and could have fitted easily into its great interior. It probably began near the center of the present nave, filled much of the present transept with its jutting wings, and terminated between the second and third bays of the choir, where it was stopped by the Gallo-Roman rampart of the island, and where traces of its apsidal foundations were found during the last century. At the roughest estimate it was sixty yards long, slightly longer than Saint-Etienne, and a little less than half the length of the present Cathedral. Its width remains a mystery.

Really, there is no way of knowing what it looked like. Probably the traditional basilican form was conserved, if only because of the poverty of ninth-century Paris in material and imaginative resources. But revolutionary pre-Romanesque plans were cropping up elsewhere. The most original naturally were found at rural abbeys such as Centula or Fleury, where intellectuals had retreated for calm and safety; but the cities too had their share of interesting churches. At Chartres, where a new cathedral was also replacing one destroyed by the Normans, there was an innovation from Auvergne: an ambulatory that enabled the pilgrim to make a tour of the famous relics in the apse. Slowly, with such developments, a national architecture was creeping to life, evolving along with a national religion, language, and culture.

And now every impulse is drawn toward the great twelfth-century flowering of French life and French art, just over the horizon. And splitting that horizon, here in Paris, is the abbey tower of Saint-Germain-des-Prés, which still looks down on the existentialist cafés of the old faubourg and is fast approaching its one-thousandth birthday, which is more than the cafés may ever hope to do. This austere old tower and the nave behind it, both of them excessively restored and disfigured, may be dated roundly at the year 1000, a perfect date for a history of any sort. Actually they may not have been completed until 1010 or 1021, neither year is sure, when the new church was dedicated by the again prosperous abbey. For Saint-Germain, like the Cathedral, had devoted protectors in the rising family of Capets, who had begun to call themselves hereditary Kings of France although a score of powerful barons laughed at their presumption.

Much had occurred since the triumph of the Normans one hundred and fifty years before. The final blow, Lewis Mumford has called the Norse invasions, and the first step toward recovery. Men organized the harsh give-and-take of feudalism from the simple need for survival. The cities learned to defend themselves, and soon would insist on their rights as virtually independent political units. Trade routes were re-established, and, thanks to the Italian war fleets, merchant ships were again crossing the Mediterranean to Asia Minor. Spain was being slowly reconquered in the first of all the Crusades. A system of pilgrimage routes covered France like a net, leading to Rome and Jerusalem, to Compostela, to the Mont-Saint-Michel in Peril of the Sea. In Hungary the converted Magyars were doing their best to hold off new pagan invaders from the steppes. Gradually, painfully, stability was born. Business revived and theology flourished, and it might be interesting to trace the connections between the two, as radicals have attempted since the Reformation. Population increased. Every art found itself on the upswing.

It was not a paradise. The poor starved and wandered naked. When they rebelled the nobility amputated their hands and feet, as Merovingians might have done. A multitude of tiny lords oppressed the weak and hindered the strong, and for most of the eleventh century, in fact, kept the Capet king immobile at Paris. The clergy was venal. The principle of dissent was discovered, and immediately declared a crime. The essentials of civilized life, as understood today, were lacking in the richest castle. To travel from Paris to Orléans was to pass through a wilderness peopled by brigands and madmen loose in the woods.

Yet when the soldiers of the abbey climbed the new tower of Saint-Germain, they could have looked out and seen a vast program of experimentation underway. After the year 1000, in the phrase of the monk Radulfus Glaber—Ralph the Beardless—France was suddenly cloaked "with a white robe of churches." In the royal domain of France, in Burgundy, in Auvergne, in Provence and Languedoc, in Poitou and the Dordogne, above all in Christian Normandy, men were building and carving and making startling progress in original techniques. To be sure, some areas lagged. The Rhineland, for one, would never regain all its lost ground in the medieval race for beauty. But each region had its particular strengths and loveliness. At Paris, significantly, the new architecture stood side by side with the old at Saint-Germain-des-Prés. The formidable abbey tower was both a religious and military feat of daring, but the adjoining nave, in spite of the novelty of its sculptures, held timidly to the archaic basilican formula. It was roofed in wood, like a church of the Dark Age.

Vaulting in stone—vaulting of wide central vessels—was the most admirable discovery of the eleventh century. In the South, men for the first time in ages looked carefully at the ruins of great Rome and commenced throwing roofs of stone across the naves of their new churches. Burgundy, which for another century would lead the Ile de France as a home of the imagination, in churches such as Tournus, was perhaps even more precocious than the Midi. But for every revolutionary development in structure—for vaulting, buttressing, equilibrium, and pure monumentality—as in political organization and military genius, it is necessary to travel to the bold western peninsula, where the Normans, caught with their terrible Duke Rollo in the same mysterious webs of Christianity that had ensnared every barbarian invader since Clovis, were now building churches of their own.

Westward from Paris the first stop would be Chartres, where a crypt which supports the present church like a toy is all that remains of the cathedral dedicated by Saint Fulbert in 1020. Then, from Chartres, the road leads directly to the shrine of the Archangel Michael on the island in the sea, where, in 1023, there was a church building on the Mount. From Mont-Saint-Michel the way is clear to a dozen cities and country abbeys, to Coutances, Jumièges, Avranches, and Bernay, or Rouen and Lisieux and Evreux, where important construction was in progress in the first half of the century. Everywhere, as Duke William prepared his adventure against Harold, the Normans were attacking Heaven with their spires and mining the earth with their crypts. They learned architecture quickly and thoroughly, as they learned all things, and pushed off as fear-lessly in every enterprise as the rugged oaken boats in the tapestry at Bayeux. At Bayeux too, before 1047, a new cathedral was begun, and beneath the northern tower is one of the oldest true ogive vaults in Europe. The major Norman undertakings, however, were reserved for their new capital at Caen, which William and his Queen Mathilda endowed in 1064, two years before the Conquest, with monuments that are still overpowering in ambition and execution: the abbey churches of Saint-Etienne and the Trinité. Through their twin-towered façades and spacious interiors, largely completed before 1100, the route opens wide on the France of the Gothic Transition, and will lead, in sixty years, to Notre-Dame of Paris.

"the renewal of all things"

And the earth was without form, and void; and darkness was upon the face of the deep. . . .

And God said, Let there be light: and there was light.

And God saw the light, that it was good: and God divided the light from the darkness.

GENESIS 1:2-4

Chapter Four

DAWN IS A lovely moment along the Loire. There are few places in the world where the day begins with such freshness and tranquil strength. Quite suddenly, in the early morning light, the reflection of birches appears in the water near shore, and over the birches the heavy shoulder of a castle, or a church spire, reflected in the clear stream as in a photograph. The slender river and the gentle country through which it flows are French as nothing else is French, just as the language of its people is the purest to be found in the entire nation. Well back from shore, the stone farm buildings stand in groups, set at handsome angles with each other, the slate roofs wet with dew. All is solid here, in the center of Gaul, and built to endure, like the granite well in the farmyard or the bullock waiting patiently to be harnessed. But the solidity is not at all the morose Norman lasting power or toughness of the Auvergnat sort. It is the large health of a friendly and generous people who are pleasant the year round. There is a happy energy here, like that of the rooster who at this moment steps across the sill and crows.

Some thirty miles above Orléans, on the southern bank, is the château of Sully-sur-Loire, a strong point in the region since the Romans. The castle, like the country it governs, is rich with history, and beneath the superb wooden roof of its great hall are memories that range from Jeanne d'Arc to the young Voltaire; but as far back as the present fortress goes, to the middle of the fourteenth century, it is a good two hundred years later than the period when France was alive with the spirit of the First Crusade and waiting for the Second, and a rugged twelfth-century donjon stood in the wide moats. This grim earlier castle was the seat of the Sires de Sully, who, although ruling barons of an extensive fief, were nevertheless vassals of the Bishop of Orléans, and compelled to support the prelate's litter on their shoulders during his investiture. The Bishop in turn owed homage to the King in the complex feudal mosaic. If, in the first decades of the twelfth century, any man of the region was asked where he lived, he would have answered to his first allegiance: the Sullias. Only with prompting would he have said the Orléanais, and it was much too early for him to sense his growing attachment to France.

About the year 1120—the exact date is missing—in the village of Sully or on one of the estates nearby, certainly not in the castle, a boy was born to peasant parents, who named him Maurice in honor of the martyred commander of the Theban Legion. Little is known of the family except that it was common and poor, but not necessarily bound to serfdom. The mother's name only has been found in an ancient obituary: Umbergie, or perhaps Umbergia, as humble as a radish compared with Eleanor or Alix. Her son eventually became one of the great self-made churchmen of the century—he rose to be Bishop of Paris and built Notre-Dame.

Information is sparse for Maurice's childhood. There is no way of discovering when he first left Sully or where he acquired his earliest education. It is not hard to guess. In the Middle Age the one avenue of success for an ambitious commoner, in theory if not always in practice, was the Church. The boy must have turned to it as early as he could. A short five miles away, on the opposite bank of the river, was the Abbey of Fleury, Saint-Benoît-sur-Loire, one of the oldest foyers of Christian learning in Europe. In accordance with the Rule of their patron, Saint Benedict, whose bones were the treasure of their church, the monks of Saint-Benoît took it upon themselves to educate the young. If Maurice did attend their school, he learned more than Latin. The curriculum of Fleury was extensive and prepared men of the world. The abbey also furnished an architectural lesson that is a liberal education in itself.

Except for the incomparable edifice at Cluny, Saint-Benoît was the greatest church in the North when Maurice was a boy, and a pilgrimage shrine as venerated as the crypt at Chartres. The monument was new, and indeed not yet finished, for work on the nave would continue throughout the century. But in the completed rear of the church—the broadly massed apse and transept, with the heavy

lantern rising at the croisée, and a smaller tower on either side—
Maurice could see the Romanesque in full triumph. The interior was
equally lordly and filled with sculptures that still delight and amaze.
And at the front of the church, begun a hundred years earlier, was
the monumental porch whose heavy piers and robust round arches
awed the pious child approaching on the plain.

To arrive at an understanding of the religious mood of the period
it is essential to visualize the intellectual and material strength of this
famous monastery in the first half of the twelfth century; to see the
long lines of pilgrims waiting to be cured and saved by the relics of
Saint Benedict, drawn by the same attraction that compelled Philip I
to be buried there rather than at Saint-Denis in 1108; and to appreciate the theocratic force of Fleury in the surrounding territory,
dwarfing the power of the Sires de Sully. It was the great final moment for monastic life. The most impressive buildings of the time all
belonged to abbeys: Cluny, Conques, Moissac, Saint-Sernin of Toulouse, Saint-Etienne of Caen. Such monks as Suger and Abélard and
Peter the Venerable dominated the artistic, intellectual, and political
spirit of the first half of the century in the same way that the most
dedicated monk of all, Saint Bernard, launched the Second Crusade
in 1146 with a passionate address from below the abbey church of
Vézelay.

Yet the centralized political power that the monks had helped
create, the Capetian Dynasty that they had sustained for one hundred
and fifty years, was now destroying all reason for the superb rural
existence of the abbeys. Now the cities would have their turn. They
were asserting themselves everywhere, demanding charters of bourgeois enfranchisement, from Amiens to Poitiers. A rise in trade and
manufacture, safety in travel, the growth of guilds and banking, the
new dignity of the royal house, were simultaneously causes and effects
of a revolutionary atmosphere in France. A national sentiment was
developing, and with it would come the cathedrals. No city and no
cathedral would reflect the period of consolidation more faithfully
than Paris and Notre-Dame. In the first half of the twelfth century
every road led to the capital of France.

Louis le Jeune took the throne in 1137, a good enough year to
assume that Maurice left the Loire to attend the schools at Paris.
The young sovereign, who, like Maurice, was only seventeen years

old at this time, would one day become a fast friend of the future bishop; but in 1137 Louis VII was too busy with his high-spirited bride, Eleanor of Aquitaine, and too occupied with a rebellion by the citizens of Orléans, to have noticed, as he rode past with his armored nobles, the penniless student going to Paris on foot.

The roads were safer than at any time since Charlemagne; still, it was not yet wise to travel alone, and for security Maurice probably joined a band of pilgrims going north from Fleury. The first leg of the journey followed the river to Orléans, and then the party turned almost due north on the antique Roman road, the same route to Paris that Leudaste had taken five hundred and fifty years earlier. Then, as now, it must have been a great temptation to continue down the Loire toward Tours and Angers, through the delicious Vouvray country, but Maurice, anxious to begin his studies, could do no more than wistfully glance downstream. Few of the famous châteaux of the Loire were yet built. There was the little stronghold at Beaugency, which provides an idea of the castle Maurice knew at home at Sully, and there were the fortresses at Loches and Chinon, but the pleasure houses of the French Renaissance—Blois and Chambord and Chenonceaux—were not dreamed of. They cannot be related to Notre-Dame except for purposes of contrast, and that contrast, in structure and motive, may be damaging to the later work.

North to Paris then. It is not hard to picture the pilgrims with whom Maurice traveled. The roads of Europe were crowded with them for five hundred years. The same general types were extant when Geoffrey Chaucer set out for Canterbury from the Tabard Inn, and Maurice's companions may have related the same fabliaux as the Reeve and the Miller to pass the time. North of Orléans they were on the great thoroughfare that belonged to "Monsieur Saint Jacques"—Saint James of Compostela, whose famous shrine was on the Atlantic coast of Spain. Returning pilgrims proudly displayed their cockleshells, attaching them to their leather pouches as amulets against ill fortune; and they carried staffs, as Saint James did in his statues, along the route. With these sacred emblems protecting them they traveled the length of France, everyone on foot save nobles and wealthy merchants and the important clergy, stopping at hostels and abbeys, praying at the wayside shrines, finding their way at dusk to the sound of friendly bells.

Some pilgrims had been farther than Spain. They had trekked to twelfth-century Rome, which was without question a City of God; to the lofty shrine of Saint Michael on Monte Gargano, where the Archangel's footprints were vivid in the rock; to Venice, which not only possessed the relics and church of San Marco but ships to transport voyagers to Palestine. Those who made this greatest of pilgrimages, by sea from Italy or overland along the Danube, and lived to return were privileged to carry the most sacred emblem of all: an image of the cross on which the Redeemer had perished. Compared to the possible misfortunes of the journey, death held no terror. For to die marching toward Grace was to be certain of Grace. On the western door of Autun, where the Elect are lifted upward through the floor of Paradise by immense angels, are seen two smiling human creatures, ravished with joy and wonder, stepping toward Heaven over the exotic flowers of the route. They are naked except for charming little caps and their shoulder-slung purses blazoned with the Cockle of Compostela and the Cross of Jerusalem.

Talking, looking, poking into every curiosity along the way, reflecting on what he had seen and singing patriotic epics such as the *Song of Roland,* the pilgrim learned. From Chartres and from Saint-Benoît, from Limoges and Bordeaux, new travelers poured onto the roads. For such famous fêtes as that of the Virgin at Le Puy they came by the thousands, to climb the steep rocks and sleep in the nave of the church. They fervently stopped, as they had for centuries, at the shrine of Saint-Martin of Tours; they made the marvelous excursion to Mont-Saint-Michel on its island in the sea. They were joined by worldly merchants, whose long business trips were only incidentally religious. They discussed the East with Crusaders who spoke knowingly of Byzantium. After Roland, Alexander the Great was their favorite literary figure, now that he too had become a feudal knight. All the past was suffused, transformed, and exalted by the limitless Christian religion. Constantine and Charlemagne emerged as contemporaries, a pair of venerable and friendly twelfth-century sovereigns. The world was opening, enlarging, discovering its capacities. The gods were everywhere, symbolizing everything, and their oracles could once again answer every question that was properly put.

All this the pilgrims carried with them—and more: an additional something which scholars are still pleased to call naïf. Whatever it was—and the indefinable quality was never more purely expressed than in the radiant faces of the Elect at Autun—it built churches of a bewildering beauty and bewitching youth. It sang in allegro, like a spring or a bird.

Possibly the fresh twelfth-century energy sprang in part from the wilderness. The land through which Maurice and the pilgrims traveled was still largely uncleared. The route scarcely resembled a Roman road. Timbers were thrown across the muddiest places, as in a corduroy road in the American West. The stretch from Orléans to Paris was crude and fearful; from necessity some of the party were armed and all were vigilant, terrified by real and imagined ogres in the dark woods.

Danger existed, yet it was impossible not to detect a pioneer spirit abroad. Almost every *Villeneuve* dates from this period. New towns were being founded everywhere, hacked from the forest like settlements in Daniel Boone's Kentucky. Liberated and escaped serfs were commencing new lives where their former masters could not reclaim them. The King issued generous charters to the new communities and demanded their undivided allegiance in return. The Bishop's Men and the King's Men collected tithes and charged tolls, and both incidentally patrolled the road against brigands. Where a noble had poisoned an area with rapacity, the royal forces laid siege to his donjon, inevitably took it, and dismantled the towers.

Halfway between Orléans and Paris, the frontier town of Etampes was an impressive example of the twelfth-century will to construct. To call Etampes a frontier town, though it is now situated in the heart of the modern Republic, is not to exaggerate. It was the bastion of the southern boundary of Capetian France: the man who held Etampes held Paris. But Etampes was also an outpost on the artistic frontier. When Maurice visited it, four important churches were building within the walled town, as well as a massive château on the dominating hill outside the ramparts.

The medieval verve of Etampes has degenerated into a backwater sleepiness, but fortunately what remains of the twelfth-century city is as exciting as the day it was built. From far off is sighted the beautiful spire of the Collegiate Church of Notre-Dame, a pinnacle of pale gray stone that has been a landmark for eight hundred years. It

Sketch of original flèche destroyed in 1792
(Collection Gilbert, Carnavalet. *Joly*)

belongs to the same family of *flèches* as the old tower at Chartres, and if it is not as perfectly conceived or built on so grand a scale as its taller brother, it is nevertheless a masterpiece in its own right. The clocher at Etampes lifts four-sided above the roofs of the town, narrows slightly at the belfry story, and then flies upward in a light fantasy of gables and pointed corner turrets that mask the transition into a single octagonal spire of grace.

This is French. The flèche is so different from what is found south of the Loire in the middle of the century that its novelty astonishes. This is a new architectural world. The motive of transition from four to eight sides, merging and rising to soar as a lance of imagination in the sky, is particularly welcome and charming. Although every arch is round and the sculptural detail archaic in tone, the tower is no longer truly Romanesque but, as its weightless structure implies, the Gothic Transition. Where the Romanesque stops and the Gothic begins in such a work is impossible to say. The question is as delicate as the light which plays upon the steeple. Happily, academic terms did not concern the artist who built it. For him it was the *new* architecture, and nothing more; he did not have professional art historians in mind when he drew up his plans, and, like all great creations, his does not classify easily.

Perhaps the first architectural lesson at Etampes does not belong to the church but to the castle. The burly donjon, called the Tour Guinette, is dated by decoration which was carved during the second quarter of the century, precisely when Maurice went north to Paris. Today it is a shell, a thick-walled ruin through which a search must be conducted for the secrets of its vanished interior, such as the crossed pair of ogives that supported the vaulting in the round chamber of the castellan. The traces that remain of these strong arches should satisfy any doubt that the fundamental purpose of the ogive was structural rather than stylistic, as some claim. In the plain-spoken military architecture of the castle there was no need for frills or idealized vertical line. What was wanted was support, and the ogive provided it. (Fig. 2.)

Etampes is thirty-five miles from Paris, and from the battlements of the castle Maurice could have taken a long view of the forested territory that surrounded the capital. Woodsmen have been clearing the Ile de France since the time of the Gallic god Esus, but there are

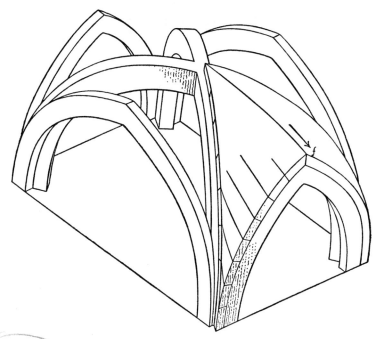

Fig. 2. Schema of a crossing of ogives. The arrow shows the lateral line of force which exerts a strong thrust, but which the eye might overlook. (After Choisy.)

still enough big oaks and dense thickets to give an impression of wildness. Until a few years ago boar were hunted near Etampes—heads of the tusked monsters are mounted in cafés—and the newspapers speak of lovers who elope to the woods and hide there from their parents, as Aucassin and Nicolette did. No large modern city has been so fortunate as Paris in keeping its surrounding woodland. On weekdays, at least, it is possible to camp in utter privacy within twenty miles of the capital, in the Bois de Meudon or near Saint-Germain-en-Laye. In the twelfth century these woods were as wild as the far Sierras and filled with wolves, bear, and leaping stags. The forest continued to the gates of Paris, where a new world began for Maurice.

Chapter Five

PARIS IN GOTHIC TRANSITION: SUGER
AND SAINT-DENIS

*t*HE ROMAN road swept out of the forest and over the hill of Sainte-Geneviève into the most exciting capital in the West. Paris was a crossways rather than a blind terminus. Two great routes, the road and the river, crossed east and west, north and south, from Champagne to England, from Flanders to Provence. Dozens of secondary roads and streams also led to the city from every point on the horizon. Paris lay like a pool of energy where the currents met. The long era of stagnation was over, and an epoch of dynamism at hand. The Ile-de-la-Cité was beginning to realize its natural position as the center of France. A new power concentrated on the fortified island, where the Palace and the Cathedral stood, and the size and scale of each building indicated a social importance which would increase mightily during the next one hundred years. At the same time the Parisians would forever abandon the timid security of the island. The capital was breasting outward to either side in faubourgs, which, in the year 1140, were not yet walled. The rural Left Bank, whose schools would soon be called a university, was covered with vineyards and farms; the commercial Rive Droite was beginning to be known as the Ville. Paris was booming, in new ideas and trade. Pack trains of goods, wagonloads of produce, barges filled with salt and grain, came to the busy market and left as laden as they entered. A new class had arisen, the bourgeoisie. Population was doubling with each generation, and the people were building with feverish haste to keep pace with the expansion.

This was the Paris to which Maurice came to study—the "oven," as one contemporary called it, in which the world's intellectual bread was baked. The Left Bank and the Cité were crammed with thinkers and artists. Five thousand students thronged the schools, arguing, fighting, shouting, singing, drinking, sleeping with respectable men's wives. The outrageous Latin they spoke has given its name to the quarter in which their successors still crowd the cafés, armed with Sartre instead of swords, but Latin then was often the easiest tongue in which scholars could converse. The students were German, Spanish, English, Italian, as well as French; when they came from the Midi they spoke an unintelligible Langue d'Oc; and when they came from Brittany they chanted a melodious tongue that was better for songs and curses than rational discussion. Latin it was then, and the Latin Quarter roared with argumentative life.

In the twelfth century even the most unorthodox schools belonged to the Church. They were scattered up and down the Mont-Sainte-Geneviève, where any clerk with authorization from the chancellor of the Cathedral could set up his own classroom. He taught any variety of subjects he wished: theology, philosophy, jurisprudence, belles-lettres; and if he had something of interest to say, as many as two or three thousand students might crowd to hear his lectures, and pay for the privilege. Saint Bernard called this irregular academic city a "Babylon" and invited the students to join him in the solitudes of Clairvaux; but only twenty seem to have followed, and this alone indicates that the lectures were fascinating. Perhaps, as Bernard charged, they were also heretical. A young man who hoped to rise in the Church may well have been wary of the avant-garde; he would be more prudent to attend the Cathedral School in the cloister of Notre-Dame.

This Notre-Dame was of course the three-century-old basilica that replaced the one destroyed by the Normans. Maurice must have been shocked and touched when he saw it, since it could not compare with Saint-Benoît-sur-Loire or the new church at Etampes. Its wooden ceilings, its rude sculptures, its coarse masonry, made it unworthy to serve as the shrine of the Virgin of Paris. The Cathedral was hopelessly out of date and much too small for a building age. On feast days thousands were turned from the doors, and the pressure within must have been intolerable. The hysteria of modern stadium crowds should remove all doubt of medieval accounts of packed masses in which women fainted and men held them aloft to breathe. The expanding population required a˙cathedral five times larger. Beyond this, the profusion of wood—in a structure lighted by candles and open lamps—was a hazard. Carolingian Notre-Dame was a *"monument historique,"* redolent with antiquity, but an encumbrance for a new Paris.

The twelfth century, by the time Maurice arrived in the capital about 1137, had already displayed impatience with the aged basilica. In 1124 the King and the Bishop shared the expense of a new roof, built of wood and covered with tiles; and shortly afterward an effort was made to renovate the entire building. This work was financed by Etienne de Garlande, archdeacon of the Chapter, and a more unprincipled and rapacious politico-churchman is not to be found in all the Middle Age. He stood at the opposite end of the moral spectrum from the man who was at this moment replacing him as chief counselor to the Crown, Abbot Suger of Saint-Denis. Politics should be taken into account, for they usually concern art. How limited Etienne was in fundamental taste and vision—and he represented a type—would be seen instantly if the Notre-Dame he restored were erect to be compared with the remarkable church built under Suger's administration of the Abbey Royal. The new Saint-Denis made Carolingian Notre-Dame forever obsolete, and whatever improvements Etienne sponsored were written off as a total loss by the next generation. He could have done little more than decorate and temporarily preserve the dilapidated monument.

The rest of the episcopal community was in as poor condition as the Cathedral, although its holdings had now expanded to cover the entire eastern end of the island (Fig. 1, p. 33). In front of the Cathedral was the Merovingian Basilica of Saint-Etienne-le-Vieux, a full six hundred years old, fallen in ruins, roofless, and unused. Nearby were the Hôtel-Dieu and the episcopal palace, both scarcely changed since the great siege of the Normans. North of Notre-Dame was the cloister, which in no way resembled the tranquil retreat of a monastery. Its boisterous school was the first true University of Paris, with hundreds of students learning theology in the open courts.

It seems likely that Maurice, who was to make his career in the Cathedral Chapter, studied here. But it is equally possible that he enrolled at the school of the intellectual Abbey of Saint-Victor, which had close ties with the Cathedral and for which Maurice felt strong affection the rest of his life. Today Saint-Victor is destroyed, and the Jardin des Plantes and the Halles aux Vins stand on its site; but when Maurice knew it, the abbey was a powerful walled establishment, heavily endowed by the Capets and made richer still by the endowments of its faculty.

In these years about 1140, when Maurice was beginning his studies, Paris was a town of fifty or sixty thousand people. The Left Bank may still have been rural, with its schools rising in the midst of vines and wheatfields, and the forest standing darkly beyond the crest of the hill; but the Abbeys of Saint-Germain-des-Prés, Saint-Victor, and Sainte-Geneviève were storehouses of wealth. Hundreds of serfs worked their fields and did chores within the walled properties. Their barns were loaded with produce, for a monastery was a serious business establishment that marketed grain for a profit. Beneath the walls of each abbey clustered a village of perhaps a hundred dwellings, which stood apart from the main body of the town. The only fortification on the Rive Gauche, aside from the defenses of the monasteries, was a châtelet guarding the Petit Pont.

This bridge was surmounted by the houses of intellectuals, and to cross it to the Cité was like passing through a street of the mind, where marvelous talk could be heard in every doorway. One leading dialectician went so far as to take the bridge's name for his own: Adam de Petit-Pont. But beneath the bridge—and this is revealing—were the mills of the abbeys, great grinding machines that were powered by the Seine. Moored alongside were barges, which carried the finished grain downstream to Rouen; and if the bargemen occasionally had reason to complain of the latrines that were installed on the bridge above them, the Parisians did not. The latrines, emptying directly into the river, were a perfectly reasonable way to provide sanitation. Lewis Mumford and other open-minded critics have perceptively commented on the general cleanliness and wholesome atmosphere of the medieval city. It was no more a dark pool of filth than old-fashioned country villages today in France, and its odors were scarcely more disagreeable than a farm's. Its baths were used for bathing, and did not become "stews" until the Renaissance. There were open squares and gardens, and the air was fresh, something which cannot be said for the slums that now occupy the historic neighborhoods.

The Ile-de-la-Cité, the kernel of France, was a microcosm of the total scheme of feudal society. Belted by its antique rampart, the island was divided equally between Church and Crown, the two separated by the central commercial street that ran from bridge to bridge. Eventually the merchant's thoroughfare would widen until it absorbed the Palace and the Cathedral, but then the Middle Age would be over. In 1140 it was comparatively narrow, and called the Juiverie, because of the fifty-odd Jewish families who lived in this most strategic of mercantile locations, with the synagogue facing the busy road. Although they had suffered in the past, and were to be persecuted again before the end of the century, the Jews were enjoying a calm and prosperous respite under tolerant Louis le Jeune.

The eastern end of the Cité was dominated by the Cathedral; the western half belonged to the Capets. The royal stronghold on the site of the present Palais de Justice had been enlarged since the Norman invasion. The Capets cherished and improved the castle continually, for, more than any single holding, it symbolized their transformation of a sprawling suzerainty into a united kingdom. Philip Augustus, who at last made the theoretical national realm a reality, also made the first step from the island when he created the Louvre about 1200. But none of the Capets would ever abandon the family fortress in the Cité. Under their rule the Louvre remained what Philip Augustus planned it to be: the key outer defense of Paris. In the full Capetian power of the thirteenth century, Saint Louis lived by preference in the Palace on the Ile, and he built the Sainte-Chapelle in its great court. At the end of the dynasty his grandson Philip the Fair, king from 1285 to 1314, still lived there, and constructed the Conciergerie. It was this rugged medieval castle, and not the Louvre, that symbolized government while Notre-Dame was rising; and from its battlements the Capets carefully supervised the creation of the Cathedral a few hundred yards away. The Louvre could not tempt the Capets. Properly it is the home of the Valois kings, as Versailles is the home of the Bourbons.

From the Cité the business energy of the Juiverie spilled over the Grand Pont to the Right Bank, which has never since lost its commercial character. Its guilds and corporations had begun to direct France economically in the same way that the Palace on the island had started to rule politically. It was an immense market-place. The narrow streets were lined with the elegant shops of merchants. The squares were loud with the cries of fishmongers and vegetable hawkers. Meat was sold in the Boucherie. The Halles already stood where the great glass and iron sheds stand today. Off to the right the Knights Templar were establishing the Paris Temple, one day to become a colossal amalgam of chivalry, religion, and finance, and the richest bank in the West. Beyond the Temple, in the fields, was the fortified priory of Saint-Martin-des-Champs, founded ages earlier by the saintly embrace on the highway. There was a cemetery farther off, and a leprosarium, and a fairground for annual festivals; and across the marshy plain rose the Hill of Montmartre with its abbey at the summit.

Such was Paris in the middle of the twelfth century. A treasure has been lost in its perished vernacular architecture, the homes of ordinary people, which invariably provide a better indication of the health of a community than its public monuments. Imperial Rome, in the age of the corn riots, was largely a bitter slum, with a wild rabble huddled in its tenements. Twelfth-century Paris was in many ways a more pleasant dwelling place for the majority of the populace. Hundreds of simple and lovely dwellings went up at this time, and to judge from fragments of twelfth-century homes elsewhere, in such towns as Vézelay, they were surprisingly well lighted and practical places to live.

The homes are gone, but happily vestiges remain of the churches. For a small city, Paris had a staggering amount of religious architecture: perhaps two hundred parish churches, chapels, priories, and oratories, not to count abbatial buildings and Cathedral dependencies that served non-religious purposes. It is amazing how little is intact, spared by the taste and violence of later ages. On the Left Bank, except for the oldest portions of Saint-Germain-des-Prés, there is only the base of the "Tour Clovis" of the Abbey of Sainte-Geneviève, now part of the Lycée Henri IV; not the Gothic upper portions, mind you, but only the foundations and first story. The monuments in the Latin Quarter generally considered very old—

Saint-Julien-le-Pauvre and Saint-Séverin—are comparatively not so at all. Saint-Julien was begun after Notre-Dame, about 1170, and there is not a visible stone in Saint-Séverin from before 1200.

On the island, where dozens of churches stood, destruction has been even more tragic. Now there is only the little Chapel of Saint-Aignan off the rue de Colombe, dated at 1120, which is now forgotten and used as a storeroom by an antique dealer. Its heavy groin vaults are invaluable as an example of Parisian art before it swung upward in the Transition.

On the Right Bank, luck is somewhat better. Hidden in the apse of Saint-Germain-l'Auxerrois, the fine late-Gothic church at the rear of the Louvre, is the formidable base of another Romanesque tower; nearby, at Saint-Martin-des-Champs, is a much richer discovery: the chancel of a church in full Gothic Transition—one of the most interesting in Paris. Here, for the first time within the city, the ogive was used according to its potentialities, the strong, slender lines running upward to give a fluid grace to the apse. When the great choir of Notre-Dame was planned in 1163, its architect looked very carefully at the ogival vaulting of Saint-Martin, severely criticizing its faults, which are many, and admiring its precocity. For this church is young. It was built between 1130 and 1142, and was the most elaborately modern piece of architecture in Paris when Maurice arrived—a small monument, full of devices to hide its awkwardness, but a crucial one.

It is a short excursion from Saint-Martin to Montmartre, where at the crest of the butte the tiny church of Saint-Pierre is now overshadowed by the dome of Sacré-Coeur. If for no other reason, this neglected structure, dating from 1137-1144, is made imposing by the proximity of the white Basilique. Sacré-Coeur, which shows the full artistic capacity of modern Catholicism, performs a greater service by placing in relief the beauties of the unassuming monument beside it.

And here, from the top of Montmartre, circles the wonderful city: Paris lighting its lamps in the smoky dusk, shrugging its shoulders at the moon. The Cathedral, Saint-Sulpice, the Panthéon, are toy buildings far across the Seine. There are dark chuggings in the railway yards. The Tour Eiffel has vanished, and a red signal hangs alone in the sky. And neon Paris, vanquished, nervous, formal in the twilight, takes its apéritif glass and drinks.

Imagine the green Paris of Maurice, and the human ease with which it accepted evening. Imagine its ancient Cathedral, its granite Palace, its churches and homes, its schools and mighty abbeys. And the boy walking through the courtyards at evening, excited, talking, learning, looking, staying up late. The conversation was filled with politics and naïve theology and architecture, especially the vast enterprise of Abbot Suger, who, a mile on the far side of Montmartre, where it now hides invisible among the factories, was rebuilding the royal basilica of Saint-Denis.

II

On a rise in the fields, commanding a wide view of the Seine, the Abbey of Saint-Denis was a living symbol of the grand medieval alliance between Church and Crown. It was guarded by tawny battlements, filled with wealth, a religio-political fortress that dominated the French Middle Age. For here, at the royal monastery, from time immemorial to the twelfth century, had resided the sacred franchise of the sovereign. The Capets were anointed and crowned at Reims, and after victory offered thanks to the Lord in the Cathedral of Paris, but in the dark crypt of Saint-Denis, where the bones of the Patron Martyr were encased in a marvelous shrine, lay the secret of their strength. They governed France as vassals of this saint, were girt with his blessed sword, and in battle charged forth beneath his Oriflamme. And when kings died, with rare exceptions they were buried near Denis in the basilica. Later the kings forgot Saint-Denis and came to hate its medieval architecture, and the alliance ceased. The people too, over the centuries, forgot the vanished wonder of the abbey and that it had ever meant more than pure oppression. Then the people rose like Hercules, devastated the Augean stable of the clergy, and crushed the king who, like Antaeus, had lost touch with the earth.

The Middle Age had few illusions about the political nature of Saint-Denis. "This place has been of royal dignity from ancient times," remarked Saint Bernard bitterly in 1127; "it has served for the legal business of the court and for the soldiery of the King; without hesitation or deceit there were rendered unto Caesar those things which are his, but there were not delivered with equal fidelity unto God those things which are God's." Bernard's famous comment was made, ironically, while the Abbey Royal was in the midst of reform under its new Abbé Suger. In the eleventh century the conduct of its monks had been outrageous, and Saint-Denis had been threatened with ruin. The abbey had regulated its finances so badly that priceless altar vessels were in pawn. The four-century-old abbey church was in as sore condition: fissures appeared, columns cracked, the towers became unsafe. While still a student at the abbey school the boy Suger resolved that, if the opportunity were given him, he would one day put an end to the decadence and restore the splendor of Saint-Denis. His success was to provide a perfect model for the career of Maurice de Sully, the foremost constructing prelate of the next generation.

In 1122, when Suger was forty-one years old, the "mother church," which, in his words, had suckled him as a child, held him upright as a stumbling youth, and mightily strengthened him as a mature man, set him among the princes of the Church. Election to the abbacy of Saint-Denis was a most uncommon honor for a commoner. Princes of the blood had held the post before this short, almost undersized, but utterly charming son of unknown parents who called himself a beggar lifted from a dunghill. But *"in brevitate sua noluit esse brevis"*—in his smallness of birth and stature, Suger refused to be a small man. As Abbot of Saint-Denis he directed three cities, seventy-four villages, twenty-nine manors, more than a hundred parishes, innumerable scattered chapels, tremendous rented acreage, and fifteen forests. All was in decay or chaos when Suger assumed control. He immediately embarked on a program of reconstruction and resettlement as bold as it was vast, and, as in almost all he did, it ended in victory. Within a decade Saint-Denis was prosperous enough to rebuild its central mother church, a project from which flowed four hundred years of European architecture.

Work commenced about 1130. Focillon says the summer of 1129, Marcel Aubert prefers the later date of 1132. It makes little difference since actual construction was preceded by a general refurbishing of the interior, which must have required a year or two. Suger wrote that he "summoned the best painters . . . from different regions and reverently caused the old walls to be painted with gold and precious colors." There is something in this of the spirit of the Dark Age from which France had just emerged. Suger had a weakness for show. The parvenu was alive in him, openly seeking display. But at the same time he was the most glorious exception to the rule of parvenu vulgarity. His taste was provided with the keenest intelligence. It looked limitlessly forward, established new canons for itself, wanted what was most new, most audacious, what most possessed the chance of influencing the future.

And so the abbot, unlike the officials of the Cathedral, decided that a simple renovation was unsatisfactory. Nothing less than a total reconstruction would please him. The painters were followed by a veritable army of craftsmen—stonecutters, masons, carpenters—and a corps of master artists, the men who designed the glass and carved the portals, who were "invited" from every part of France rather than "summoned," as were the lesser workmen. Together they would rebuild the ancient church by sections—first the façade, then the sanctuary, and finally a nave linking the two extremities. Directing them all, insisting on universal use of the ogive, exhorting, making innumerable suggestions, criticizing with the eye of a connoisseur, and probably filling them with annoyance because of his meddling, was Suger. But, like Molière's *Gentilhomme,* he paid. He wished his church to be as sumptuous as Sancta Sophia, and polite travelers from Constantinople assured him that it was.

Characteristically, Suger began the reconstruction of Saint-Denis with an imposing new façade. Against strong protest, he resolved to raze one of the treasures of the Carolingian Age, the porch that sheltered the tomb of Pépin le Bref, and extend the front of the church some eighty feet westward. Today this façade dominates the square of a slum town. On a winter's day the effect can be indescribably sad. Paul Eluard, who was born at Saint-Denis, could not forget it. The poor shuffle past, wearing their sullen lives, rachitic, cornered, so outraged and brutalized by present society that, if they would not again take arms against the basilica they wrecked in 1793, they might against the foppish intellectuals who come to admire it. Ordinary tourists do not come to Saint-Denis. They are frightened by the neighborhood and confused by the church. In truth, it requires some imagination, aided by a study of old gravures, to re-create the grandeur of the abbey. Few medieval structures have been treated more savagely by the intolerance of later ages. The mutilation at Saint-Denis is a living wound, a terrible hole in the sky, where the tall northern spire, now gone, once rose two hundred and seventy-three feet.

Capture, nevertheless, the strong diagonal movement running upward to the southern tower. The eye is lifted crossways above the central portal, through the rose, over the battlements, and directly upward in the open, rising bays. The diagonals are never at rest but sweep from portal to window to tower, so that one marches upward, from whatever perspective the church is discovered, on the great steps of the architect's mind. Yet the façade also thrusts straight upward vertically, in each of its three divisions, like a Gothic fountain of aspiration. Here lies the profundity of Saint-Denis. The round arches are Romanesque, and their perfect proportions reveal the Romanesque at its most complex, in its full and vigorous mature moment, its essential problems solved, its motives turning toward subtlety. Nevertheless one would swear that the arches are more pointed than they are, that they rise steeply and break in a precocious point.

The immense battle of the Gothic Transition is visibly being fought on the face of the wall. Four massive buttresses hold the façade erect and lift it away and upward from the square. As one concentrates on them, it is possible to forget the galaxy of rival diagonal themes. The buttresses are straight upward power. Those at either end, however, are doubled by a necessary side member. These side buttresses give the composition a powerful reinforced frame, but at the same time they widen the wall and resist the skyward motion. The two elements are at war: the horizontal and the vertical. The heavy battlements and dozens of level moldings and inscriptions break the vertical rise. They break it, but they cannot halt its climb. The upward motion is the stronger, and it conquers. Up, up, in columns and arches, in the tall lancet windows, in the open bays, in the dynamic closed masonry, the façade asserts its restlessness. The swift diagonals, the monumental doors, the sculptural detail, the strong beat and the weak beat of the windowed arcades, the focusing rose and the tower overhead, add to an impression of enormous wealth.

Archaeologists have written a long pedigree for this façade. The tradition of a symmetrical, twin-towered façade is ancient. It may be traced from pre-Christian temples to the great Romanesque churches of Normandy; but none had received this lavishness of design, and none was constructed, as this one was, with a masterly and scientific use of the ogive. The façade of Saint-Denis is the first of its kind in France. It rose like a giant child in the heart of the royal domain, fully grown at birth.

Its basic dispositions, of course, had already received a chaste and lovely treatment in Normandy, at such churches as Saint-Etienne of Caen. There the architect of Saint-Denis found his four powerful buttresses and twin towers, his three great doors, the meaningful windows, combined in a formula whose simple elegance could not be improved. But the spareness of the Norman wall was strange to Suger. His façade, which the austere beauty of Saint-Etienne has never obscured, had to be as rich as the rest of his church; it must charm as well as overpower. Hence the French architect, or the Norman who came to France at Suger's invitation, was compelled to vary and enrich the Norman scheme, at the expense of purity, to suit the broader Gallic temper. The stories were juggled. A crucial innovation —the rose—was set in the wall like a gem. The doors were filled with a carved celestial population.

Suger imported sculptors from the talkative South to accomplish these wonders. Today their central achievement, a powerful Last Judgment, is ravaged and melancholy, so battered by the Ancien Régime and the Revolution, and then transformed by the restorers, that it is almost beyond recognition as medieval art. In spite of these depredations a minuscule Suger may be perceived crawling into the aureole of the Redeemer with a pious gesture. In the twelfth century he would have been seen a second time, prostrate before Christ, in the reliefs of the cast bronze doors immediately below. In the apse there is a third portrait of him, this time in glass, at the foot of the Virgin. His name also appeared in dozens of Latin inscriptions that were effaced long ago but remain vivid in his writings. He could not bring himself to ignore the one enemy his religion assured him was not to be feared: Oblivion.

No man stood further from Bernard of Clairvaux. Suger was a sincere and devout Christian, he wept passionately when mysteries were sung, but he was not a saint. The age of such divine constructors as Saint Hugues of Cluny had passed. After the twelfth century, art was no longer considered a miracle. Yet, unsaintly as the abbot was, his flat materialistic bias made possible the most spiritualistic architecture; a similar point of view would later enable Maurice de Sully to build Notre-Dame. Suger dared dream, as the twentieth century, which prides itself on philosophic materialism, has been afraid to dare, of an art that excites (*excitans*) "from the material to the immaterial"—"*de materialibus ad immaterialia!*"

All France took his motto as it followed the Oriflamme of Saint Denis. The ordinary people understood the summons gladly and rushed to fulfill their artistic responsibilities. These were enormous, in the days before the machine. Hand-hewn stone, for example, has a private beauty unattainable by the power saw. The entire local community, swollen by pilgrims, shared in the humble tasks that together thrust towers into the sky; and by June 9, 1140, in the warm French spring, the façade was advanced enough to be dedicated. It is possible that twenty-year-old Maurice neglected his studies for a day to witness the impressive ceremony.

A month later Suger was ready to lay the foundations of the new *chevet,* which was to be his masterpiece. If the façade was a portentous creation that appeared as if by magic on the soil of France, the sanctuary was an even rarer stroke of legerdemain. It was so weightless and soaring, bathed in such mysterious light, that it was like nothing ever seen in Europe. Its influence was felt wherever the Gothic wandered, from Spain to Sweden, as far eastward as Hungary, and of course in England.

Never, in none of the famous cathedral apses which were to follow, was the ogive employed with more grace and confidence than by the architect of Suger's ambulatory (Fig. 3). The true Gothic was born in his vaulting. If he was the same man who constructed the façade, he undoubtedly profited from his bold experimentation there. The apse of Saint-Denis is free from the rudimentary heaviness of the forward part of the church. Its nervures have great strength, but they are profiled with refinement and seem calculated to perform exactly their assigned role and no more. There is no waste —the first crime in architecture as in the other arts. The pillars, if anything, are dangerously spare and reveal a perfectionist's desire for precision. The ambulatory has two wide aisles, the second rounding

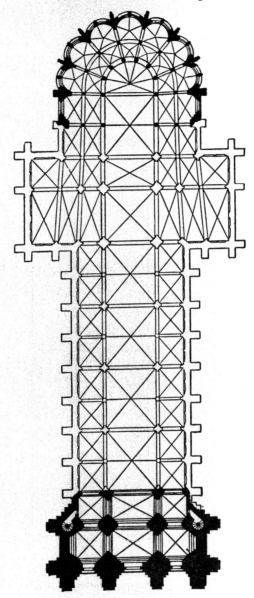

Fig. 3. SAINT-DENIS: The portions in black indicate the façade and apse spared by the thirteenth-century reconstruction. (After Dehio and Bezold.)

into chapels along the circumference. This exceptional width not only provides a splendid stage for processions, it also ensures the broad stability of the upper mass. Two spines of pillars, eight in each, receive the direct thrust from above, while the heaviest strain of all, flowing to the outer shell of the monument, is carried by the massive piles of the exterior wall. And so, with astonishing ease and simplicity, the architect succeeded in mounting an enormous mass above a 180-degree turn, using materials of not one-hundredth the elasticity of steel.

Such an arrangement would have been impossible with old-fashioned groin or barrel vaults; their flexibility was too limited for the diverse pressures of the double aisle. None of the greatest Romanesque churches, neither Conques nor Saint-Benoît nor Saint-Sernin of Toulouse, had attempted the apsidal double aisle; nor did any of them have fenestration to compare with the fourteen spacious windows of these chapels. The ogive, on the other hand, adapted easily to the complex plan. Here it is obvious why the revolutionary new system of construction should be called ogival architecture rather than "Gothic"—applied as an insult by smug Raphael.

Astonishing, this sudden profusion of ribbed vaulting at Saint-Denis; more astonishing, the speed of construction. From crypt to the roofs, the apse was erected in three years and three months—time symbols that Suger, like any man who believed in a numbered universe, found mystical. The abbot was fully aware, too, of the historical importance of the consecration of the sanctuary on June 11, 1144. Nineteen prelates, led by the Archbishops of Reims, Sens, Rouen, and Canterbury, took part. So did the King, twenty-four-year-old Louis le Jeune, and his beautiful and temperamental Queen, Eleanor of Aquitaine; the Queen Mother; peers of the realm, diverse "counts and nobles from many regions," and "ordinary troops of knights," who, Suger remarked with an Olympian air, were too many to be counted. And, of course, there were the common people, pushing to enter the church with such force that the King and the nobles personally kept them back with sticks and canes.

Did Maurice de Sully, twenty-four years old like his sovereign, join the throng which walked from Paris for the occasion? From Suger's description, Paris was empty that day. The entire populace seems to have made an architectural excursion. In the Middle Age there was a special way to Saint-Denis. One did not simply stroll out from the northern faubourg, if one was devout. A complex ritual, involving six pilgrimage stops, called the Stations of Saint Denis, was performed by the pious. A serious young clerk like Maurice would not have neglected this obligation to the Holy Martyr. The route followed the Passion of the saint. It began high on the Left Bank, in the crypt of Notre-Dame-des-Champs, which was thought to be the underground chamber in which Denis assembled his congregation. Thence Maurice crossed what are now the Luxembourg Gardens to the lost church of Saint-Etienne-des-Grés, considered the site of the Roman house in which Denis and his followers had worshiped for the first time within the city limits. Next Maurice went to another vanished church, Saint-Benoît, off the rue des Ecoles, where Denis had been seized; then he continued to the eastern tip of the island, behind the Cathedral, to the priory of Saint-Denis-du-Pas, on the spot where Denis had been tortured. The fifth station, Saint-Denis-de-la-Chartre, was on the other side of the Cathedral cloister, near the present Flower Market; it was a chapel built into the ruins of the *carcere Glaucini,* the Gallo-Roman jail in which Christ had administered Holy Communion to the saint. Finally Maurice and his fellow pilgrims climbed, at least part of the way on their knees, up the steep slope to the Martyrium on Montmartre, which legend had made the place of decapitation.

From Montmartre the crowds hurried to the abbey, singing hosannahs and praying, occasionally discovering that they were no longer blind or paralyzed, that they could see or walk by the Grace of Christ, and they were lifted on shoulders and held high for the masses to touch and admire, as if they held further cures in themselves. It was a festival of religion, and, being French, of meat and wine. The great Parisian fairground was alive with attractions, but the most spectacular of all was reserved for the sanctuary of the new church. In the crypt and the ambulatory the nineteen bishops simultaneously celebrated a Mass of Masses before the gilded altars. In their hands they held jeweled vessels, which are now broken and scattered and sought by the museums of the world. Suger hoped the moment might never be forgotten:

You might have seen . . . how so great a chorus of such great pontiffs, decorous in white vestments, splendidly arrayed in pontifical miters and precious orphreys, held the crosiers in their hands, walked round and round the vessel and invoked the name of God so piously that the King and the attending nobility believe themselves to behold a chorus celestial rather than terrestrial, a ceremony divine rather than human.

You might have seen, too, his round face flushed with pride and excitement, his jaw firm, his lips set with dignity, his eyes wide and alert, his monkish hair cropped in a beautiful line across his forehead and exquisitely combed, his robes pleated in lovely folds, his expressive hands extended in gentle piety, as he appears in his stained-glass portrait: Suger at the highest moment of his career—the King, the peers and prelates of the realm his guests, the vaults soaring above, the colored light shifting its intensities, and, outside, the people of France gratefully shouting his name.

Chapter Six

*t*HE CENTURY advanced at a quickened pace. It was filled with artistic revelations, in song and cut stone. The polished Burgundian splendor of the Romanesque burst forth in the nave of Vézelay. In the Ile de France, the private domain of the Capet king, the Transition rushed down the center of Saint-Denis as Suger strove to link his façade and apse. This was the *opus modernum* par excellence, the brief Latin phrase that became the watchword of an epoch. The impulse to construct broadened, deepened, spread with husky roots through the people. Towns and villages modestly adapted the ideas of the episcopal cities. At Chartres, after fire destroyed most of the city in 1134 but spared the Shrine of the Virgin, a new façade was replacing the damaged front of Saint Fulbert's cathedral. This project, in which chanting multitudes hauled stone from the quarry of Berchères, occupied the entire middle third of the century. In 1145 the work was in full progress.

Medieval inspiration now soared three hundred and forty-three feet into the air to the summit of the southern flèche at Chartres. Come to the gray pilgrimage city on its stark hill in the Beauce and watch the many faces of the spire as they receive the same sun as the wheat. Row in a flat-bottomed boat through the silent moats, past women scrubbing laundry on the stone landings, then continue far down the Eure, where the tower appears, miles away now, through openings in the willows. This is the twelfth-century strength, the century of the soldier, the priest, and the architect, a century of immense injustice yet as civilized as the tower that changes shape and concentrates in a lonely dynamic point without losing honesty and vigor.

Students still make an organized pilgrimage from Paris to Chartres, walking the distance in a conscious intellectual gesture, sleeping in barns, reading Péguy, following the route in the June sunlight. Maurice went too, with his classmates, on foot from altar to altar of the sixty-mile road, hearing Mass in the wayside chapels, sharing Parisian ideas with young people in the rural towns, thanking farmers for apples and milk, until he reached the underground altar of the Virgin in the crypt of the cathedral, next to her pagan well. There he could ask what he wished of Mary. The boy, who had witnessed the triumph of Suger, may have requested a boon. His century was young enough for him to beg Mary to make him great.

Suger's was only one of a striking group of medieval success stories—almost all victories within the Church—which provided encouragement to a commoner as ambitious as Maurice. The usual bishop, of course, was still an aristocratic, and frequently unprincipled, seigneur, like Gaudri of Laon, who during the furious municipal uprising of 1112 was beheaded in his wrecked cathedral by a serf. But at the same time a number of intensely practical sons of the poor, Maurice among them, were elevated to eminence and wealth. The Church took them early from their families, trained them in the schools, and, when their preparation had been completed, assigned them to high executive posts. Early in the century, in 1113, the dialectician William of Champeaux received the important prelacy of Chalons-sur-Marne. Gilbert of Auxerre, also common born, was named Bishop of London in 1127. Still a third commoner, Gilbert de la Porrée, was elected to the venerable see of Poitiers in 1142. There were dozens of others, including Maurice de Sully's predecessor on the episcopal throne of Paris, Peter Lombard. Like most self-made men, they were economic conservatives.

Cash was vital to this age, which has been described as too lofty for money interests. Economic policy dictated most of its wars, including the proto-colonialism of the Crusades. Innumerable manuscripts deal uniquely with real estate and finance; and so chivalrous a figure as Joinville's Saint Louis gave thought to his treasury balance. And then as now, it was a hardship to be poor in Paris. The chroniclers agree that Maurice de Sully, when he arrived in the capital, had a most difficult time. He begged his bread, they relate, and possibly also served wealthy students as a sort of batman. There was nothing unusual in this; thousands of scholars supported themselves by such means. What was quite rare was Maurice's grave dignity and determination. In one legend he proudly rejected alms that were offered on the joking condition that he renounce his hope to be bishop.

Maurice seems to have risen quickly. By 1142 the signature *"Mauritius clericus"* appears on a charter of the Cathedral. A second charter, dated 1147, was witnessed by a *"Mauricius subdiaconus"*— subdeacon. Maurice de Sully seems to have been concerned in both cases although final proof is impossible because of the missing surname. If he was born, as supposed, in 1120, and if these signatures were indeed his, Maurice was a clerk in the Cathedral Chapter at the age of twenty-two and a subdeacon at twenty-seven.

The Chapter of Notre-Dame deserves a book in itself. It was a powerful independent organism, frequently involved in bitter disputes with the Bishop and Pope, governed by its own officers, controlling its own land and communities, and enjoying an annual revenue of some eighty thousand Parisian livres. Its cloister spread over the northeast corner of the Cité, breaking through walls and arcades until it resembled no other in France. Its disorderly lines, which in spite of the changes of eight hundred years may still be studied from the towers of the Cathedral, were already chaotic when Héloïse lived with her uncle Fulbert on the rue des Chantres. By the 1140s the clandestine embraces of Héloïse and her tutor Abélard were already more than two decades in the past; but the lost songs Abélard wrote for her in 1117, to believe his own claim for them, must still have been resounding through Europe. Certainly they were not forgotten on the Ile-de-la-Cité, even after Abélard's death in 1142. Nor were the details of their romance: their secret marriage in 1117 or 1118; the child born to Héloïse when she went into hiding in Brittany; her uncle's furious revenge upon Abélard when he discovered their secret; and the entrance of both husband and wife into religious orders in 1119. Héloïse survived Abélard by twenty-two years, until 1164, spending the end of her life in seclusion as abbess of the Convent of the Paraclete, in Champagne, Abélard's retreat from the quarrels of Paris. But her fame lingered in the capital; and

Maurice de Sully and the other clerks in the cloister must have thought of her whenever they passed the house whose twelfth-century foundations remain intact.

The cloister was a city within a city, suffering only its own jurisdiction and jealously guarding its privileges. Most information concerning this stronghold of the Chapter comes, in fact, from various royal, papal, and episcopal edicts that attempted to discipline it. There were wild doings in the forty-odd houses of the canons, and the sergeants of the diocese often had difficulty maintaining order. Strange pets—stags, monkeys, crows, and bears—were tethered in the courtyards. Women, some wise and some foolish, passed through the gates to bathe and dine. There were copious deliveries of wine and mutton. The canons adored colored slippers, beards, and long coiffures—which were eventually forbidden. They threw dice in a gambling game called *griesca*. During the holiday season erupted the *Fête des Fous,* and sausage was eaten on the altar of Notre-Dame.

The cloister was also the home of the school, and although it might seem a bizarre place for reflection, a quiet individual who sought privacy may have been able to find it. The Cathedral possessed a library that was large for the Middle Age, when a book cost as much as a house and was chained to its lectern. Its several hundred volumes are now largely destroyed, although some remain at the Bibliothèque Nationale. Leafing through the illuminated manuscripts, studying the Fathers and the Commentators and a few scientific documents that had been translated from Greek and Arabic through Hebrew or directly into Latin, Maurice acquired a vague Ptolemaic view of the universe, a world domed by mystical spheres and so cloudy in its terrestrial outlines that Norway and Turkestan were its farthest limits.

It is fairly certain that Maurice, equipped with a thorough knowledge of Saint Ambrose and Saint Augustine, was professing theology by 1145—at the age of twenty-five!—in the Cathedral school. He may also have taught belles-lettres and philosophy—evidence is lacking. It was as a conservative theologian, in any case, that he made his reputation. In a period of audacious religious thinkers, Maurice was a champion of orthodoxy. Together with Robert of Melun, he refuted a formidable opponent, Peter Lombard, the Master of Sentences, in theological quarrels (*quaestiones*) that were altogether typical of the times. Maurice debated with Peter not only in *disputationes* but also in written words (*scripta*), so that their differences were the talk of intellectual Paris in 1150. John of Cornwall, a student at the time, later recalled Maurice's part in his education:

I should not pass over in silence two venerable masters, Robert of Melun and Maurice, today Bishop of Paris, whose theological instruction was in no way heretical. I have not read their writings on those questions and controversies, but I was present at a number of their lectures and debates in which they accused Peter Lombard's doctrine . . . of falseness, not to say error.

The Schoolmen debated before excited crowds of students, and time passed swiftly, punctuated by great events. On Christmas Day, 1145, Louis le Jeune solemnly took the Cross at Bourges. Perhaps the King was remembering the frightful day three years earlier, during his war with Count Thibaut of Champagne, when the royal troops burned Vitry and thirteen hundred people perished in the town's flaming church; perhaps he was merely yielding to the Pope's entreaty that he come to the rescue of the already crumbling Frankish states in Asia Minor. The Second Crusade was the King's, but, after his assumption of the Cross failed to arouse his barons, the movement became Saint Bernard's. The saint called a meeting at Vézelay on March 31, 1146, to which people came from every part of France; one hundred thousand are said to have come in all. Bernard addressed them from a platform set up in the fields below the town, speaking against the background of the new abbey church of the Madeleine, which, at the crest of the hill, lifted its reddish stone to the sky of Burgundy. Bernard's words have been lost, but their effect is known. His audience was enraptured. Men began to cry out, "Crosses, give us crosses!" Whereupon he cast off his white Cistercian robe so that it could be cut up for the multitude.

After this beginning, the Crusade ended in disaster. Suger ruled the kingdom for two years, while a tragedy of French arms took place in Syria and Palestine. But when Louis returned, his army decimated and his marriage about to dissolve after Queen Eleanor had displayed more than a niece's affection for Prince Raymond of Tripoli, he found France better administered and more solvent than it had ever been under his family. This was Suger's final gift to the nation. In 1151 he died, and a year later, at Beaugency, Louis divorced Eleanor of Aquitaine, whom he had once loved with "immoderate passion" (*"amore immoderato"*), and who, feminist historians forget, although she may have provided him with horns, had not given him a male heir. It was a disaster for France. Suger, while he lived, had fought desperately to prevent it. Eleanor almost immediately was Queen of England, where she found a completely different husband in Henry II; and the Anglo-Norman-Angevin "empire" was extended to Bordeaux by the addition of Aquitaine.

It was at this moment that Maurice de Sully began to establish his reputation as one of the foremost preachers of his time. His sermons, from 1150 on, were famous. They were copied and recopied in *scriptoria* and circulated in collections which the Church considered models for young priests. The language was direct and in the popular tongue, intended for a common audience whose faith could not profit from subtleties. Soon the sermons crossed the borders of France. Such Englishmen as John of Cornwall and Robert of Melun, who in spite of his name came from Hereford, carried the texts home; and in the Bodleian Library at Oxford a manuscript contains five of them, side by side in Medieval French and English.

It is possible that Maurice himself carried his sermons across the Channel. Every churchman, if he was not an anchorite, traveled on a professional basis in those days. Such a well-known intellectual as Maurice was invited to synods, feasts, and consecrations; he made the routine pilgrimages; he was dispatched to preach in areas that were attracted to heresy, the bewitching Valley of the Rhône and hot Languedoc. Distances were short. Even now, as the railway shoots through the black outskirts of Paris, the green country quickly spreads out of the walled suburban gardens in its ageless, swelling beauty. The stacked wheat, the fresh and tender hay, the carts with staunch wooden wheels, the bordering forest, the Percheron horses —which were the battle steeds of the knights—are less than an hour from the city; and then, over a hillside, appears the spire of Senlis or of Saint-Leu-d'Esserent. On the property of the Cathedral of Paris alone, a priest could ride across half the kingdom, stopping at hospitable communities in which he had an official place.

Great prelates traveled with suites; and frequently, when they attended the dedication of a monument, they were accompanied by their master builders, who left their names on parchments. The bishops of the wealthy agricultural centers of Noyon and Senlis, friends of Suger who had participated in the consecration of Saint-Denis, were struck by the brilliance of the new abbey church. When they returned to their own outmoded and shabby cathedrals they simultaneously decided to rebuild them with the ogive and on a larger plan.

During the First World War the Germans nearly destroyed the lovely Cathedral of Noyon. Its vaulting was shelled; the tops of the towers were carried away; much sculpture was smashed. Still the church holds, as Amiens holds, and stands as an unconquerable reproach to barbarism. Here the massed forms of the Romanesque have yielded with generous old strength to the first Gothic lyric; and the church smiles with youthful sincerity, like a young knight. There is no concealment, no self-conscious show; but rather the frank rhythm of the great piers of the nave; the sensitive equilibrium of the curved transept; the concerted double thrust of the western *massif*. Construction began about 1150 and terminated in 1235—slightly in advance of Notre-Dame of Paris, whose architects knew Notre-Dame of Noyon to its last details.

Senlis, smaller than Noyon, but with the same Transitional charm, was begun in 1153. Although much of the original work has been altered, enough is intact to reveal an absolute familiarity with the ogive, which is employed even in the tiny apsidal chapels, which could easily have been vaulted in a half-dome of solid masonry. Except for its famous thirteenth-century spire, Notre-Dame of Senlis was built in thirty-eight years and solemnly dedicated in 1191.

Shortly after the commencement of Noyon and Senlis, between 1155 and 1160, one of the greatest Virgin shrines in France entered the medieval race for beauty: Notre-Dame of Laon. Seen from the plain below, perched on its lofty citadel, the Cathedral of Laon has one of the most dramatic emplacements in the West. In France, the Mont-Saint-Michel alone surpasses it. The lordly flanking towers, with the great Norman lantern in their center, present a silhouette of mythological grandeur. Here it was that the Gods of Thunder dwelled, and that the last sons of Charlemagne resisted the Capets, battling history. Here too had been the bloodiest communal revolt of all, when the bourgeoisie rose up in 1112 for financial and social liberties, and the serfs rose with them for simpler freedoms. The burning, ravaged city, barricaded on its hill, was a symbol of the whole modern era to come, which is not yet over. The King, bought for a higher price by the Bishop than by the merchants, recaptured the stronghold by assault, and then there was more slaughter as the nobles took revenge. Later the peasants sacked the smoking ruins. After two years of existence the Commune vanished in violence in 1114.

It was re-established sixteen years later. The centralizing current of the times was too strong, the language of the Flemish trade route too persuasive, the industrial wealth of Laon too tempting, for the Capets not to come to terms. Then the city flourished. Its cloth was sold to all the known world, marketed as far away as Egypt, where its quality and dyes successfully competed with the fabrics of the Orient. Its wines were famous and were exported to England and the Low Countries. The bank of the Laon Temple was bursting with deposits—the rich circular chapel the Templars left on the hill, as fine as the one in London, leaves no doubt of that. The schools once again began to attract students. And by 1160 the noble bullocks, whom the grateful community honored with statues in the towers of the cathedral, were dragging stone up the steep, twisting road to the summit.

Laon and Paris are both cathedrals which are widely loved—Paris as much for its historic situation as its art. Strange this, when the twelfth century felt that Paris was far from a special place. It re-membered when the capital had received very little consideration outside its own small province. A number of other cities—Tours, Lyon, Reims—had been fully as important in the Kingdom. Laon too, for example, was an intellectual center. It too had a stirring political history. It could be a remarkably pleasant place when the sunlight ripened the grapes on the southern slope of the hill. Its stone houses were solid, its people hospitable. More, its cathedral incorpo-rated all the poetry of the age.

From a distance the towers of Laon play tricks. Head on, they are as concrete as the mountain beneath them; at an angle, they are as open as the air, and clouds float through their apertures. The entire structure is like that: sound, honest, responsible, and then suddenly playful with magic. How did the stone oxen fly one hundred and fifty feet into the towers? Ah, monsieur, how was the cathedral built at all! Laon will not tell. It smiles and dances away. In a moment it is back, garrulous as a child, showing sculpture and glass, and hiding them once more in the deep round arches.

The Middle Age considered Laon a masterpiece. Villard de Honnecourt, the traveling thirteenth-century architect, sketched the western façade in his notebook and remarked that although he had been in many countries he had nowhere seen the equal of its towers. The interior too, in truth, leaves nothing to be desired. Purists might demand a circular chevet rather than the rectangular sanctuary; but the present scheme, with its flat wall and great rose dominating the altar, in reality replaced an earlier curved apse, which seems to have been wrecked by a structural disaster about 1200. This round chevet, dating from 1155-1160, must be imagined as erect if the church of the Transition is to be visualized. Otherwise the elevation is similar to Noyon's, but executed with more mastery; and the lantern, a Norman feature which is rare in France, floods the heart of the structure with light. The vaulting is seventy-eight feet above the floor, as tall as any church attempted until, a few years later, in 1163, Notre-Dame of Paris would jump half again as high.

Saint-Denis, the western face of Chartres, Noyon, Senlis, Laon—the century moved on in its unprecedented outburst of construction. All France was building, and, as a great man must, Maurice de Sully moved with his country and his times. Now he was called "Magister," and advanced to the highest posts in the Chapter of Notre-Dame. Sometime near the end of the decade he was named a full deacon and canon. In December 1159 he became an archdeacon, one of the five most powerful men in the Cathedral after the Bishop—his old antagonist, Peter Lombard. It was at this time, according to the chroniclers, that Maurice's old mother, Umbergia, came from the Loire to visit him. She was brought to his residence in the cloister by a group of wealthy ladies of Paris, who had first taken care to dress the peasant woman in elegant new clothing. Maurice affected not to recognize her. "My mother," he said, "is a poor woman who has never worn anything but homespun." Only when she changed to her old clothes did he throw himself in her arms.

In July 1160, Peter Lombard died, and the episcopal throne was vacant. There are two versions of the election of Maurice, one by the sweetest liar of the Middle Age, Caesarius of Heisterbach, which is certainly apocryphal. The Chapter, asserts Caesarius, was unable to agree on a new bishop. Accordingly a committee of three canons was delegated to select a candidate. But the committee disagreed too, and in despair appointed one of their number to act with the proxies of all. This lucky fellow, Caesarius claims, was none other than Maurice, who elected himself, declaring, "I know neither the thoughts nor the designs of others; but as for me, with the Grace of God, I propose to administer my diocese irreproachably."

The second version is closer to probability. It involves a case of royal interference in the affairs of the Church, a frequent tactic of the Capets, who liked to be sure of their bishops. In the account of Stephen of Bourbon, who, like Caesarius, wrote long after the fact in the thirteenth century, the Chapter indeed could not reach a decision. The canons were deadlocked between Maurice and a theologian with a ferocious appetite for texts named Pierre le Mangeur. Perhaps after a strong hint from the Palace, the advice of Louis VII was requested.

The King asked which of the two was the more steadfast, the more zealous in all that pertained to the salvation of souls, who was the more active preacher and the more interested in good works. The canons replied that Maurice was the more fervent preacher, the more concerned with practical affairs, and the more worthy of praise in connection with the saving of souls; as for Master Peter, he was the more devoted to knowledge of the Holy Scriptures. To which the King replied, "Choose the more zealous for the supervision of souls; save the more learned for the direction of the schools."

This is actually what happened. Peter the Eater, digesting his theological tracts, remained an academician and later became chancellor of the Cathedral and head of the schools; Maurice was Bishop of Paris for thirty-six years and constructed Notre-Dame.

The election has been dated: October 12, 1160. Shortly afterward Maurice traveled to Sens for his consecration by the Archbishop, for in the hierarchy Paris was still suffragan to this venerable ecclesiastic city of the Gauls. Notre-Dame did not become a metropolitan cathedral with an archbishop of its own until the seventeenth century.

Inside the Roman walls of Sens, on the northern border of Burgundy, was another superb new piece of architecture—for Sens is early, and in some ways the most original church of the Transition.

This majestic cathedral, as broad as Chartres, as tall as Laon, is older than Saint-Denis. It was planned before 1130, work was surely in progress by 1135, and when Maurice was consecrated bishop there in 1160 the choir and nave were virtually completed.

Bishop Maurice returned to Paris in an ancient ritual of triumph. He spent the night before his arrival at a nearby town, so that he could enter the city at daybreak, on a white horse. Then, after an elaborate service at the Abbey of Sainte-Geneviève, a great procession made its way down the streets of the Left Bank, the monks of Sainte-Geneviève marching before, the people shouting from the windows and roofs, the students joining, the city hung with banners, as the *Te Deum* rose to the sky. The Bishop, in pontifical robes, was carried in a litter by the fourteen major vassals of the Cathedral—vassals of the Holy Virgin, in whose fief they held lands. Their number was made up of the Counts of Blois and Nevers, the Count of Brittany, the Count of Alençon, the Counts of Saint-Paul, Meulan, and Bar-le-Duc; the Lords of Bourbon, Montmorency, and Beaumont, of Saint-Marc, Chevreuse, and Brunoy; and the King of France. Maurice was their feudal seigneur. He was deputy on earth for the Virgin of Paris and collected homage in her name. The procession crossed to the island, hymns ringing out to the Lord, the monks in silken capes, the barons in samite and furs, the ordinary people wearing flowers or sprigs of autumn leaves. The Chapter of Notre-Dame came out to meet them, the dean, the precentor, the chancellor and archdeacons, the canons and clerks, the choir breaking into music. They passed the ruin of Saint-Etienne-le-Vieux, its roof gone, its magnificence forgotten; the Hôtel-Dieu; the episcopal palace, antiquated now too; and in the center of its dependencies, the three-hundred-year-old Carolingian Notre-Dame that Maurice would destroy. At its western portal he swore allegiance to the Church of Paris. And then the pageant passed into the Cathedral: priests, monks, the singing choir of boys; Bishop Maurice, the Archbishop of Sens, the prelates of the realm; the King and his new queen, Alix of Champagne; the barons and their ladies, the lesser nobles and knights; the merchants and artisans and, striving to enter, the common thousands. Then Maurice was enthroned, and there was a long day of prayers and rejoicing, and a feast that night.

notre-dame

Take you up every man of you a stone
upon his shoulder . . . that this may be
a sign among you, that when your children ask their fathers in time to come,
saying, What mean ye by these stones?
Then ye shall answer them, That . . .
these stones shall be for a memorial unto
the children of Israel for ever.

JOSHUA 4:5-7

Chapter Seven

THE DECISION TO BUILD
1160 - 1163

IN HIS MOMENT of triumph Maurice de Sully decided to rebuild the Cathedral. The project would fill the rest of his lifetime, but when he died thirty-six years later, in 1196, he left his work nearly completed. He was able to look up in the towering choir and the even greater nave and see the long chain of keystones in place. The roofing was paid for in his will, and of the original plan the western facade alone remained to be undertaken. If Notre-Dame is owed to any single man, it is to Maurice, who owed all to the Virgin. She had lifted him from the dunghill, as Suger had been lifted by Saint Denis, and the Cathedral was Maurice's personal offering of gratitude.

And so the Cathedral of Paris entered the medieval race for beauty at a moment when competition was most intense. The royal domain, which had lagged throughout the Romanesque, surged ahead mightily after Suger's reconstruction of Saint-Denis. Like the strong bow of Nimrod, the ogive curved in the French sky. Noyon, Senlis, and Laon were building in the Transitional style. At Chartres the western tower cloaked the rest of the shrine in a proud modern shadow. The impulse grew tall and wandered, persuasive, restless, refusing to pause, walking the roads with the easy power of youth. The Romanesque, an elderly man, for a short time accompanied the new hero. Then he turned away to die slowly in the South, with a smile in the cheerful villages, occasionally with a stiff, bitter grimace, amounting to fury, blind and facing the sun, in Saint-Gilles and wealthy Arles.

The Gothic, in those later days, did not remember him. But in the middle of the twelfth century the two walked hand in hand, like Athenians, the old man giving more than he received; spending wisdom the youth never fully learned, for when he in turn grew old he had no wisdom to give, but only pride.

The image is not altogether a conceit. The Shepherds of Chartres, carved about 1150, are its most delightful illustration. They are posed, of course, in the fields near Bethlehem. One is well along in years, his head protected by a hood, his weight resting on a staff, his finger pointing instructively to the Star. He is the soul of the later Romanesque, this old shepherd: his glance averted from the spectator; distracted by thought, cold, and the significant night; yet gentle, with the trace of a smile. Beside him is a boy, already taller, his hair tousled and uncovered, his cape thrown jauntily back, and his walking stick—a curved plaything—light in his hand. He is the most winning personification of the young Gothic. Both figures were exceptionally dear to the Virgin, and she commanded that both be placed near her baby in his manger, so that their lambs might delight him. But if Mary had a smile for either herdsman, it was for the boy, whose gesture is irresistible. He is playing a rural pipe, straight out of Theocritus! Rather, he has just broken his melody and is silent with wonder, holding the flute in a wide-eyed dreaminess. In an instant he will again place the pipe to his lips and play.

A note of this early Gothic music now enlivened the old Cathedral of Paris. About 1150, while the Shepherds were being carved at Chartres, Suger presented Notre-Dame with a stained-glass masterpiece from the workshops of his abbey. The courtesy was made more exquisite by its subject. According to the Neo-Classicist Le Vieil, who found its manufacture "very crude" and destroyed the scene in the eighteenth century, the window represented *"une espèce de Triomphe de la Sainte Vierge."* What sort of triumph this was will be seen in a dozen cathedrals, in stone as well as glass. The drama of Mary's enthronement in Heaven beside her Son received its most classic treatment, in fact, here at Notre-Dame, after 1200, in sculpture that has been likened to the Phidian Greek. Be that as it may, if the glass of 1150 had survived, it might be preferred to all its imitations. As Le Vieil smashed the panes, he could not help admiring the "brilliance of the colors, particularly the blue," which he thought equal to the intense blues of Saint-Denis.

As a decade passed swiftly, this blue empress looked down at the worn pavements of the old Cathedral, waiting like a royal lady for a champion. Then, as she knew he would, Maurice de Sully was elected bishop and resolved to build a palace worthy of her.

For three years, from 1160 to 1163, he mobilized his resources. From Champagne to Brittany, and south beyond the Loire, forming a great block of properties in the center of the nation, and in isolated holdings as far away as Provence, the Cathedral of Paris possessed fiefs, castles, towns, farms, mills, and forests. It charged tolls on roads and bridges; it collected tithes and a variety of other taxes. It was also the largest single holder of real estate in Paris and received a full third of the municipal revenue. The Cathedral owned not only half the Cité, but the Ile Saint-Louis, which was then called the Ile Notre-Dame, as well as hundreds of dwellings and shops, the Grand Pont and part of the Petit Pont, fields and vineyards on the Left Bank, and on the Right a tract of land called the Bourg-l'Evêque, which extended from the Louvre to what is now the Etoile, and then was still given to agriculture and falconry.

Hundreds of parish churches, chapels, and priories, each with land of its own, helped swell the episcopal treasury. And although such major abbeys as Saint-Denis were independent and answered to the Pope alone, the Cathedral controlled a score of smaller monasteries and religious communities, most of them thriving. Year after year wealth concentrated on the tip of the island. The Cathedral had its own river port, where barges deposited corn, wheat, oil, and wine for the storehouses of the cloister. Flocks of cattle supplied the Chapter with meat. And performing the necessary manual toil were thousands of serfs, whose flesh was as tenaciously held as their souls by the Virgin. These unfortunates could not marry, change their residence, or even peacefully die without the authorization of her priests.

How zealously the Cathedral guarded its property rights may be seen in a single episode. One night in 1155, finding it too late to return to Paris, Louis VII stopped at the suburb of Créteil, and in accordance with custom lodged there with his retainers at considerable expense to the inhabitants. He had forgotten that the village, although it was less than ten miles from his palace, belonged not to the royal domain but to Notre-Dame. When he returned to Paris the next morning and tried to enter the Cathedral, the doors were locked. Bewildered, the sovereign demanded an explanation, and was sharply reprimanded by the canons for his offense against Mary and her Church. He was ordered to make a public apology, which he did, and then to kneel throughout the day before the closed portals, praying forgiveness. This he did too, like "a very gentle lamb."

As soon as Maurice de Sully was placed in charge of the domains of the Virgin he revealed that he was as superb an administrator as Suger. A line of his obituary—*"redditus episcopatus multipliciter ampliavit"*—is an indication of how he increased the wealth of the diocese. Episcopal revenues climbed; and Maurice saw to it, in accordance with Church tradition, that at least one fourth of this income should be used for construction and maintenance. Schools and hospitals were built. Roads were improved. The Petit Pont and other bridges were rebuilt in stone. Large sections of the forest were cleared. Harvests increased, and the standard of living mounted dramatically. The feudal organism began to function with an efficiency that was rare.

Money for Maurice's project—and a glance at Notre-Dame shows how much was necessary—also poured in from outside sources. The House of Capet naturally was the greatest lay contributor—Louis VII donated two hundred livres *"ad fabricam ecclesiam";* but the nobility, clergymen with private means, the flourishing bourgeoisie, and workers' confederations all did their part. If the glass of Paris were intact, like Chartres', marvelous little scenes of medieval life would be seen tucked in the corners of the windows, which were actually signatures of the donors. A glance at the signatures of Chartres (which alone of the cathedrals has kept its ensemble of glass) shows that the total community has never, in any part of the world, or in any era, been so strikingly represented in the creation of beauty.

Every social class, from bankers to blacksmiths, had a place in the medieval church. Quite literally, the butcher, the baker, the candlestick maker participated. They would have taken to arms had they been excluded! So would the furriers and the cloth merchants, depicted in their elegant shops; the tanners curing hides; the water carriers and their vases; the wine merchants and vintners, advertising even then by showing some two dozen uses of the grape, of which the Eucharist was the highest. There were fishmongers and pastry-cooks; cobblers at their workbenches; sweaty plowmen; carpenters and wheelwrights; haberdashers and apothecaries! The list goes on and on. It even includes bureaucrats—*"de camera regis"*—playing chess on the job; the clergy too—bishops, deacons, ordinary chaplains. Delightfully, there were the artists themselves—the weavers, the sculptors, stonecutters, and masons, all those who had a hand in building and decorating the church—sometimes hard at work, lugging pink mortar and deep green stones, or relaxing with a goblet of wine. And everywhere in the Cathedral, prominent in the high roses but far from ruling absolutely, were portraits of armored knights and barons on battle steeds, kings and gowned ladies.

Not only great ladies gave. The Virgin laughed at snobbery. The humblest gave too, as much as they were able, if not in money, then in kind—*"sive in pecunia sive in alia re."* There was a saying in the Middle Age that Notre-Dame was financed by the ordinary women of Paris—mothers who were grateful for the ease Mary gave them in childbirth, wives to whom the Virgin had returned husbands from Crusade.

These gifts to the Virgin, it should be emphasized, were made freely. The clergy did not extort them by theocratic force. Some pardons were offered, but Notre-Dame and the other cathedrals were not financed by sale of indulgences: the Gothic belongs to a spiritual world different from that of Saint Peter's of Rome, for whose construction, to the fury of Luther, Grace was marketed throughout Central Europe by the Dominican Tetzel. When hard money grew scarce in medieval times, as it often did, the Church suffered in much the same way as everyone else. Credit could be obtained only from usurers; and when Maurice de Sully saw his ready cash expended at intervals during the construction, he was forced to borrow in the Juiverie.

The truth about the past is invariably more amusing than fancy, and it is high time, now, that the facts have begun to be told about the building of the cathedrals. Yet legends persist, and one of the most charming depicts an emotional army of volunteers, each with a stone, all singing strongly, arriving from every direction to deposit rock upon rock as the churches rose in a haphazard surge of common will. Like most fables, this one is literally false and poetically quite true. The volunteers did come, of course, to some shrines—Chartres and Saint-Pierre-sur-Dives in Normandy among them. They did speak a single religious language, as in the days before Babel; and their canticles were a perfect blend of voices. The whole age pursued its artistic passion like the dancing children of Hamelin, decoyed by beauty. The flute of the Gothic piper was more persuasive than Pan's —indeed, his music was often confused with the hornèd god's; and it drove popular enthusiasm to the sky itself, until at Beauvais it could go no higher, and the walls came tumbling down. But the chanting volunteers, in the end, formed a small portion of the corps of work- ers—and probably the least effective portion at that. Also, there was nothing haphazard in the construction of the cathedrals. No projects on the grand order have been more lucidly conceived and executed.

Paris, particularly, was no *opus pietatis*. If it had been, the chron- iclers would not have lost the opportunity to say so. Erwin Panofsky is altogether correct in describing the "Cult of the Carts" as largely a symbolic action, resembling a group of citizens driving the first car across a new American bridge. Granted, the first stones for Notre- Dame may have been drawn by teams of pilgrims, crying out sins and being shriven by an escort of priests, but the impulse did not last. The work, from start to end, was organized on the same prosaic professional basis as almost everywhere else in France, including the stupendous undertakings at Bourges and Amiens. The human drays of Chartres were a spectacular exception to a calm general rule. At Paris, as at Laon, beasts drew the stones—as beasts should—and were driven by paid teamsters. Unskilled labor was performed by thousands of *operarii,* who depended on their toil for a livelihood; and the actual laying of mortar and placing of stones, to say nothing of quarrying and carving, were done by specialists of the highest competence.

Never has the irrational been dealt with so rationally, the impos- sible made so possible. The Acropolis was planned with no greater sanity than Notre-Dame. The Cathedral was conceived with a lavish- ness that the mercantile mind has come to call waste, since it shows no immediate profit and turnover, in spite of an enormous invest- ment of cápital; perhaps two or three billion dollars of our own money for all the French churches of the twelfth and thirteenth centuries, and one hundred million for Notre-Dame alone. But one might re- mark that Notre-Dame, after eight centuries of harsh treatment, seems ready to stand for eighty more, while Versailles, less than four hundred years old, is falling to pieces. Notre-Dame was built throughout with a moving sincerity. Its workmanship was of rare excellence even for the Middle Age. Its materials, whose sumptuousness may be seen from the foundations to the towers, were perhaps the finest employed in any Gothic cathedral. Hidden parts of the monument were given the same elaborate care as the great façade. Expense was sought rather than spared.

Maurice, probably with Louis VII attending, conferred with the officials of the Chapter, and together they decided on the scale of the new Cathedral. The ambitious Bishop had his way. Both the Merovingian and the Carolingian basilicas were to be demolished, and the Gallo-Roman rampart broken through, to allow the church to find its full dimensions. There is no more striking symbol of the twelfth century's willingness to dispense with the confining past than the breaching of this ancient wall. A new age was at hand. After three years of preparation funds were available for ground-breaking by 1163, and it remained only to select a master builder and commence work.

The term architect is not to be used. Poor Mr. Pecksniff—his craft was not included in the liberal arts! Architecture was a modest subdivision of geometry, and the architect was what he should be: an accomplished builder with a dislike for frills and with a lifetime of practical experience. The Middle Age gave him a number of practical titles: master mason or stonecutter (*magister lathomus*), or simply *lathomus* or *cementarius,* but the best was *magister operis:* master of the work. The common people called him maistre or mestre.

The name of the first master builder of Notre-Dame must be considered lost, although there is a tantalizing signature on an act of the Cathedral for the year 1164: "Ricardus cementarius." Was this Richard the supreme Master? It would be a hazardous assumption. A few years later a carpenter named Symon also witnessed an act from the chancellery of Bishop Maurice. Doubtless many documents, carrying signatures of other workmen, have vanished over the centuries. It is only after the year 1250 that the names of the chief architects of the Cathedral are known, but it is certain that the preceding "anonymous" masters were famous in their time. The men who designed the cathedrals were as celebrated as princes and often were called across half of Europe to assume commissions, as were Villard de Honnecourt, who built churches in Hungary, and William of Sens, who went to Canterbury, and died there like a prince, falling from a high scaffold. Just as the Middle Age had no special love for darkness, filth, and disease, it had no particular liking for anonymity.

The cathedrals were blazoned with the names of their creators. Scores of monuments and innumerable pieces of sculpture and glass are signed, often with a prideful flourish. A Toulousain sculptor named Gilabertus described himself as *"vir non incertus"* to show the world how sure he was of himself. Architects too were happy to sign their work. Sometimes the signature was modestly inscribed at the base of a pillar; sometimes it extended in a magistral line across a wall or façade; there was never a fixed rule. The greatest cathedrals —Chartres, Reims, Amiens—were signed in the center of the laby- rinth, the twisting route of stone in the nave on which the devout crawled to a figurative Jerusalem. The medieval pavements of Notre- Dame have been destroyed, but it too almost certainly had a similar maze. At the heart of the labyrinth the name of the Master Builder as Daedalus was engraved in bold, uncial letters, and the maze itself became known as the Maison de Dalus, as close as the Middle Age could approach classical spelling.

Modern research has discovered a good deal about the master builders. The typical master was apprenticed early to the craft of masonry and served his father or an uncle. At the same time he learned draftsmanship, stonecutting, quarrying, lime-burning, and a host of related skills, whose secrets were carefully 'guarded. In every city the masons formed a jealous and exclusive corporation, with a strict code. The number of apprentices was limited, and al- though a master might have dozens of helpers and "valets," he could teach his trade to only two. Like the master sculptor, master weaver, and master glassmaker, he belonged to the working people and was not, in a narrow class sense, a gentleman. Still, he was paid more generously than a simple *operarius,* and his standard of life may have been near the bourgeois level. If his actual money wages were low, they were augmented by payment in kind—food, and even lodging and attire for himself and his family, since in most cases the master builder was a responsible married man who took his wife and children with him on long professional journeys. Invariably the clothing he received included a symbolic pair of leather gauntlets, so that taking an assignment was commonly referred to as "putting on the gloves."

Notice that by this time, except in rural areas, the architect had ceased to be a monk or priest. He was a layman, with the French emphasis on *laique,* as opposed to *seculaire.* This, of course, is not to support the Romantic theory, first advanced by Victor Hugo, and later elaborated by Eugène-Emmanuel Viollet-le-Duc, the great nineteenth-century architect who restored Notre-Dame, that the builders of the cathedrals—three centuries before the Reformation—were anti-clerical libertarians. Far from it. The master builder was a pious Catholic who particularly adored the Virgin, his special patron Saint Blaise, and Saint Thomas the Apostle, whose mission in India was performed under the credentials of a traveling architect. The master worked well wherever he toiled, on a castle, house, mill, or bridge, but nowhere did he release the same fire as in a church.

What, then, if the skill of the layman created Notre-Dame, was the role of the priest? It was enormous. The starting impulse and sustaining force in these undertakings came from the Church. Maurice de Sully is a case in point. He was a model *évêque bâtisseur.* The Bishop was the controlling executive and overseer. Like a powerful modern entrepreneur—Henry Kaiser, say, at Boulder Dam— he made the great decisions of policy and assumed the great risks. He personally selected the leading artists on whom the success of the venture would depend. He directed the financing. He purchased materials in massive quantities. Details were handled by his priestly subordinates, who supervised incidental hiring and firing, the weekly payroll, and the very real problem of discipline among the workers. Finally, a priest dictated the complex program of iconography. Maurice, one of the foremost theologians of his time, certainly did not confide this task to a rival. But if he prescribed the subjects of the sculpture and glass, the execution was not his. The imagination which set stone angels flying was the artist's, who adapted freely from the theme provided even when the priest had given him a specific manuscript or ivory to copy.

Possibly Maurice conducted a formal competition to select his *magister operis* and the other masters. It was usual for ateliers to compete for important commissions by submitting drawings, wooden models, and budgetary estimates. But the most careful study of Notre-Dame will not reveal exactly where its artists came from. Many famous ateliers were at work in the Ile de France when Notre-Dame was begun; the Paris workshop shows similarities but no final rapport with any of them. A safe guess is that the majority of the men who built the Cathedral had been trained in the guilds of Paris. The Parisian masons, stonecutters, and quarrymen had participated in dozens of local projects in the preceding three decades; Suger, for example, mentions that he summoned the carpenters to assist in the construction of Saint-Denis. Most of these experienced local workmen were now free, in 1163, from another project completed that year, the reconstructed choir of Saint-Germain-des-Prés.

Under the broad supervision of the Bishop and the immediate direction of the masters, a robust army of craftsmen assembled on the island. Parchment after official parchment was being issued from the episcopal palace: deeds, acts, delimitations of terrain, options, contracts and agreements of every sort, which were witnessed by the foremen immediately concerned and stamped with the Bishop's great seal of which a few impressions are conserved at the Archives Nationales. The die was presumably cut during the first weeks of Maurice's episcopacy and shows him as he looked to an engraver of the year 1160. He is posed in the sanctuary of the Carolingian Cathedral, stark and stiffly erect before his ceremonial throne. In his left hand he holds a crosier; his right hand—and this is the outsized hand of benediction of the Christ of Vézelay—is lifted to bless. The posture is as taut and elongated as a statue column at Chartres, and the feeling is strongly architectonic. Indeed, this miniature is closely related to the sculpture of the late Romanesque. It is at once dignified and lively, clear and mysterious, distorted and accurate.

Maurice's face is the powerful Romanesque head. The nose is heavy and prominent, the lips drawn, the eyes half closed and near ecstasy. Cast in dark red medieval wax, the portrait seems extremely remote. Maurice's miter, for example, belongs to a style that was already becoming unfashionable in the twelfth century. Its crowns are set to either side rather than fore and aft. A few years later, when he sat for his portrait in stone for Notre-Dame, he was attired in the new Gothic mode and wore the miter that many European prelates still prefer.

The hot wax was poured again and again over the scarlet ribbons and the seal brought down on the legal papers, which, had they endured, could have told the story of the Cathedral's construction like a log-book. A considerable number of houses—*"multis mansionibus,"* says the chronicle—were purchased for demolition. A new road, the rue Neuve Notre-Dame, was cut from the parvis to the north-and-south highway, with which it made a T-intersection near the Petit Pont, so that materials could be easily carried through the crowded Cité (Fig. 1, p. 33). Most of the quarries were located on the Left Bank, and from the Butte Saint-Jacques and the Plain of Montrouge, as far south as Bagneux and Arcueil some ten miles away, stone was being extracted for Notre-Dame. Not since Roman days had the Parisians taken so much rock from the earth as they would for their Cathedral, and in the course of the work they would become superlative quarrymen. The stone was selected by the knowing eye of the master builder and then cut from its beds along the natural seams. It was dressed on the spot, hoisted out of the pit by winches and levers, and loaded on long, two-wheeled oxcarts like the ones seen in the French countryside today. For one hundred and fifty years, to the cracking whips of the teamsters (*bubulci*), the oxen would make the slow trip down the Rive Gauche, across the bridge, swinging off to the right on the rue Neuve to the workshops, until, in the first years of the fourteenth century, the Cathedral stood complete.

As work got underway in 1163, all available space in the cloister, in the Bishop's courtyard, on the parvis, in all the area surrounding the Carolingian Cathedral, was taken by worksheds, dormitories, dining halls. Timber was carted from the forest and stored to dry. The smiths were hammering clamps and hinges. A foundry was set up in which the bells would be cast. The lime kilns were smoking briskly. The glassmen were laying out patterns on their chalked tables. The roofless Merovingian Basilica of Saint-Etienne, long abandoned and a ruin, was again filled with vitality. It became the major workshop, and within its ancient walls stone was at last being carved for the first portal of Notre-Dame.

Although the western façade would not be undertaken until 1200, its decoration had already been planned. The south portal was to be given to the Virgin in Majesty, the Empress of the Christian Earth, who ruled in the name of her infant Son. With either a Byzantine enamel or ivory for a model, almost identical with a model used fifteen years earlier at Chartres, the Master Sculptor of Paris addressed the great curving block of limestone that was to be the tympanum of the portal. The mallet and chisel he used, the elegant gloves that protected his hands, the embroidered cap he wore on the job, the flagon of wine he kept on a little shelf, may all be seen in the Sculptors' Window at Chartres, as well as the young, happy expression with which he worked. After he completed the central Virgin and Christ, the master carved a pair of tremendous angels to protect them; and then, in the space remaining, he added the founders of the Cathedral, Maurice de Sully and Louis VII, as they posed for him about 1165. Although the Bishop and the King sat as patrons do always, with a desire for recognition, neither lived to see his portrait joined with the wall of the church. The tympanum waited in the atelier thirty-five years, and only when its portal was at last ready, in the thirteenth century, did workmen lift it into place. After nearly eight hundred years it still looks down on the parvis with the grand manner of the Gothic Transition. (Plate XII.)

The Virgin, enthroned above the doorway, is herself a throne for the Child who lifts his little hand and blesses. The angels adore the Mother and Son from either side, and beyond, in what would be a human world, the Bishop stands erect and confident, and the King kneels. On the left, crowding beneath the angel's wing, Maurice de Sully is in the staunch prime of life, forty-five years old if he was actually born, as supposed, in 1120; and his full-bearded vigor is impressive. The beard has been grown, it might be remarked, in the four or five years since he became bishop and posed for the much less imposing portrait on his seal. Now one of the most powerful prelates in France, he looks with the clear, worshiping eyes of an intellectual at the beauty of the Virgin, who has made him a Prince of the Church. Can he be recognized as the peasant boy from the Loire? Yes, if only because of the visible strength, resolution, and ability that the soil of France has always given its most gifted sons. But the peasant boy has become a lord. He has the pastoral majesty of Saint Augustine. His episcopal robes rival the Byzantine gown of the Virgin. The eye loses its way in their delicate pleats and embroideries, the lovely fold of the chasuble, the fringes of the stole, the exquisite collar. But now one is drawn to the strange figure of the King.

His very foot speaks. Royalty has rarely been depicted with such grace and, again, idealism—excessively idealized, a severe critic might add. Yet the characterization is not exaggerated. The man is very nearly a religious fanatic. He has often knelt barefoot, here at the doors of Notre-Dame, for real and imagined offenses against the Lord. Although he is the same age as Maurice, he looks older. The events of a tumultuous lifetime have left their mark.

He is no longer Louis le Jeune, but Louis le Pieux, an elderly mystic who prefers no diversion to Mass in the Cathedral. He is preeminently "Eldest Son of the Church"—traditional role of the French monarch; Defender of the Faith but a poor Protector of the Realm. Since his divorce from Eleanor and his defeats by the Plantagenets, he has lost half his kingdom. Rouen, Poitiers, and Bordeaux have all been incorporated in the Anglo-Norman-Angevin "empire" of Henry II and Eleanor. Frederic Barbarossa presses him on the east, threatening Champagne and Burgundy and commanding the Rhône at Arles. A narrow strip of territory, which includes Paris, Orléans, and Bourges, is all that remains to the Crown of France. The moment is grave, but in an astonishingly short time the tide will change. While the façade of Notre-Dame is building, Louis' son Philip Augustus will reconquer most of the lost domains.

What is Louis remembering as he implores the Grace of the Virgin? In his old age he has become so gentle and courteous that he is a subject of ridicule to foreign students at Paris, but neither he nor the French people have forgotten the cruelties of his youth. The burning church at Vitry and the screaming hundreds inside had sent him marching to the Holy Land. The Crusade failed, as did every one of his military undertakings from that time forward. War, of which he had been fond, ceased to interest him. He became increasingly reflective. He read easily in Latin. He sympathized with the peasantry and earned their love, so that he was not afraid to nap in the forest while a single knight guarded him. His concern for the oppressed extended even to the Jews, who prospered in peace throughout his reign. He was an ideal Christian king—much more Christian, say, than Coeur-de-Lion—and his piety rivaled his great-grandson's, Saint Louis. But piety made him no match for Saracens or for hard-headed Plantagenets who ignored Christian niceties. This "tame" French King—*"mansuetus rex Galliae"*—accomplished little as a warrior, and the barons reviled him for it, but while he reigned the Cathedrals of Paris, Laon, Sens, Noyon, and Senlis rose from the earth, and nothing in Barbarossa's Germany or Henry II's England compares with them.

Perhaps Eleanor of Aquitaine was right when she reportedly complained, in the heat of their separation, that she had married not a monarch but a monk. Louis was raised in the cloister of Notre-Dame, which he thought of as a maternal bosom (*maternali gremio*); he was trained by the canons. He possessed the ecstatic temperament to an exceptional degree. The luxuriousness of the penitent's robe that he is wearing here, and the sweep of the royal cape, which mingles with the angel's, must be charged to the sculptor, for this King meant them to be models of austerity. The same may be said for the beautifully trimmed beard and elaborate coiffure that so lightly supports his crown. Idealized, this irrational monarch. Perhaps. Yet even the raisonneurs of the Enlightenment, had they taken time to examine the portrait, might have agreed that the artist treated him with an objectivity that was almost cold. The Middle Age was too realistic not to face irrealism.

The man who knew the unpredictable Louis best, and could explain his vagaries if anyone could, is by the happiest of chances here too. He is seated quietly behind Maurice on a little chair that curves with the tympanum—one of the minor touches that make for the monumental effect—and, as does his seat, he bends to conform with the lines of his beloved Cathedral. He is Barbedor, a priestly aristocrat who was Louis' personal chaplain and confessor and intimate friend. Here he sits as a scribe, recording the foundation of the Cathedral with an expression of such charm and—one hesitates at the word—sweetness that it is impossible not to be endeared to him at once. Anyone would confess to this beardless clerk.

After the King and the Bishop, no individual contributed more to the early construction of Notre-Dame than Barbedor. He had large private means, and his gifts seem to have been made when they were most needed. When houses had to be cleared, he purchased them for demolition. Periodically, when funds ran low, he gave large sums so that work could progress. In the choir, which was being erected as these sculptures were carved, he endowed the priceless stained glass for the high windows. It would seem too that he acted as Maurice's chief aide in supervising the work, for from 1168 to 1184 he was dean of Notre-Dame and one of the principal dignitaries of the Chapter.

The story of Barbedor's appointment as dean is worth a moment's digression. It opens a large window—of twelfth-century blue—on the personal feeling of the Middle Age. Naturally all three men in the tympanum were directly concerned. The episode began in 1163 or 1164, when Louis sent the following note to the Bishop, abbreviating the name of Barbedor for reasons of discretion:

Louis, by Grace of God, King of the French, to his friend Maurice, venerable Bishop of Paris, greetings and affection.

It is frequent practice, and a wise policy, for those who through God's Grace have risen to high station, to be well disposed toward those who have helped them succeed, so that in the fullness of their own success they may return kindness for kindness.

We are both aware that our clerk and yours, Bar., devotedly hoped and is now devotedly happy for your present eminence, and has in fact done all he could to help you succeed as you have. We have already solicited your aid for him in the past, and have good hope of your help. But, because of his hard-working attention to duties at court and the fact that he lives in our personal entourage, he cannot often present himself before you. Therefore, we take the occasion to repeat our request, and beg you to keep him in mind . . . so that, if some worthy post were to become available, you might think of him.

The letter, in addition to showing the manner in which a Capet addressed a common-born Prince of the Church, reveals typically the mood in which medieval politics were conducted. Maurice, of course, did not forget Barbedor, and four years later, in 1168, as soon as the deanship fell vacant, the clerk received the appointment.

Who *could* forget this absolutely delightful scribe? He is industriously attached to his duties even here, writing forever in his open book on the wall of Notre-Dame. What entries he is making are a mystery, but it is certain that the Virgin noticed them, as she did not fail to notice his forthright chin and amusing haircut, or the bold modeling of his lips and eyes. And although in daily life his capuchin may have hung less richly than it does here in Mary's presence, the Virgin—like any woman of regal taste—would nevertheless have been intrigued by the robe's broad clasp, spread as a butterfly on his breast.

The Virgin did not stir, but she noticed all. Nothing escaped her, and no one entered the exclusiveness of this portal without her wish. Her Son, a child of five, was delighted by everything, and was perhaps indiscriminate on occasion, as he looked out on the parvis with happy interest. The Mother was too lofty and remote for the thought of discrimination to occur to her. She stares straight ahead, turning neither left nor right, with the calm glance of eternity. Yet she saw and felt. She saw her clerk Barbedor and Bishop Maurice and King Louis, and, to judge from the skill she allowed the sculptor, she was pleased with them. She adored the grand scale, this twelfth-century empress, but she had an eye for detail. Wherever she held court she took her favorites with her. On the lintel immediately below the tympanum, carved at the same time, are the old and the young Shepherd.

How they differ from the pair at Chartres! These Shepherds are a Parisian's ideal of country life, and their graceful little dogs run and play, but do not govern flocks. There is a striking difference in tone between the two cathedrals, between city and country, capital and province, merchant and farmer; between Parisian limestone and rough Chartrain granite; between—if it is possible to speak so of Chartres—sophistication and naïveté. There can be no question which is the more charming. Chartres is the more warm, innocent, and spontaneous in every way; Paris the more aware. Any tourist may decide which is more lovely.

Did the Virgin smile? She seemed to signal. She, of course, enthroned beneath the dome of Heaven, knows the answer to every perplexity. She counsels against excessive questioning. There is not much to know, even where she came from. She sailed to France from Ephesus and Byzantium, and found her image already celebrated in the hills of Auvergne: a tough and sober woman of the back country who welcomed the Magi in a plain wooden chair. By the tenth century she had a garish cousin at Conques, who placed flowers in her earrings: the golden idol of Saint Foy. But the nearest relation of the Virgin of Paris is the Virgin of Chartres, who sprang from the stone fifteen years before her. The Paris Virgin, like any woman impressed by a lovely elder sister, has jealously copied some of her mannerisms. Both she and the Virgin of Chartres, for example, love jewelry and wear massive finger rings. Both their gowns are golden silk. The swirling pleats belong to the same fashion, collecting like plumage at their feet. Only the embroideries differ. The goddesses are sisters, unmistakably. They are not twins. It is surprising that Emile Mâle could once have thought they were carved by the same hand. The Paris Virgin is less robust. She belongs to a gentler climate. She is accustomed to a somewhat higher standard of life. Her tastes have formalized with the times. She sees the Transition moving quickly to the full Gothic.

She *is* Notre Dame of Paris. Literally dozens of other Virgins will be seen in the Cathedral. None will be so overpoweringly lovely and inaccessible. None will possess a majesty so absolute. Some will be great queens, none will be an Empress of Heaven. For as modern times approach, the Virgin becomes an ordinary woman or less. Here, however, in the twelfth-century portal, she enjoys her complete éclat and splendor. She is the Patroness of all Patrons, the only begetter, the only Founder of Notre-Dame: she and the Child in whose name she rules. It was she who discovered Maurice de Sully in his village on the Loire; she who disciplined Louis VII after his early wildness; she who was so taken by Barbedor that she took him from the King's service and placed him in her own. It was she who collected the workmen, who quarried the stone, who encouraged the apprentice on the dizzy scaffolds, she who mixed the blues and reds of the glass. She, again, who organized the farms and forests of the kingdom, who punished rapacious barons, who policed the roads, who stored wheat, pressed wine, baked bread, cobbled shoes, and sold cloth that the Cathedral might rise. She was, when the nation was worthy of her, medieval France. The world should stand to either side, like her tall astonished angels, swinging a censer and drunk with the smoking spice; or letting the vessel fall to clasp hands in admiration.

Chapter Eight

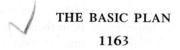

THE BASIC PLAN
1163

ENTER! THESE vaults, these pillars, are Mary's. This is the Virgin's world, and its serene terms must be respected. The darkness is hers, the silence, the cool peace, the pearl-colored light that drifts downward like snow. And suddenly the perspective opens.

No church seen thus far possesses the specific grandeur of Notre-Dame. None anticipated the magnitude of its premise. The Cathedral of Paris unexpectedly took world architecture to so grand a scale that it astonished citizens of the twelfth century as much as citizens of the twentieth. They, who had seen the church at Cluny, had never seen vaults this high. They had never seen this blending of refinement and power. The Cathedral is pure upward thrust, rising to God, nearly one hundred and ten feet to the main vault. At the same time it lances horizontally to the east, in colonnades and galleries, which travel some one hundred and thirty yards (122.5 meters) to the rear of the church. Statistics mean little, since the apparent size of a structure is all that matters, but it has been calculated that the floor surface is more than sixty-five thousand square feet, the interior volume no less than 7,700,000 cubic feet. The Cathedral can comfortably receive nine thousand people, including fifteen hundred in the upper galleries of the choir and the nave; twelve or thirteen thousand can crowd the church on extraordinary occasions, such as the Liberation of Paris in 1944. There is room here for all.

Thus to conquer space, to thrust such a mass upward and make it live, required a single overriding creative intelligence. Henry Adams fancifully insisted it was the Virgin's. He may have been right. Since the time of the impersonations in the *Iliad,* the great gods have often amused themselves in human actions. The clear gray eyes of the Master Builder were Mary's eyes. Her wisdom entered him divinely, as Pallas would enter a Greek.

Earthlings of the twelfth century were not literary enough to suspect this. Instead they took the human achievement at face value and called the artist Daedalus. And, indeed, it should be assumed by the present age of great architects that the constructive genius belonged to the Master Builder alone. But if he traced his plans independently of the Virgin, who allowed him to proceed as he wished so long as what he accomplished was beautiful, the Master nevertheless was not entirely a free agent. Priests are invariably less generous than gods, and so the Church supervised him closely.

In particular the Master was affected by the personality of the Bishop. He was goaded by Maurice de Sully's ambition and checked by his orthodoxy and very French sense of "mesure." The rival elements are reflected throughout the work, and perhaps most clearly in the basic plan itself.

The fundamental cross shape was dictated by a set of conventions which religious art had been developing for centuries; and it was the Bishop and his assisting clergymen who interpreted those conventions for the lay architect. Like Carolingian Notre-Dame and Merovingian Saint-Etienne before it, the Cathedral is oriented toward the rising sun, so that the warmth of Christ pours into the sanctuary at matins. Not until the Jesuits revised the canons of Church aesthetics, as they revised so much else within the Church, was this typical dogma relaxed. By that time, however, the Church had conducted its own Reformation at the Council of Trent, after 1545, and the Middle Age was ended. But while medieval faith was intense, every church was planned like a fantastic compass, with the east as its dominating pole of magnetism.

The rising sun meant Life. The sun sinking below the western horizon inevitably suggested Death. And so the western façades of the cathedrals became enormous lessons in morality, which showed the alternative routes to Heaven and to Hell. For the central door the theologians prescribed a tableau of the Last Judgment, which turned gold at sunset like blazing Domesday.

A secondary axis of north and south crossed the major line from east to west. North, the dark country, the region of Night, of primordial emptiness and dread, had the special significance of the Old Testament. To the Middle Age, the north wind blew from the chilled biblical land of the patriarchs and prophets: gaunt, bearded Abraham and strident Elijah. Northern light entered the transept, as it does still in Notre-Dame, through a breath-taking blue rose, like a stark dawn in Genesis. The northern God, who lived near the pagan wastes, was the unforgiving God of the Ten Commandments.

Confronting the Old Law was of course the New, with its brilliant promise of salvation. In the opposite transept, the south held the warmth of total love. It flamed with the sun-filled glory of the Evangel. To pass beneath the reds of the southern rose, as the sun floods downward at noon, is a baptism of light, a fiery meeting with the Redeemer. But more than the hot embrace of Christ, this is the warmth in which to find Beatrice, and Mary. The medieval man could give himself completely to the symbol, like a guest at Cana.

After wandering through the church, across the transept, and around the wide curve of the apse, it is good to return to the entrance, far down the nave, and take a place among the thousands of empty seats. The full length of Notre-Dame extends eastward, and for the first time it is necessary to consult M. Aubert's guide. For although the first rush of beauty was best met unaided, help will henceforth be needed to decipher its mysteries. The mysteries are never petty or academic, but they are sometimes technical, and so the floor plan (Fig. A) must be unfolded to solve the most obvious problems.

The first impression of Notre-Dame is that it is a great hollow cross, but the plan shows that, on the contrary, it is a horseshoe! The middle of the horseshoe is cut by the transept; its open end is sealed by the western façade. Since, at ground level, the transept scarcely juts beyond the exterior wall, the cruciform lies virtually hidden within its perimeter. Only in the uppermost portions of the Cathedral does it boldly emerge as a cross. Below, the angles of the cross are completely filled.

Look closely at the plan. On either side of the nave are three parallel bands, which, after being broken by the transept, continue around the choir like a triple rainbow. The two inner bands are the side aisles; the outermost is a chain of chapels tucked between the exterior buttresses. These chapels were an afterthought which was not entirely happy. They were not foreseen in the original plan of Maurice de Sully's architect but were added in the thirteenth and fourteenth centuries, and in turn led to other modifications and difficulties. The transept, for example, which originally stopped at the line of the outer aisle, had to be extended an extra bay on north and south to compensate for their presence. But the chapels should not intrude now, nor do they affect the Cathedral's basic structure.

Before the chapels were added, the buttresses stood vividly free along the entire outside wall, and the interior consisted of only four major elements:

1. The choir and its aisles.
2. The transept, minus the thirteenth-century additions at either end.
3. The nave, also flanked by a double aisle.
4. The western façade, with its three portals.

With a unity of style that was rare for the Middle Age, these elements were constructed in a sustained campaign of eighty-seven years. Architects changed, and bishops, but the grand original design of Maurice de Sully remained dominant. Maurice himself, from 1163 to his death in 1196, saw the choir, the transept, and the bulk of the nave completed. He supervised two different masters: the man who built the Transitional choir, and his successor who devised what was perhaps the first true flying buttress, and with it created the Gothic nave. After Maurice's death, probably two, but conceivably as many as three or four additional architects worked on the façade, whose superb harmony would at first glance seem to be the creation of a single master. The classic western wall was begun in 1200 and stood finished by 1250.

In spite of the unity of Notre-Dame, each change in architects is detectable. The various phases of the construction are not only visible in the monument but in the plan drawing as well. Examine the plan again. You will notice that Notre-Dame is far from being absolutely symmetrical. The giant horseshoe contains irregularities that might make a smaller monument chaotic. But in so large a building variations are necessary to avoid monotone, and hundreds of melodies run through the Cathedral to relieve its massive themes. The Renaissance, which made a cult of symmetry, and even the

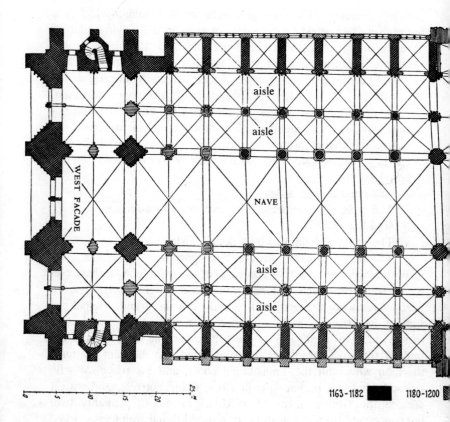

aisle

aisle

WEST FACADE

NAVE

aisle

aisle

1163 - 1182 ■   1180 - 1200 ▨

Fig. A.

showing the dates of construction of its parts. The shifts in the central axis and

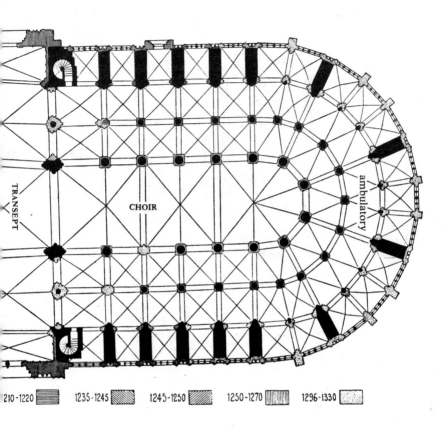

PLAN OF NOTRE-DAME,

the lack of absolute symmetry are particularly noticeable. (*Marcel Aubert*)

Figs. A (adapted) and E are from *Notre-Dame de Paris, Architecture et Sculpture,* Paris, 1928, by permission of the publisher, Morancé.
Figs. B, C, and D are all taken from Marcel Aubert's *Notre-Dame de Paris, Sa Place dans l'Architecture du XIIe au XIVe Siècle,* Paris, 1928, by permission of Laurens, Editeurs.

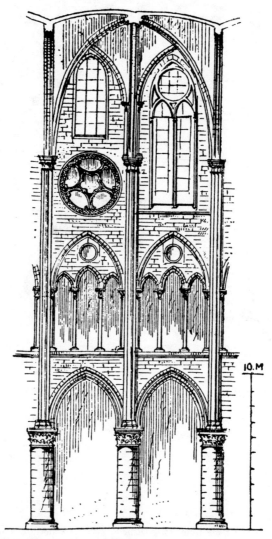

Fig. B. ELEVATION OF THE NAVE. The left-hand half shows the 12-c. design; the right-hand half shows that of the 13 c., made possible by the flying buttresses of Fig. E (*see pages* 132, 133).

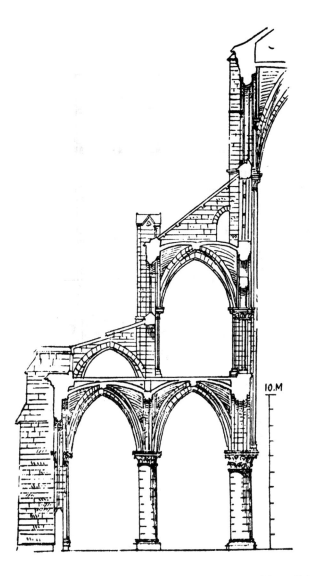

Fig. C. CROSS SECTION OF THE CHOIR, in its 12-c. state, without flying buttresses (*see pages,* 133, 153).

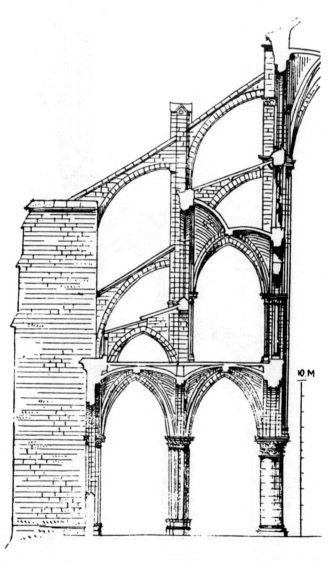

10. M

Fig. D.   CROSS SECTION OF THE NAVE, in its 12-c. state, with an intermediate support for the flying buttresses (*see page* 153).

Fig. E. CROSS SECTION OF THE NAVE, showing the daring leap of the 13-c. flying buttresses and the elimination of the intermediate structure above the tribune (*see pages* 153, 243).

Skyscraper Epoch, could have profited from this lesson. The Middle Age, for example, made no effort to conceal breaks in the campaign of construction but, on the contrary, displayed them frankly. If the east-west axis of Notre-Dame is sighted from the foot of the nave, it is easy to see that the church markedly shifts direction at the transept. The choir slants perceptibly north. But since the choir was built first, this means that it is the nave which diverges from the original axis and was begun on a new alignment.

This is one of the more obvious secrets of Notre-Dame, and it is charming enough, but the nineteenth century, which was rarely satisfied with a simple medieval truth, felt obliged to complicate it with a fable. Romantic archaeologists believed that the fault in alignment intentionally symbolized Christ on the cross, leaning to his right in agony. They contended that the Portail Rouge, the little door on the north of the choir, signified the wound of the Roman spear in the Savior's side. M. Aubert, disposing of this theory briefly, remarks that the Portail Rouge stands beyond the transept, and if it is a symbol of the wound, it is above Christ's shoulder and not below it.

The disalignment may indeed have been intentional, but for non-symbolist reasons. The plan shows that there is not one break in the axis, but two, the second somewhat more difficult to see. The nave also fails to coincide exactly with the façade where they are joined. Why this second inaccuracy? Perhaps poor calculation was the reason, although the medieval surveyor could be precise when he wished. No, both breaks seem to be due either to faults in the terrain, which are now undetectable, or, more likely, to the danger of collision with structures on the southern side of the Cathedral. If the axis of the choir had been extended, Notre-Dame might have butted into the episcopal palace or the Hôtel-Dieu.

In fact, the Cathedral was hemmed on every side by adjoining structures (Fig. 1, p. 33). On the north, near the façade, stood the Baptistery of Saint-Jean. The cloister ran along the entire northern flank. On the east was the priory of Saint-Denis-du-Pas, a pilgrimage station, which could not be moved. Space was severely limited, and the Master Builder had to make the most of the land at his disposal. This was his reason for adopting the horseshoe plan rather than a frank cruciform. Henri Focillon has termed Notre-Dame *"une église continue"*—an unbroken church—and no better description has been offered. The unbroken outer wall has the chaste line of a Cistercian chapel, and the medieval builder admired its severe possibilities. It enabled him to utilize all the available terrain, to expand interior floor space to a maximum, and to give his church majestic dignity and calm.

And so, artistically and spiritually, it must be recalled that Notre-Dame was not intended for its modern isolation. It was meant to thrust out of the walled Cité and tower above its low roofs. From a distance the upper portions of Notre-Dame alone were visible, and in the high air the cross shape stood out with splendid force. On ground level the Cathedral claimed every inch of land it could. It is easy to criticize this plan in the abstract and to argue that Paris lacks the dramatic transept of Chartres or Laon. But Chartres and Laon were not constructed in the crowded Cité. Their rural situations, although compressed, were more flexible than a water-locked island.

Unified, self-confident, serene, and powerful, dominating Paris, looking out over France and the West, Notre-Dame would seem to have been a scale model of the Church Triumphant, of Saint Bernard's Church Universal. The generality is tempting, but it cannot be made. This was the time of a schism. Christendom was cut in two by the cold Alps and by a foul moat of politics. The German Emperor and the French King each had his own Pope, and the whole course of European history—and European art—was affected by the fact that, in the end, the French policy won. It is also the reason that Alexander III was in Paris in 1163 to lay the first stone of Notre-Dame.

Mahomet had come to the mountain. As an exile in France, Alexander found churches with which the ancient sanctuaries of Italy could not compare. In the Cathedral of Sens, where he set up his refugee court, he had a mansion of the Lord that dwarfed his Saint Peter's of Rome. But more than Sens—every new splendor of the Transition was his. Wherever he traveled in France the pontiff was welcomed in churches of such audacity and confidence that he must surely have felt that he was suzerain of the world and that there was no other Pope than he. In the spring of 1163 he swept into a cheering Paris to consecrate the reconstructed choir of Saint-Germain-des-Prés.

The Pope stayed in the capital a month, from March 24 to April 25; and, according to tradition, he also dedicated the new Cathedral during his visit. There is no documentary proof, as there is for Saint-Germain-des-Prés, except the word of late medieval writers, but the legend would seem to be correct. Maurice would not have missed this opportunity to inaugurate his great enterprise.

The scene at the tip of the island may be imagined from accounts of similar ceremonies. A great procession made its way beyond Carolingian Notre-Dame, through the breach in the Gallo-Roman wall, to the deep foundation trenches. The Pope or whatever prelate presided mixed holy water with mortar and blessed the project. Then, in his brocaded robes, he descended into the excavations and with a trowel set the first stone upon another. The throng thereupon burst into the *Fundamenta Ejus;* no one has been closer to the moving thunder of the Latin than John Milton:

> Among the holy Mountains high
> Is his foundation fast,
> There seated in his Sanctuary
> His Temple there is plac't.

Stirred by the anthem, awed by the labor before them, did these twelfth-century creatures give way to total ecstasy? Two decades earlier, at Saint-Denis, Eleanor of Aquitaine and Louis le Jeune had wrenched the rings from their fingers and cast them into the diggings. Bishops and lords had done the same, throwing gem after gem into the hardening mortar, laying stone upon stone upon stone, as if they would build the church in a day, weeping, chanting, crying out sins, stretching crosswise on the ground.

But if the foundations were cemented with God's own mortar, they were laid with human skill. When the celebrities departed, anonymous workmen took their place. The cavity was filled with a bed of stone ten yards deep, on which the Cathedral might thrust its pressures until Domesday. The base would not give. After eight hundred years it rests as solid, as plumb, without fault or crevice, as the bedrock from which it was taken. Viollet-le-Duc, who at one time or another examined the substructure of every major church in France, was struck by the broad power of the foundations of Notre-Dame. Only Amiens and Bourges compare with them. A massive retaining wall runs beneath the entire perimeter of the monument, following its horseshoe shape. This shell widens as it descends and enters the earth in steps a meter tall, half as high as a man. Its stone, the *lambourde ferme* of Montrouge, is among the finest employed in the Cathedral and is laid with the utmost care in natural beds. The heavy blocks were placed beneath the Cathedral in the same position that nature placed them in the quarry, so that their full geologic resistance comes into play. All this stone is of course below the surface and was never meant to be seen, but it is dressed as fastidiously as any visible masonry above. It set a tone of integrity for the entire structure.

Behind the retaining wall is an immovable mass of filling—flint, ashlar, and cement, plus wreckage of the Carolingian and Merovingian basilicas, and the deep remains of the Gallo-Roman city, its rampart and pagan altars. The twelfth century fused the past with volcanic heat. The filling of the foundations was packed so hard, and then pressed down farther by the weight of the church, that it became as homogeneous as lava. The whole rests like a fact of nature on the rough green sand of the floor of the Seine.

Chapter Nine

THE CHOIR AND THE APSE
1163 - 1182

O N THE MIGHTY foundations the first master builder of Notre-Dame erected a structure of the utmost simplicity: the twelfth-century chancel, or chevet. It would grow complex with time. Like a creature of the deep, moving slowly through history, its shell would accumulate a variety of life, some parasitical, some necessary and lovely as sea flowers. Successive ages have rebuilt and augmented, harmed and restored, the sanctuary of Notre-Dame, until the Gothic Transition would scarcely recognize its own labor. Today, seen from across the Seine, the apse appears a model of late Gothic eloquence. The white arms of the flying buttresses surround the dark Cathedral with a weightless, dancing motion, and a charm that is almost literary. The buttresses are considerably younger than the venerable walls they support; they are a full century later than the central vessel, which was originally conceived without them. Had the flying buttresses not been added, Notre-Dame might have collapsed and vanished, for when the choir and apse were begun in 1163 no one dreamed of the cage of exterior supports that was to give medieval architecture its incessant outward movement.

From the Left Bank, on the quays where twelfth-century intellectuals watched summer pass pleasantly, as the river flowed westward and sunlight played on the stone rampart of the island across the narrow stream, it was easy to see the new Cathedral taking form. The rampart, dating from Roman times when the Ile was half its medieval size, curved northward where the second bay of the choir stands today, not far beyond the transept. And crowded in the curve of the fortifications, its roofs hardly surmounting them, was Carolingian Notre-Dame. Through the wide breach in the wall teamsters were driving wagon after wagon past the old church to the clear ground at the eastern end of the island, where they would deposit their loads of stone before turning back through the Cité, and across the Petit Pont, to the quarries. Hundreds of workmen, who had been hard at it since dawn, were scurrying over the foundations, finishing stone, carrying hods of mortar, and already climbing the scaffolds. They would not knock off until sunset.

The site, with its eastern end free, was thus ideally given to construction of the sanctuary before all else. This was precisely what Maurice de Sully wished. The nave, the transept, even the façade of his Cathedral were secondary. In Paris, as almost everywhere in Gothic France, the choir and apse came first. Architecturally, as they were socially, the common mortals in the nave might be neglected. The Virgin, who dwelled in the rear of the church, could not; nor could her priests; nor the Capet King, who ruled by divine mandate and therefore had a special place in her shrine.

The Virgin spoke through her priests and governed through her earthly seigneurs, but it was she alone, in the twelfth and thirteenth centuries, who dominated French society. With few exceptions, the greatest cathedrals of France are hers: Amiens as well as Paris and Laon, Chartres and Reims, Strasbourg and Bayeux. It is a surprise to find a church such as Bourges dedicated not to Mary but to Saint Stephen. The Virgin was more than any saint. In the three hundred years since the Norman invasions she had become the most powerful deity of the Occident. Where she once commanded a small local guard, fighting desperately for her life and its own, she had armies at her disposal, which she now hurled repeatedly against the Saracenic East. Where a dozen clerks had tended her embattled altar at Paris, scores sought space in her shrine.

The sanctuary of Carolingian Notre-Dame could not nearly contain this host of priests. At least fifty clerks would appear for an ordinary Mass; one hundred and fifty or two hundred would empty the cloister for important services. Nor could the aged basilica provide a suitable stage for the ceremonies of the court—a vital consideration, since Paris, like Reims and Saint-Denis, was a royal church. Throughout their dynasty Capets were baptized and married and thanked God for victory at Notre-Dame; and it was from the

Cathedral that royal funeral processions set out across the capital to Saint-Denis.

And so the chancel was not only given priority as the most precious element of the new church, it was also provided with dimensions as formidable as the site would permit. Its great curving structure extends no less than one hundred and seventy feet (52 meters) eastward from the transept. Its over-all width is one hundred and fifty-seven feet (48 meters). It covers an area as great as the total ground surface of a good-sized abbey church such as Saint-Germain-des-Prés. Yet its central vessel, flanked by a spacious double aisle, is relatively narrow: only forty-three feet (13 meters) wide against a length of one hundred and twenty-one feet (37 meters).

For liturgical purposes, this slender vessel was divided in two distinct portions, much as it is today. The first four bays compose the choir, where the Chapter is seated during the Mass. The extremity of the vessel, separated from the choir by a flight of three steps, is properly the sanctuary itself, where the master altar is located, beneath a great semicircular vault of eight ogive ribs. The double aisle that surrounds the sanctuary constitutes the apse.

With the old Carolingian apse on its west, jutting timidly among the scaffolds, the chancel of Notre-Dame lifted from the earth. Cluny, the culmination of the Romanesque, without the ogive, had pushed its vaults ninety-eight feet (30 meters) above the pavements of its rich Benedictine shrine. Before Notre-Dame, the ogive had tried nothing in this class. It had reached only seventy-nine feet (24 meters) at Sens and Laon. The Master Builder of Paris boldly decided that he could go half again as high as Laon, surpassing Cluny, to one hundred and seven feet (32.5 meters).

To appreciate this step it must be remembered that this was a period when structural disasters were frequent. Vaults cracked, even Cluny's, and mortar showered down dangerously. The ribbed vault was too recent a feature to have stood any test of time, and to lift it almost thirty feet was an act of courage. No church would go higher than Notre-Dame in the twelfth century, and few afterward. Chartres, rebuilt a generation later in 1194, went to one hundred and eighteen feet (36 meters). Bourges and Reims, both after 1200, advanced a meter beyond Chartres. Then the fully developed Gothic, at Amiens, leaped to one hundred and thirty-eight feet (42 meters). The tallest cathedral was Beauvais, whose vault is higher than Saint Peter's of Rome. Yet it marked the point where grandeur became grandiosity, and ambition, show. At its zenith the Gothic decayed. Beauvais marked no real structural advance beyond Amiens. It sacrificed stability for effect. Its materials were chosen for economy. Begun in 1247, when Notre-Dame stood largely completed, its keystones rose one hundred and fifty-seven feet (48 meters)—half again as high as Paris! In 1284, less than forty years later, it fell half to pieces, and remains unfinished. The other great cathedrals, from Paris to Amiens, were completed and have held.

The chancel of Notre-Dame, then, in Focillon's phrase, inaugurated the "Age of the Colossal." How the young ogive was raised to such a height is worth studying in some detail; for although technicalities may be boring they lie beneath the poetry of the monument like a solid Shakespearean pentameter. Also, no matter how lovely the exterior of the Cathedral, the architecture must be considered first from within. In the Gothic, as in the twentieth-century International, in all structure with moral integrity, outer appearance is governed totally by interior dispositions. This truth the Master Builder knew better than Le Corbusier. He knew too that his building could not stand unless it was strong, and that it could not please unless it was beautiful, and he proceeded from these assumptions alone.

Stand at the entrance of his choir and study the towering vessel as it appeared when it stood completely open on the west. From arch to pointed arch, Notre-Dame rises in three distinct and separate surges; and this is the basic elevation of the Cathedral, which will be seen again in transept and nave: the lowest element is the grand colonnade of the double aisle on either side, with its massive pillars and heroic arches, curving to meet at the rear of the sanctuary; next is the intermediate story of the tribune, the open spectators' gallery, which, like the aisle beneath, makes a turn around the apse; here the major arch has become an *arc de décharge,* or covering arch, with a charming double arcade nested beneath it; and finally, filling the wall above to the vaults are the high windows of the clerestory. The tracery of each window defines two lancets and a surmounting rose, the whole contained in a third great pointed arch.

In spite of the dimensions of these windows—they are thirty-two feet tall—it is apparent to anyone who has seen Laon or Noyon, not to mention a thirteenth-century cathedral such as Amiens, that Notre-Dame is an exceptionally dark church. One reason for this is the narrowness of the central vessel: the light of the high windows strikes the opposite wall rather than descending at a diagonal to the floor of the church, as it does in a vessel such as Noyon's, which is only two-thirds as tall, but almost as broad, as Paris. Yet dark as Notre-Dame appears today, it was darker still in the twelfth century, before the present windows were installed. They date from the thirteenth century, when the whole top of the church was rebuilt to provide it with more light and stability. In the eight bays immediately adjoining the transept, however—the last two bays of the choir, the first two of the nave, and four in the transept itself—may be seen an approximation of the clerestory of the twelfth century, reinstalled as a Romantic caprice during the restoration of Viollet-le-Duc.

In these bays there are not three levels but four, and it is the clerestory alone which makes the difference. Instead of totally occupying the upper wall with tracery, the high window is a small lancet, severely pure in outline. Immediately below, between this modest clerestory and the tribune, in a space that was filled by the lower part of the window in the thirteenth-century scheme, is a rose. The roses were not windows but lightless apertures that opened on the roof of the tribune. They were intended merely to strengthen the construction with their round frames and to give scale to the wall—which they do admirably. They provided an enchanting bouquet for Mary's shrine, yet light was more important to the Middle Age than dark charm, and the twelfth-century fenestration was dark indeed. For this reason the thirteenth century cut the roses from the wall, lowered the roof of the tribune, and replaced the small lancet windows with the immense sheets of glass which are seen today. If the two elevations are considered side by side (Fig. B), the difference made by the reconstruction may be appreciated easily. The expanded clerestory admitted twice as much light as its timid predecessor.

Yet in the end, after the great windows were installed, Notre-Dame remained darker than its contemporaries, and the Middle Age had to concede that the fault was incurable. It lay in the church's own precocious grandeur. Notre-Dame, like blind Samson, was too tall for its age. To illuminate adequately a vessel of this height, the flying buttress was necessary to shore the upper walls, so that the intermediate tribune could be eliminated and windows opened which filled the entire wall between the colonnade of the aisle and the main vault, as at Amiens. The First Master of Paris did not have the flying buttress. The Second Master—the man who built the nave after 1180—would develop it in the course of the work, possibly the first architect to do so; but even he would not realize its full potentialities. He too would use the tribune to support his upper wall.

Buttressing is part of the larger subject of equilibrium, impressive sounding but given to simplification. It is necessary only to give a half-turn to the elevation drawing (Fig. B) to place the choir in cross-section (Fig. C), and see how it was held erect in the twelfth century, before the addition of flying buttresses.

Here is the calm, grand unity of the Romanesque. There is nothing of the striving uneasiness and shooting independent line which would characterize the Gothic in less than twenty years. Instead, the scheme is of such compact simplicity that it seems the work of the preceding architectural age. The Transition has moved with feverish haste, but its youth should be remembered. Scarcely thirty years have passed since its birth at Saint-Denis; and the new system of building has not yet freed itself from its aged parent. A glance at the cross-section shows how a Romanesque feature—the broad and open tribune gallery—received central importance in a church of the second half of the twelfth century, as it did in Norman churches of the eleventh. The tribune serves as a prism that focuses the pressure from above and transmits it in even waves on the double aisle below.

Follow an impulse downward from the topmost key. The ogive curves and plunges into a group of slender colonnettes whose shafts fall sixty feet, without a break, clinging elegantly to the wall, until they reach the great columns of the aisle far below. The colonnettes enhance the scale of the church but assume a minor portion of its thrust. The major stress flows outward and diagonally downward through the tribune, where it is absorbed and split on another web of ogives. From each key the forces of the monument again jet downward, like brooks in the Alps, flowing and curving, hurrying through channel after channel, deepening, widening, streaming broadly through the wall, pouring into the double aisle. Here, on the vaulting of the aisles, the dividing action of the tribune is twice repeated. The pressure from above is again absorbed on an ogive frame, and again split in four, eight, sixteen, thirty-two branches to the colonnade.

This grand colonnade is one of the most splendidly ordered of the Middle Age. Its pillars are models of strength and optimism. Although they have supported the Cathedral for eight hundred years they appear young, and cheerfully share their round power with the entire monument. They are not monoliths, it may be remarked, but superimposed drums of stone. Each drum is roughly half a yard high, a yard and a half in diameter, and would seem to weigh four or five hundred pounds. The stone itself is as hard and resistant as any in France: the bedrock of Bagneux and the Butte Saint-Jacques. A dozen such drums, set on a heavy base, and surmounted by a magnificent capital, make up a typical pillar.

At confident intervals, yards apart, spaced with complete audacity, the pillars show the young Gothic at its most robust and honest moment. The ogives, leaping from capital to capital, frankly reveal the diverse flow of pressures. There is no strain, no sign of weakness anywhere; no pretentious detail, but only serene and unhurried strength, even as the aisle approaches the great turn of the apse.

The circular apse is rivaled only by the western façade as the most spectacular element of Notre-Dame. It was without doubt the most difficult part of the church to design and build, to maintain the equilibrium of the choir as it makes its tremendous 180-degree turn. To mount a gigantic structure above a turning aisle was at best a risky undertaking before the Age of Steel. At worst it was sheer hazard. Masonry, when its weight becomes prohibitive, resists unusual shapes; and the round apse of a cathedral—pressing inward toward the void of the transept—taxed the ingenuity of the Master Builder as no other portion of his church. The primitive round choir of Laon collapsed in short order, before the year 1200; and Laon attempted only a single aisle. At Paris a double aisle was planned, and the risk became considerable indeed. For safety, the Paris Master might have compressed his turning colonnade (as many masters did), so that the interval between the pillars of the *rond-point* would have been no wider than the pillars themselves; but he might as well have conceded his unintelligence utterly and thrown up a solid wall.

There was, of course, another alternative. The Master could have abandoned the circular scheme and adopted the safer rectangular plan, which the Cistercians preferred for their ascetic creations and which was also popular in England. The flat wall was cheaper to finance, easier to construct, and child's play to buttress. Singularly, the Master who rebuilt Laon was the only French cathedral architect who found these advantages worth while, even though the flat wall offered the additional temptation of a great rose, like that at Laon, above the altar of the Virgin. The Paris Master and his Bishop, Maurice de Sully, did not wish to give the apse the broad grandeur of a façade. A façade is a public thing, the most accessible of images. The apse was altogether private. It was filled with the ineffable presence of Mary, suffused by her tenderness, alive with her secrets. If a church was to possess mystery anywhere, it needed it here. And so, to serve as a marvelous religious tunnel for the pilgrim making a tour of the famous relics, and, more important, because of the effect produced when the Litany was sung from altar to altar on its sweeping curve, the apse necessarily had to be round. If the master had the courage to establish a double aisle rather than a cramped single one, so much the better.

Without the elastic properties of the ogive vault, the problems of the round plan in a large structure might have been insuperable. Happily, when he drew up his plan in 1163, the Master of Notre-Dame had a full local tradition of ribbed-vault apses to instruct him. During the previous thirty years Paris had seen three important Transitional structures erected. Two have already been seen: Saint-Martin-des-Champs, in the fields on the Right Bank, and Saint-Denis. The third, completed at the moment Notre-Dame was begun, is the choir of Saint-Germain-des-Prés.

Saint-Martin-des-Champs (1130-1142) and Saint-Denis are contemporaries, but, as Focillon has pointed out, the two seem decades apart. Saint-Martin, a modest building, might have disintegrated had it been much larger. It bears terrible marks of improvisation. At Saint-Denis, on the other hand, for the first time in the ogival style, the apse was approached by a master in full control of his art (Fig.

3, p. 79). As one would cut a pie, Suger's architect divided the ambulatory into seven equal sections, each falling wedge-shaped across a double aisle. The inner aisle he vaulted with simple crossings of ogives. The outer aisle was more difficult to vault, not only because its perimeter had grown to very considerable length, but also because each exterior bay was rounded to give it a chapel form. It is worth looking at the Master's technique here to see how fluently, in the year 1140, an architect could speak the Gothic language. In each crossing of ogives he merely added a fifth rib and carried it to a supplemental pier set between the windows. With the thrust of the monument falling to either side, the windows could find their desired size and fill the wall.

After the rebuilding of Saint-Denis, Saint-Germain-des-Prés had been quick to react with a reconstruction of its own. The two formidable Parisian monasteries had been at artistic war, not to mention political conflict, since Merovingian times. In the Gothic moment, eying each other jealously across the Seine, their rivalry was intense. Consequently, when the monks of Saint-Germain dedicated their new choir in 1163, they were thinking of revenge. In a sense, they had it. Saint-Germain, after Sens, was the second ogival monument to omit the tribune. But otherwise Saint-Germain attempted less than Saint-Denis, and its problems were less complex. Not only is its apse somewhat smaller, it is also simpler in basic plan. Instead of the double aisle, the Master of Saint-Germain decided on a single one and a ring of chapels inserted between the exterior buttresses. The result gives the possibility for private worship which Christianity has appreciated in all its diverse eras, but the clarity of Suger's church is missing.

Thus the highly individualistic spirit of the Transition is alive in three Parisian churches—and a fourth: Notre-Dame. Maurice de Sully's Master Builder was as experimental, as courageous, and his approach as fresh as any of his predecessors. The Gothic was still expanding, and he rose on its swell of beauty. Even if he had wished to borrow ideas, few existing ones would have fitted his church. Notre-Dame was almost as large as Saint-Martin, Saint-Denis, and Saint-Germain together; and as no French architect before him, the Paris Master was forced to consider the apse on an epic scale. Instinctively he realized this must be in terms of simplicity, strength, order, and space.

This sounds Greek. And indeed it is not impossible that the Master had been reading Euclid, translated through Arabic to Latin, and then conceivably to the French popular tongue. There was, after all, a Vitruvius in the library of the Cathedral of Rouen. In any case, the Paris Master reduced the problem of the apse to the simple Euclidean theorem of concentric circles: the larger the circle, the longer its minute of arc. Granted, the dimensions of a church might expand at a frightening rate as the radius from the rond-point lengthened, in the same way that waves broaden quickly as they flow outward in a pool of water, but at least the expansion in a stone monument would be predictable and regular.

The Master knew that the regularity of the plan was dependent on pure line. Clean unbroken circles were necessary for perfection. But could an ideal purity be maintained? An important conference with the Bishop must now have taken place on the subject of chapels. Might chapels be dispensed with, the Master asked, to avoid complication of the plan? Maurice de Sully's decision was Yes, and many amateur theologians have since disagreed, saying that chapels had to be added, ultimately, for proper conduct of the services. To this it may be replied that the chapels of the apse of Notre-Dame were not added until the fourteenth century, one hundred and fifty years later, when medieval architecture, and with architecture all things medieval, had begun its decline. In the twelfth century chapels were far from being essential. Notre-Dame was not the only church planned without them. Bourges, Mantes, and a number of other monuments fall in the same category. Presumably there was no objection to placing altars against the wall of the ambulatory and isolating them, if necessary, by tapestries and cloths.

The elimination of chapels enabled the Master to conserve his unbroken outer wall: the continuous perimeter that gives Notre-Dame such chaste external power. But purity of apsidal line also had a major effect within the church, where the Master boldly flung the main colonnade, without any reduction in strength or spaciousness, around the perilous curve. He maintained as wide an interval between pillars as in the straight portions of the aisles; and at the same time he preserved the majestic size of the pillars themselves. As the apse is approached, there is no weakening of tone, no hesitation in visible line. The ogives move outward above like spokes in a great hastening wheel.

The calm regular splendor of the apse is one of the chief beauties of Notre-Dame, and one that has not always been noticed. The fourteenth-century Master Builder nearly ruined it by the addition of chapels. The Neo-Classicists, who thought they knew about order, were so ashamed of its lines that they hid them with stucco, which has since been washed away. The apse remained unappreciated until Viollet-le-Duc, at last, analyzed its mastery:

The architect of Notre-Dame of Paris resolved the problem by breaking completely with Romanesque tradition. Since he wished the interval (A) between the pillars of the rond-point to be as wide as the interval (B) between the pillars of the straight aisle, it followed that the first radiating bay of the apse provided an inner space (LMGH) which was difficult to vault, and an outer space (HGFE) which was impossible. For how could an arch be established from F to E? Even the key of a round arch would have risen much higher than the key of the pointed archivolt LM. Since the second radiating bay opened still wider, it presented even more difficulty. The Builder therefore decided to insert intermediate pillars (O and P) in the central line of columns (H, G, and I); and also inserted an intermediate pier (Q) between the exterior buttresses of the first bay, and two intermediate piers (R and S) between the buttresses of the second larger bay.

This disposition of two pillars on the inner radius, three on the central, and four piles on the outermost, made it impossible to vault the aisles with conventional crossed ribs of ogives. Such a system requires an even number of pillars in each line, forming squares or parallelograms across which the ogives may pass as diagonals. But the Builder was not stopped by this difficulty. He abandoned the system of crossed ribs; and after he had established simple transversal arches between MG and GF, and between NI and IK, he connected NP, MP, GR, PR, PS, and IS with a triangular system of ribs which passed easily from an even number of pillars in one aisle to an uneven number in the next.

"Creative genius," exclaimed Viollet-le-Duc in admiration. The Master had made the vital discovery that a V combination of ogives was as resistant as an X; and his apse, with its remarkable triangular vaulting and severe strength of form, immediately joined the apse

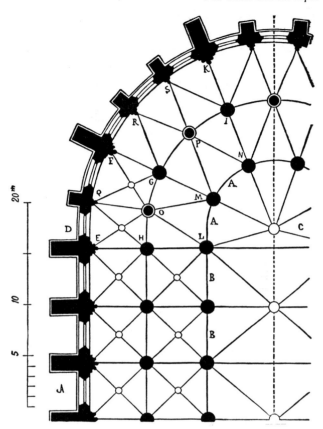

Fig. 4. NOTRE-DAME. Section of the apse in the twelfth century, before the addition of chapels. (Viollet-le-Duc)

of Saint-Denis as a model for the classic Gothic to come. From Saint-Denis came the apses of Vézelay, Chartres, and a score of thirteenth-century cathedrals. Notre-Dame influenced Bourges and Le Mans, a widespread group of smaller French churches, Spanish cathedrals such as Toledo, and the Cathedral of Nicosia in distant Cyprus.

At Bourges, both in the crypt, where the V-vaulting of Paris was partially copied, and in the ambulatory above, it is possible to grasp the effect of the apse of Notre-Dame before its chapels were added. For although Bourges has been disfigured by the addition of five tiny chapels, it has not suffered a disaster equivalent to that of Paris, where the entire rear of the church has been robbed of light by the later chapels. At Bourges light flows directly into the aisles and floods the sanctuary with the blue brilliance of the glass. The effect at Paris, before the source of light was moved the width of another aisle from the heart of the church, must have been very similar.

Le Mans, begun less than two decades after Bourges, in 1217, adopted many features of the continuous Parisian plan but was designed from the start with a circle of splendid jutting chapels, which are small churches in themselves. Le Mans was also one of the last cathedrals to use the double aisle. As churches continued to grow in size, the double ambulatory no longer seemed essential or even desirable. The single aisles of Amiens and Beauvais, well over twenty feet across, provide almost as broad an ambulatory as the double aisle of Notre-Dame.

And now, from 1163 to 1182, the choir and apse rose in nineteen years. Tales that the cathedrals required several centuries for their actual construction are simply not true. Except for superficial additions, a typical cathedral was built in less than one hundred years. Notre-Dame took only ninety; some went up in less than fifty. Although the master builders operated in a preindustrial age they had a variety of technical equipment at their disposal: the winch and the windlass, the inclined plane, the lever and the jack. They were expert riggers of block and tackle. They handled stone quickly—certainly as quickly as it is handled in France today.

As soon as the heavy drums of rock were carted from the quarries they were finished and hoisted in place, one upon the other, and the colonnade lifted. The tough and slender arches were sprung across the aisles, and the tribune mounted above. Since space was limited, the roofs of the lower portions of the monument became workshops, as the scaffolds rose higher. By 1177 the choir was completed except for its main vaults, and its furnishings were being prepared. Albert, Precentor of the Chapter, who died in 1174, left twenty livres for the stalls. In 1175 Archbishop Henry of Reims made a characteristic bequest of a friendly prelate (and of a Capet: he was brother to Louis VII) when he endowed twelve lamps that were to burn perpetually. Barbedor donated fifteen livres for an expensive window. Such treasured possessions of the old Cathedral as Suger's blue Virgin were dismounted and carried to the new. Window after window was being set in lead frames: a haunting ensemble of glass, which was destroyed in the eighteenth century and replaced with white glass to admit more light. Today the white glass is gone too, supplanted by colored windows of Viollet-le-Duc.

Finally, in 1182, the main vaults were sprung. The chancel stood completed, and on the Feast of Pentecost, May 19, the master altar itself was consecrated by Henri de Château-Marçay, the papal legate, who was the highest ranking churchman then in France. Maurice de Sully assisted him in a ceremony which the chroniclers describe as splendid. But three years later Notre-Dame was the scene of the first of the grand historical episodes which, over the centuries, would make it the most important single building of France. To the new Cathedral on January 17, 1185, came Heraclius, Patriarch of Jerusalem, to preach the Third Crusade to the people of Paris and their young soldier king, Philip Augustus.

Chapter Ten

THE NAVE
1182 - 1200?

n OTRE-DAME was already famous. Itinerant merchants and priests, pilgrims, diplomats, foreign students, traveling knights and crusaders, freed serfs seeking new homes —the whole wandering human fabric of the Middle Age passed through the capital of France and admired its Cathedral. And when they proceeded on the long roads they spoke with wonder of Notre-Dame, of the height of its vaults and the beauty of its sculpture and glass. Sometimes, if they returned to a calm monastery or castle, the travelers would mention the church in chronicles. In their descriptions Notre-Dame is called quite simply the *ecclesia* of Paris— the cathedral church par excellence, in a city of many remarkable churches. News of the monument spread through the West with a speed any modern project would envy.

And so the tourists, who have never ceased to come, began to arrive on the island. Among the first was the Abbot of the Mont-Saint-Michel, Robert de Torigny, as distinguished a churchman and as ambitious a builder as Maurice de Sully. Abbot Robert made many improvements on the Mount, some of which survive to challenge anything at Notre-Dame; yet, audacious constructor though he was, the abbé was nonplused by the nearly completed choir he saw in Paris in 1177. "For some time now," he noted in his journal, "Maurice, Bishop of Paris, has worked hard and made much progress in erecting the Cathedral of that city, whose chancel is already terminated, except for the main vault. If this work is ever brought to completion, no other church on this side of [the Alps] will be able to be compared with it."

Not every critic was so enthusiastic. If Notre-Dame was admired and famous from the first days of construction, it was also notorious to the puritan mentality. The Church Protestant, still speaking as part of the Church Catholic, objected bitterly to Maurice's creation. Half a century earlier Saint Bernard had thundered against the Romanesque, attacking its rich churches as "Synagogues of Satan." Now, in the cloister of Notre-Dame, a voice rose angrily against the Gothic. One of the dignitaries of the Chapter, Pierre le Chantre, came to grips with what he called the *"morbus aedificandi"*—the "disease of construction"—which had seized France; and he caustically denounced his Bishop and his Cathedral on grounds of luxury and pride.

"To build churches as is done at present is to sin," Pierre wrote in his *Summa Ecclesiastica* about the year 1180. Then, in an elaborate play of words that was actually an argument against the spacious Gothic church plan, he continued: "The chevets (*capita:* i.e., heads) of our churches should be more humble than their bodies (*corporibus*) because of the mystery they symbolize. For Christ, who is at our head—the head of his Church—is more humble than his Church. Yet today chancels are built higher and higher."

At a time when the choir of Notre-Dame stood strikingly alone above the roofs of the Cité the reference was unmistakable; but Precentor Peter went on as angrily as before: "And for what good are palaces erected, and fortified towers, and ramparts? It is forever this passion to build. . . ." Maurice must have felt this gibe keenly, for he had just constructed an elaborate residence. While the choir had risen he had transformed the episcopal palace from a primitive Carolingian fortress to a powerful twelfth-century château, complete with donjon and crenelations. Today the palace is gone, destroyed in the Revolution of 1830; and there is a pretty park on its emplacement between the Cathedral and the Seine.

The lost palace may be seen vividly in the seventeenth-century gravures of Israel Sylvestre or in the drawings of Viollet-le-Duc, who, as a child, saw the building intact; but it may be visualized best by a trip to a cathedral that has kept some of its dependencies—no cathedral has kept all. In the Bishop's courtyard at Laon, where larks hop in the summer grass, the scale of the episcopal residence at Paris and the formidable thickness of its walls may be appreciated easily. At both Laon and Meaux are approximations of the personal chapel that Maurice de Sully consecrated to the Virgin, to his patron Saint Maurice, and to Saint Vincent and all the other martyrs. Also at Meaux, and remarkably preserved, are the lower rooms of the palace in which the official business of the diocese was conducted; and at Sens are not only the lower rooms, but above them a great hall of the thirteenth century, which makes it possible to picture Maurice's great hall of the twelfth. The hall of the Bishop of Paris was an unobstructed vessel, ten yards across and nearly forty yards long, with a line of lancet windows on either side. This lordly room, in 1179, was the scene of an event that marked a turning point in French history: the advent of Prince Philip Augustus.

Since the August night in 1165 when Paris awakened to revelry at the news that a male heir had been born to the throne after a wait of twenty-eight years, the Capet Dynasty had looked to this child for its salvation. The Crown was in a position of grave weakness: a disastrous series of wars with the Plantagenets had reduced the kingdom by half. It mattered little that Henry II of England owed Louis VII a vassal's homage. Henry was Duke of Normandy and of Aquitaine and Count of Anjou, and possessed as much of France as the King. Nor was Henry Plantagenet the only enemy of the Crown. All the leading feudatories—the princes of Champagne, Flanders, Burgundy, and Nevres—cantankerously abused the royal dignity. Louis, more mystical than ever, would not stand up to his barons.

The boy Philip did. The loyal bourgeoisie of Paris chuckled over tales of his precocity. When Philip was four years old, in 1169, he accompanied his father to a meeting with Henry Plantagenet at the crest of Montmartre. There, through the good offices of the French King, a reconciliation was being attempted between Henry and Thomas Becket, once Henry's friend and chancellor, but now his hostile Archbishop of Canterbury, who had taken refuge in France. For the first time, Philip was presented to the strongest monarch of the West. Henry, preoccupied by his quarrel with the Archbishop, regarded the prince irritably, spoke a few words to him, and galloped off. But with the singular courtesy which seems to have belonged to the Gothic Age alone, Philip called him back and beseeched him to "love his father, France, and himself, Philip, and so obtain the good Grace of God and men." The eyewitness who recorded this speech was Becket himself, who added: "It seemed that the Lord had inspired the mind and tongue of that chosen child."

The child was chosen, and yet throughout the 1170s he was needlessly exposed to danger. Hitherto the Capets had prudently practiced infant coronation as soon as possible. Inexplicably, however, Louis postponed anointing his son; and without the ceremony at Reims, Philip was scarcely more regal, before the medieval lord, than a number of nobles—all relatives—who coveted the throne. Those loyal to the royal house were astonished by the delay. Maurice de Sully, who had baptized Philip, repeatedly urged Louis to crown his heir so that divine succession might be guaranteed. At last, in 1179, the peers and prelates of the realm were convoked to Paris, where they met in the great hall of Maurice, which for some reason the King preferred to his own Palace a short distance away. They waited patiently as Louis first prayed alone, to Mary, in the Bishop's private chapel. Then he emerged and announced his intention to crown Philip on the next Feast of the Assumption. Whereupon the assembly cried out, "So be it! So be it!" But the single important personage in France to be absent from the ceremony was Louis, who lay paralyzed and dying at Paris, while the boy king at Reims, like Shakespeare's Prince Hal, wore his father's crown and ruled in fact and name for nearly a year before the old king's death in 1180.

A new period in French life followed, accompanied by territorial expansion and centralization of royal power, which would lead, ultimately, to the absolute state of Louis XIV. Philip was a child, but a most gifted and determined child. He knew not only how to fight but how to intrigue; and for the five years before his twentieth birthday in 1185 he so manipulated existing rivalries (with the aid of clever advisers) that, for a time, even the Plantagenets were helping him control his rebellious nobles. A feudal coalition led by Champagne and Flanders was defeated in a major civil war; and then, with a singleness of purpose which was rare for the Middle Age and which could not be diverted even by the Third Crusade, Philip turned westward for his savage battle with the Plantagenets that would culminate in the taking of Normandy.

Philip Augustus was no mystic, and his piety never achieved the intensity of his father's or of his grandson's, Saint Louis; but he was nevertheless devout to an extent the modern world can scarcely appreciate. Strong as he was, Philip bent like a reed before the wind of Heaven. He too was a Capet, or "Chapet," the nickname that means "clad in an ecclesiastical cloak"; as did all the family, he held official Church positions, such as the Abbacy of Saint-Martin of Tours. He experienced ecstasies that have been described as "hallucinations." His special protectors were Saint Thomas Becket, murdered through a gross political blunder in 1170, canonized in 1173, and honored almost immediately afterward with an altar in Notre-Dame, who, like a celestial lawyer, now defended Philip's interests before the Court of Heaven; his personal patron, Saint Philip the Apostle, who, according to the Golden Legend, "preached Jesus Christ among the Gauls"; and, of course, Saint Denis, the Patron of France, and the Virgin, Patron of all the World.

As it had been to all his family, the Cathedral of Paris was "exceptionally dear" (*"specialem nostre dilleccionis"*) to this emotional child; and very early in his reign he decided to enlarge and honor it (*"ampliare volumus et honorare"*). The resolution was made good. During Philip's forty-three years on the throne the church's proportions would expand in direct relation to the enlarged national state. The nave of Notre-Dame, larger and more complex if not more lovely than the choir, corresponds exactly with the first twenty years of his reign: the Third Crusade and the struggle for Normandy.

The nave also belongs to a Paris that benefited greatly from the sovereign's improvements. In 1186, the chronicler Rigord relates, Philip was resting in his palace after a victory over the Burgundians:

He was strolling in the great royal hall, thinking over affairs of state, and walked to the Palace windows from which he often looked out on the Seine for diversion. The horse carts crossing the city, cutting up the mud, stirred up a mess which he couldn't support; and he decided on a difficult but necessary piece of work which his predecessors had not dared to undertake because of the crushing expense. He summoned the burgesses and the provost of the city, and ordered by his royal authority that all the roads and streets of the city should be paved with strong, hard stone.

Only the major streets, leading to the gates, were paved; but the Parisians thought so much of the innovation that one street is called the rue Pavée to this day. At about the same time the cemetery of the Holy Innocents, in the Marais on the Right Bank, where Goujon's fountain stands, was enclosed by a stone wall, probably out of respect for the dead, but—at a time when plague erupted from burial grounds—representing a victory for public health nonetheless. The Hôtel-Dieu was modernized and enlarged; and the Schools were incorporated in a university. The financial condition of the entire city was bettered by a stroke of high-handedness typical of Philip: he exiled the Jews in 1182 and abrogated all debts owed them, except for twenty per cent which he claimed for the Crown. Population continued to rise and was approximately one hundred thousand. The capital had become a metropolis; and to protect it from surprise attack, Philip walled its perimeter on both sides of the river, the Right Bank in 1190-1200, the Left Bank in the ten years afterward. Fragments of his stout rampart, which was surmounted by towers every hundred yards, may be seen throughout the center of the city; and a long section stands independently, high on the Left Bank, behind the Lycée Henri IV.

Without doubt King Philip had much to say about the construction, and above all the financing, of Notre-Dame. His move against the Jews, for example, appears to have been inspired, at least in part, by the heavy indebtedness of the Church during this period of unprecedented building. Pierre le Chantre, in another attack on Bishop Maurice, wrote with heat against churches constructed through the "usury of avarice" and the "avarice of usury"; and there is other evidence to indicate that Maurice, like the Abbots of Saint-Denis and Saint-Germain-des-Prés, indeed borrowed from the Juiverie or from Christian usurers when funds ran low. For collateral these prelates did not hesitate to leave jeweled altar vessels, ivories, and even illuminated Bibles, in pawn.

Philip Augustus became the chief adviser in the building of the Cathedral, as his father had been, but Maurice de Sully continued as director and leading spirit of the project. Every major decision in policy and aesthetics came not from the royal, but from the episcopal, palace. Yet as more and more of Maurice's time was consumed by the responsibilities of his diocese and his part in the government of France (during the Crusade, for example, he was a custodian of the royal treasure)—to say nothing of international problems of the

Church such as the Becket affair—the Bishop found that he needed a special assistant to supervise the construction. Barbedor, upon whom Maurice had previously depended, died about the time the choir was completed; his name drops out of the cartulary in 1181 and that of a new dean, Hervé, appears in 1185. Happily Maurice found a trustworthy helper in his nephew John, whom he appointed warden of the Cathedral. Another nephew, William, was appointed a canon. Such nepotism was natural in the Middle Age. It was one of the rare ways for a family to cross class boundaries.

The old generation was passing. As his nephew came to aid Maurice, and as son succeeded father in the dynasty of Capets, a new master builder took charge of Notre-Dame, perhaps also replacing a father. The Second Master's name, like that of the First, has been lost, but his personality stands out with an individualism as bold as Leonardo's in the architecture of the nave. He was the last of the Gothic experimenters, for when he in turn passed the work to another, the classic Gothic had been formed. His effort to perfect a whole phase of art may be seen in the groping line of the flying buttress.

In spite of the over-all success of the choir, two serious faults were apparent when the Second Master assumed the work in 1182 or 1183: its darkness and, what had been feared, the instability of the upper walls—the tribune was simply not enough to hold them erect much longer. The Master was determined to avoid these shortcomings in the nave, yet the faults were extremely vexing because each seemed to prevent correction of the other. A larger clerestory would solve the lighting problem, but to increase the size of the high windows would only weaken the walls where they most needed strengthening. Additional light, therefore, would have to be provided at lower levels of the monument. As for the question of stability, the Master, developing his idea from buttressing arches hidden beneath the tribune roofing of earlier constructions, including the choir of Notre-Dame, conceived a radical external support, freely flying from the other buttresses, to shore the upper walls. His was the earliest known use of the device which, like most great inventions, emerged in several regions almost simultaneously. Before the decade ended, the flying buttress appeared on a score of churches from Champagne to Normandy. Since they were all smaller and less influential churches than Notre-Dame, the Paris Master was very likely its inventor.

Thereupon he "put on the gloves" and proceeded to his task. With the surveying devices Suger mentions—*"geometricis et aritmeticis instrumentis"*—he laid down a new central axis, which, as has been seen, diverges slightly to the north from the axis of the choir. Carolingian Notre-Dame was now totally demolished, but Saint-Etienne-le-Vieux was left standing on the site of the façade, where it continued to serve as a workshop. A great rectangle of ground was thus available for the nave, bordered on the east by the choir, by the Merovingian basilica on the west, the cloister to the north, and the episcopal palace on the south. From Maurice's château it was possible to enter the choir directly, at the point where a modern gallery leads from the Treasure today.

Enter here, through the Bishop's private passage, with Maurice and the Master and walk to the transept. It is worth lingering at the croisée, as these practical men would have done at the close of the twelfth century, to compare the first and second phases of the work. From the transept crossing, at the heart of the Cathedral, both the choir and the nave may be seen to advantage; and at first they may seem quite identical. The Second Master was careful to continue the main lines of his predecessor, and there is no clash whatever between their basic elevations.

But, upon study, differences appear. The central vessel of the nave is fourteen rather than thirteen meters wide; its vaulting is a foot or two higher than the earlier part of the church. This expansion, difficult enough to perceive at ground level, may be detected in the vaulting of the croisée far overhead. The croisée is not a perfect square, as theoretically it should be, but an uneven quadrilateral, which widens as it goes westward. The inequality of dimensions is diffused, but far from concealed, by a tremendous pair of crossed ogives. These ribs form diagonals of sixty feet (18.5 meters); and their assured flight across the transept is the first sign of the skill and confidence of the Second Master. For directly above this vault is a spire weighing more than a million pounds (500,000 kilograms), as high again as the interior of the church. Yet the transept is bridged with the most nonchalant of Gothic gestures. It is vaulted as casually as an aisle. Except for the pier at the southeast corner of the croisée, which has leaned outward two or three feet during the last eight centuries, there is no indication of the mass which here presses downward upon the most vulnerable point in the church.

From either side of the transept the work of one master confronts the other's. On the east the First Master terminated the choir with two grand piles whose clustered colonnettes, without a break, mount the hundred-foot distance to the vaults. These piers set a fashion in France. They were copied at the four corners of the croisée in almost every thirteenth-century cathedral. Not so at Paris. The Second Master, as he was to do throughout the nave, considered the effect of such piers on visibility and the diffusion of light and rejected them as too bulky. Instead, he chose a support whose surface could be reduced—shaved might be a better word—to the minimum: the pilaster. The slender uprights he devised seem little more than ribbons of rock strung between earth and sky. Yet, unlike the thick piles across the way, they have not yielded so much as an inch beneath the weight of the vault and the spire.

Pilasters are rare in the Gothic. They seem out of time and space, with their suggestion of dead Rome or the unborn Renaissance. And, in truth, the Paris Master may have noticed them on a battered Roman gate or temple—the fluted pilasters on Gallo-Roman ruins at Autun were copied, with great charm, in Autun's Romanesque cathedral. But neither the Romans nor the would-be Romans of the Renaissance, nor even the Romanesque, used pilasters as they are used here. In Notre-Dame vertical potentialities are realized beyond any dreaming of Vitruvius or Palladio. The fluting has disappeared, and there is only the pure face of the rock.

The Second Master employed the pilaster again, on a much smaller scale, in the arcades of his tribunes—a subtle device but one that permitted him to open three arches in each bay rather than the two in the choir. Subtler yet, he punctured an *oeil-de-boeuf* in the tympanum of each tribune arcade on the southern side of the nave— the side of the sun—again, to increase light and to reduce the weight of the construction.

It has been calculated that the supporting members throughout the Cathedral—buttresses, piles, pillars, pilasters, columns, and colonnettes—occupy no more than fourteen per cent of the total floor surface of the building. The proportion is perhaps the lowest for any major building vaulted in stone, and is approached only by other Gothic structures. Saint Peter's of Rome, in comparison, suffers from a ratio of twenty-six per cent; Sancta Sophia has twenty-one per cent; and Saint Paul's of London, in which Wren made a conscious effort for light and space, seventeen. Since the nave of Notre-Dame is less encumbered than the choir, its proportion is even more favorable than that of the church as a whole; and it presents a superb field of vision.

The need for light motivated the Master's preoccupation with spaciousness and economy of structure; but it was the need for stability—which he found in the flying buttress—that enabled him to refine his supports with such elegance. He could reduce his weight of masonry because, at the summit of the nave, graceful stone arches were now drawing off that pressure which in the choir had rested on the interior construction alone. Nothing in Gothic art is easier understood than the flying buttress: its principle is the same as that of the timber shoring which, to the delight of tourists, holds up sagging old houses in modern France. The stone arch flew to the point where it was most needed, and thus propped not only that point but a broad area of the wall.

The flying buttress is simple in itself; in relation to the structure of a cathedral its ramifications are endless. Every line in this architecture carries a triple impulse. One current travels from the main vault outward through the flying buttress to the exterior foundations. Another does not leave the inside of the church but goes downward through the tribune to the colonnade. Still a third current, and this is the impulse that explains the whole equilibrium of the nave, jumps between the other two. It can be seen pulsing in the central pillars of the aisle. The colonnade of the nave (Fig. 5) has a rhythm which was not found in the choir. Its key lies in the central line of pillars that separates the outer from the inner aisle. In the choir these columns are uniform. In the nave their form varies. First is a column of the type found in the choir: a round shaft posed on a square base and surmounted by a capital. The next column, however, is reinforced by a dozen colonnettes, which surround the shaft with visible extra strength. A simple column follows, then a reinforced one, alternating the length of the nave. The strong beat of this alternance, sounding at intervals of ten yards, is the clearest

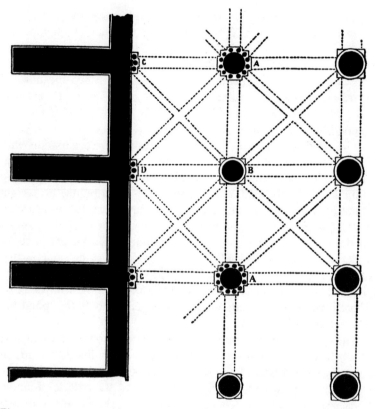

Fig. 5. NOTRE-DAME. Alternance of the aisles of the nave. (Viollet-le-Duc)

note in the symphonic architecture of Notre-Dame. And, as in contrapuntal music, its answering voice—for there must be an answer—is found some distance away.

Walk from the aisle to the central vessel and look up, nearly one hundred and ten feet, to the main vaults. Archaeologists describe the vaults of Notre-Dame as "sexpartite": that is, each pair of crossed ogives is supplemented by an arch that passes through their keystone, so that a six-ribbed figure results—an X with an I passing through its center. Each of these sexpartite vaults is separated from the next by another simple arch. Thus:

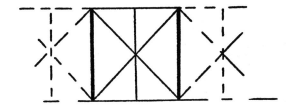

An alternating rhythm, and it is an exact response to the alternance in the distant aisles, is set up by this system. Where vaults meet, three ribs descend into the vessel. But in the middle of each vault only the supplementary arch is carried down. Therefore the vaulting alternately transmits a triple and a single stress to the structure below.

The first flying buttresses were an organic part of this metrical composition. Indeed, only through the alternance of the vaults and the colonnade has it been possible to deduce their appearance, for the bold single arches that support the nave today (Fig. E) are not the work of the Second Master. They date from the middle of the thirteenth century, when the Gothic could accomplish whatever it wished. In 1182, however, their sustained flight of forty feet was beyond the ingenuity of any architect, including a genius like the Second Master. He attempted only half that distance (Fig. D), and launched a double flight of shorter arches, on two levels, which first jumped from the outer buttress to an intermediary pier, and then from the pier to the wall of the church. The piers were mounted on the strong pillars of the aisles, and through them the alternating music of the vaults was carried sensitively to the floor of the church.

It is interesting to compare the cross-section of the twelfth-century nave with that of the choir (Fig. C). The calm which had been possible in the earlier composition has been disrupted irrevocably. The Transition is over. Line after line shoots between earth and Gothic Heaven, leaping, leaping, with an élan which foresees the sharp dynamism of steel. Here was the innovation for which French architecture had been waiting half a century. Churches now, with complete safety, could go as high as at Amiens. It is foolish to say that flying buttresses "were not strictly necessary," using for evidence the fact that the Angevin School did without them. Although Saint-Maurice of Angers is a great and fascinating church, and beautiful in its own right, its size and complexity are nothing beside Notre-Dame. Above one hundred feet, vaults needed propping. Saint-Maurice, at little more than sixty feet (19 meters), holds without flying buttresses; Notre-Dame could not; nor could Bourges, Chartres, Reims, or Amiens.

But if the flying buttress was in a strict sense necessary, the tribune was no longer. One or the other was required, not both; yet it will be seen in the cross-section that both were employed here, and that the tribune needlessly complicates the plan. The clerestory too, in the twelfth-century nave, was the same line of timid windows as in the choir. The Master was moving to perfection at what must have seemed breakneck speed, but he could move only so far in advance of his age.

In the generation that followed, perfection could be had for the asking. Or, at least, it could be had after a study of the nave of Notre-Dame. The Master of Bourges, about 1200, carefully examined the Paris scheme and then threw three double flights of buttressing arches against the wall of his cathedral. With this support, he confidently broke through what should have been the floor of a tribune and raised his inner aisle to sixty-four feet, against thirty-three for Notre-Dame, through which light pours with a freedom the Paris School must have envied.

And at Chartres, after 1194, another unknown master, again depending on flying buttresses to guarantee his wall, opened windows forty-six feet high at the top of a church whose lighting has never been surpassed, even by Amiens. Such windows, theoretically, were possible at Paris from 1182 on. It was not until fifty years later, however, that the upper wall was rebuilt and an adaptation of the Chartres clerestory installed.

After Bourges and Chartres, France moved to an age of perfect churches, to Reims and Amiens, to a monument as charming as Saint-Urbain of Troyes, which is a church of glass. All will be free from twelfth-century gaucherie; yet none will have the twelfth-century hope and its young sense of achievement; none will have the pulsing life of its alternating colonnades, from the deep beginning music at Sens, and the gracious fugue at Noyon, to the symphony of the nave of Paris.

None will have the twelfth-century innocence, from which the Transition, like a plant in April, grew suddenly tall. The floral decoration of Notre-Dame, budding in the choir, was brought to a monumental flowering in the nave. The flowered capitals of the great pillars are at the most intense moment of the Gothic spring, the rich June of the twelfth century, when Chrétien de Troyes sent Perceval riding through a perfumed forest after the Grail. In less than twenty years, after 1200, it will be summer; and the flowers of the western façade will no longer be abstract but real, recognizable as the garden flowers of the Ile de France, and delightful as the blossoms with which Aucassin pelted Nicolette, but with only autumn, and winter, before them.

The Bishop, old now, looked on as the great vessel rushed westward to completion, bay after bay of the nave; as more glass was hoisted to the high windows; as vault after vault was sprung; as the quarries continued to produce rock, and the teamsters drove their oxcarts on the newly paved roads, down the Left Bank and across the Petit Pont to the island; as son replaced father in the craft of masonry and the art of sculpture, growing more expert, more sure, more ambitious; working from daybreak to sunset; rioting at pots de vin offered by Maurice as each stage in the construction was passed, and being disciplined by the Chapter's police; and then the next day, at dawn, climbing the scaffolds again, as the morning Mass was sung in the choir, mounting higher and higher in the early sunlight, looking beyond Paris to green fields and forest; higher and higher, as the Virgin steadied them on the catwalks and cornices and smiled down at her civilization and her city.

And at the same time the army of Philip Augustus surged westward through the Vexin into Normandy, charging behind the Oriflamme, shouting, "Montjoie-Saint-Denis-Sainte-Marie!": an army of foot soldiers now, and sergeants, as well as knights; and its payroll met by the bourgeoisie of Paris as well as by the King. Philip too was older: canny, tough, prematurely bald; the Crusader who had abandoned Coeur-de-Lion and returned to war on his lands. What followed was the most improbable of Walter Scott's romances:

Richard's captivity and the songs of Blondel; Richard's prison song too, in moving Medieval French; and the English ransoming of their King. "The Devil is loose!" Philip wrote to John Lackland, and suddenly Richard's troops were surging back into France.

Maurice did not see the struggle decided; he died three years before a lucky, or unlucky, arrow—unchivalrously aimed by a commoner at a king, in 1199—reversed the fortunes of a war which Richard had seemed likely to win. While Coeur-de-Lion was battling furiously at the edges of the Ile de France and threatening to march on Paris, work on Notre-Dame proceeded calmly, as if the war, or even politics, did not exist. Only occasionally would a burly soldier, such as Guillaume des Barres, ride to the episcopal palace and make a gift of fifty livres to the church of the Virgin, who watched over him in the field. Guillaume may have won the money jousting: he was so strong a chevalier that he threw even Coeur-de-Lion at one tournament, to Richard's hot-headed indignation.

War and politics and bloody tournaments were heartbreaking and had to be ignored, or made the best of, if one was going to build a church. But as construction went on Maurice must have considered his long attachment to the House of Capet, going back to the autumn day in 1160 when King Louis and the lords of France had borne him through Paris to the door of the Cathedral; to the morning in 1162 when he rode with Louis to a bridge on the Saône and stood by the King as he called the bluff of Frederic Barbarossa and miraculously won; to the birth of Philip, and the sight of the little prince, on his pony, riding up to Henry Plantagenet. Slowly, time had passed, to 1180, at Louis' bedside, when he administered last rites as the sovereign gave his jewels and robes to the poor; he watched, too, as Philip received the crown from the Archbishop of Reims; and a few months later, he assisted in the marriage of Philip and Isabelle de Hainault, the beautiful and unhappy queen he would bury, only ten years afterward, in the apse of Notre-Dame. In time, there would be noble tombs throughout the sanctuary. Near Isabelle was Geoffroy Plantagenet, Count of Brittany, who might have been a king, but had been killed jousting, in 1186.

The road had been long, so long, from the simple heartland of France to the complexity of Paris; from the hovel of illiterates beside the Loire to a fortified episcopal palace; from his Romanesque childhood to his Gothic age. All, all had changed now. Paris was doubled in size, France was finding its true geography, the entire Occident was awakening to its artistic capabilities. The Gothic, no longer simply *opus modernum* but *opus francigenum*—the art born in France—was moving outward, to England and Spain and Germany, to Italy and Sweden, to fortress churches in Syria. And at the center of all stood Notre-Dame.

And still the old man wandered among the construction, commenting to his nephew John, or to the Master Builder, or the Master Sculptor, the Master Glassmaker, the Master Painter, and their assisting *"ymagiers";* chatting with ordinary carpenters and masons and day laborers, the common workmen who never forgot that their Lord Bishop had sprung from the same social class as themselves, or a lower one. Then he might return to the choir, if a service was beginning. A chronicler saw him, near the end:

Maurice, Bishop of Paris, vase of abundance and a fruitful olive tree in the House of the Lord, flowers among the other bishops of Gaul. I speak not of those inner qualities which are known only to God; but he shines outwardly through his erudition, his preaching of the word of God, his generous charity, and the extent of his good works. He reconstructed the Church of the Blessed Mother of God, Mary, in which he dwells as Bishop; and for a work so lovely and rich [*decentissimo et sumptuoso*], used less of other people's resources than his own means. He also opened a parvis before the Cathedral, between the two bridges, and to this end acquired at great cost land occupied by private homes. It was he who reconstructed the episcopal palace, and who built two abbeys. . . . His presence in the Cathedral is frequent, or rather, continual. I have seen him, at an unimportant service, at vespers: he was not enthroned in the Bishop's chair, but was seated in the choir, surrounded by a hundred clerks, intoning psalms with the others.

Finally, he needed rest. He was seventy-six, very old for a man of the twelfth century. The line of keystones was in place now, in all but the last double bay of the nave, which would not be erected until the façade was ready to be joined with the rest of the church. That was work to pass on.

The Abbey of Saint-Victor seemed the answer to his weariness. Maurice had always loved the monastery on the Left Bank in whose classrooms intellectual Paris had first come alive for him. After he had become bishop, Saint-Victor was the the most loyal of the epis-copal dependencies: the monks had supported his orthodox deci-sions in every theological argument; they had obeyed his judgments in lawsuits; and he, in turn, had been generous and faithful to them. At Saint-Victor, Maurice had a house and a private chapel, with a gallery from which he could glance across the Seine to the apse of Notre-Dame, perhaps the most lovely single view of the Cathedral. Early in the year 1196, without definitely resigning the episcopacy, he went there to live.

Surprisingly, Maurice found himself wealthy. The Capets had relinquished their rights to a dead prelate's fortune, and he was free to dispose of the property as he wished. "Blessed are the righteous," he wrote in his last will and testament, "for they shall have justice before the Lord." He ordered his executors to give entire satisfac-tion to anyone he may have wronged—for what bishop, in a feudal age, had not committed wrongs, and had not used clever words (*sophistica*)? He provided handsomely for his nephew John, and for John's son Philip, who had also been appointed an official of Notre-Dame. He left a very considerable endowment to the Abbey of Saint-Victor—nine hundred livres—and made large bequests to other churches and convents of the diocese. Nor did he forget the poor, especially poor clerks, for he himself had been a *pauper clericus:* he left one hundred livres for them; and one hundred livres more to the canons of the Cathedral who were assigned to the serv-ice of matins, and who arose, in all seasons and all weather, at mid-night. To the Chapter of Notre-Dame he left the bulk of his real estate, including the important fief of Ivry; his right to certain tolls; his vestments (for rich apparel was handed down from generation to generation in the Middle Age); various sums for chalices and other vessels and for the decoration of the master altar; and one hundred livres to pay for the roofing that remained to be built above the vaults.

At the end of the summer of 1196, the chroniclers relate, he ex-perienced visions and raved. Suddenly he sat up in bed and asked his attending priest for the Sacrament. The clerk could not refuse, but since he thought the Bishop's mind temporarily out of control he brought him an unconsecrated wafer. Maurice refused it, and the astonished priest ran to carry him the true Host.

Then Maurice called for the Bible, and in his strong voice read from Job: "For I know that my Redeemer liveth, and that he shall stand at the latter day upon the earth." This said, he laid the parchment upon his breast, blessed those about him, and died. It was September 11, 1196.

Abbot Robert and the monks of Saint-Victor buried him beside the altar of their church, and asked Maurice's friend, Stephen of Tournai, one of the celebrated poets of the age, to compose the epitaph. *Clamat Parisius non habuisse parem,* wrote Stephen: "The people of Paris proclaim they have not had his equal. . . . Provide for thy faithful servant Maurice, a pontiff of such great merit, O Virgin Mary":

> Pontificem tanti meriti, servumque fidelem
> Serva Mauritium, Virgo Maria, tuum.

notre-dame
the
classic
phase

Vergine madre, figlia del tuo figlio,
umile ed alta piu che creatura,
termine fisso d'eterno consiglio,
Tu se' colei che l'umana natura
nobilitasti si che il suo Fattore
non disdegnò di farsi sua fattura.

Paradiso, XXXIII

Thou mayde and mooder, doghter of
thy sone,

. . .

Thou humble, and heigh over every
creature,
Thou nobledest so ferforth our nature,
That no desdeyn the maker hadde of
kinde . . .

Translation by CHAUCER in
The Prologe of the Seconde Nonnes Tale

notre-dame

the

classic

phase

Chapter Eleven

ROM HER prodigious height, poised on the balustrade before the western rose, so remote and inaccessible that she seems to glance downward from Dante's Heaven, the Rose of the World, the Virgin, stands flanked by angels. Her son, a baby, is cradled against her shoulder and is much too young to be concerned with the capital below; but the Mother, who clearly has a predilection for Paris, points out its curiosities to the Child nevertheless, with a grave but delighted interest. Surely Paris must still please her, else she would rise up with her escort of angels, and fly straightaway to Lourdes, and remain there hidden in the grotto. But the Virgin keeps her high perch at Notre-Dame, exposed to sun and rain and the wind; and although, over seven centuries, her image has repeatedly weathered away, so that the present Mary is modern, the statue has always been replaced. The Virgin has never concealed herself from Paris, no matter what grief the city has caused her. For Mary knows not how to judge, but only to forgive; and if Paris has more or less forgotten her, she has not forgotten the Paris of the Middle Age.

By the year 1200 the capital had new status. It had become "a historic town whose fame and glory have spread throughout the world." Yet Paris was still a medieval city of twisting streets and little houses, of cloisters and gardens, vineyards, and even patches of unused land within the walls. The skyline was pierced by the steeples of parish churches. It was a city of quiet charm and middle-class respectability, but also of roaring energy and vice. On the Left Bank the students chattered their Latin, picnicked in the green valley of the Gobelins, gambled, swore, fought with swords beneath the ramparts of the abbeys, played wild pranks on the bourgeoisie, and escaped from the exasperated police; while at the same time their professors secured papal and royal recognition and a seal for the university.

The commercial Ville, on the Right Bank, was expanding prosperously to the wall of Philip Augustus, and beyond, through the gates, to the faubourg Saint-Denis and the international fairground, where the Foire du Lendit was held each June. On the west, where the wall curved to the river, the municipal defenses were reinforced, shortly after 1200, by a burly tower—the Louvre—whose foundations rest beneath the present palace. From this stronghold, where the King's military strength was centered, the garrison could look westward across fields and forest toward the Anglo-Norman enemy; or eastward, across Paris, above the Halles and the Boucherie, to the fortified Temple, where the King's treasure was stored. Between the Temple and the Louvre, the Right Bank was—as it has remained— a thriving marketplace of produce stalls, expensive shops, craftsmen's ateliers, and cheap bazaars.

At the center of all, uniting the Ville and the Université, drawing all Paris and all France together, was the Ile-de-la-Cité: the seat of the Crown. When Philip Augustus was not fighting and camped in the field, or hunting at Saint-Germain-en-Laye, or enjoying the hospitality of his vassals, he lived here, in the Palace of his fathers, where he dispensed justice, levied taxes, formulated strategy, and presided over the Curia, or royal court. Here, in politics at least, multiplicity was being reduced to something like unity; throughout the thirteenth century important feudatories would kneel in the Capetian throne room, place their hands between those of the King, and surrender privileges, wealth, and eventually their independence to Philip and his sons.

But if in 1200 political organization was gaining form and cohesion, society remained as unpredictably medieval as ever. Perhaps, at the extremities of the island, the Palace and the Cathedral were valid symbols of unity, but in the network of streets between them there was tumult. The Cité ran with Rabelaisian variety of life. It was crammed to the banks of the river with buildings, some of which walked out over the Seine on stilts. There were some thirty churches and chapels; the hospital and its foundling home; innumerable taverns and inns; brothels and baths; a wheat market, spice shops, and bakeries; and charcuteries which were famous for their ham. There were the homes of the leading burgesses, many of them fine residences which had been confiscated from Jews; and the smaller homes of the ordinary working people. Here and there, architecturally as important as the parish churches, were the solid guild halls of the drapers and the furriers.

The streets were narrow and exciting. The upper stories of houses were cantilevered outward, their gables jutting on carved wooden beams, from which gargoyles laughed when slops were tossed down in the center of the road. Construction carts, produce wagons, and mounted knights made their way through a walking populace of merchants and money-changers, artisans and laborers, serfs and villeins from the countryside, politicians, priests, begging friars, thieves, heretics, intellectuals, harlots, stout bourgeois housewives.

This was the bewildering Paris, so intensely devoted to the Virgin, which created one of the most lucid constructions of the Middle Age: the western façade of Notre-Dame. And only if the Cathedral is approached through its maze of streets may the great unifying wall be understood. The front of the church is the *summa* of medieval Paris: the total, ideal image of the society which challenged Heaven with its superlative faith and which, from the casting of the façade's foundations before 1200 to the completion of the towers in 1250, made Heaven yield. Unlike the *Summa Theologica* of Saint Thomas Aquinas, which belongs with it historically, the façade was finished by its buildings. Moreover—what the closely written quarto volumes of Aquinas could not hope for—the façade is still taken seriously by ordinary people and not merely by scholars and priests. After seven hundred years of hard use and considerable misfortune, the wall stands erect and unconquerable, with the broad, lifting strength of the Gothic Triumph.

The façade of Notre-Dame expresses a collective ideal—an ideal which in the thirteenth century was felt and appreciated by the people as a whole; and which was more or less comprehended, in its grand lines, by the total population. Yet by paradox, as long as the Middle Age lasted—or rather, as long as the medieval environment endured—no man saw the façade as did his neighbor; nor did either of them see it, as it may be seen today, in entirety. Because of the nature of the medieval city, each could see only portions of the wall, which were tantalizingly incomplete and which changed continually as the individual changed his position, compelling him to add the parts to form a total image in his mind. The façade, as a whole, like ideal Christianity, was its own mystery.

Not even the Capets from the battlements of their Palace had an unobstructed view of Notre-Dame. A spire, an overhanging cornice, intervened. Some part of the construction remained hidden. From the best position he could choose, the summit of the Left Bank, the medieval Parisian did not see the whole of the façade. Its base plunged into a confused mass of dwellings; and he had a view of the towers and the rose window, but not of the portals. When he descended the Left Bank to the Ile he frequently lost sight of the church altogether, only to find it leaping at the end of a narrow street.

A walk down from the university, the route taken by the Cathedral's great men throughout the Middle Age, is still a very remarkable way to discover the façade of Notre-Dame. How confusing this nest of Scholasticism can be, any tourist knows who has ever lost his map. The single dominating landmark—the Cathedral itself—disappears without warning, and the traveler wanders to an impasse. Yet clerks of the thirteenth century threaded their way through the labyrinth with ease, starting from the Gothic refectory of the Abbey of Sainte-Geneviève, where students of the Lycée Henri IV dine today; then down the steep rue de la Montagne, slipping on the cobbles, and catching glimpses of Notre-Dame.

It is worth noting how, seen above the old roofs, the Cathedral gains in scale and immensity; and how, after it vanishes, it invariably reappears larger and more imposing. Swiftly down the hill hurried the tonsured clerk, through the colleges of twenty European "nations"; and then, as the slope flattened to the river, through the L-shaped rue Maître-Albert, the Street of Albertus Magnus, the "Doctor Universalis" who was the Master of Aquinas; or, taking an alternative route which the Middle Age liked as well, behind Saint-Julien-le-Pauvre, through the rue Fouarre—the Street of the Straw—which Dante found so delightful a home of intellectuals that he mentions it in Paradise with one of its most illuminating residents, the dialectician Sigier de Brabant—*"Quella luce di Sigieri!"*—who did not hesitate to challenge Saint Thomas in theological quarrels. But worlds change, as they must. As early as the fifteenth century such men as François Rabelais, with reason, found these streets ludicrous. Panurge anointed the pavements of the rue Fouarre with his pungent Bourbon or Sorbonne Tart, traces of which linger in the dung-littered alleys. Today the satire of the Renaissance has been replaced by the bitter Marxism of the poor, with its own ironies and hope of salvation. All evidence of the Schoolmen has vanished, except for the ancient houses and the names of streets, but, through any of these turning little thoroughfares, Notre-Dame can be seen thrusting to the sky with the grand religious force of the Middle Age.

Once the same effect, or a better one, could be enjoyed in the Cité, before the island was razed by Baron Haussmann. Notre-Dame remained hidden as it was approached from the Juiverie, until, as a corner was turned, a portal appeared, and then another, never the three portals simultaneously, never more than a section of the surmounting Gallery of Kings; perhaps only half or a third of the rose; perhaps not the Virgin, but Eve standing a short distance to her left on the lofty balustrade; and then one of the towers. The surface revealed itself slowly, in partial glimpses, and then, suddenly, there was a small open parvis, and the great width of the façade moving directly overhead, with a crushing statement of force, more than two hundred feet to the towers.

The tourist, standing close to the portals, with his back to the modern plaza, may still appreciate this ultimate surprise if he stares straight upward at the climbing power of the wall. Then, however, he is quite likely to make an innocent mistake. He guesses that the façade may be seen more impressively from the far end of Haussmann's parvis. Alas, when he has walked the distance, Notre-Dame seems oddly less imposing. The illusion is one that only the city planning of the Second Empire could create: the Cathedral is ready to sink into the earth rather than fly. Yet as soon as Notre-Dame is again approached, the façade regains its scale with a vitality that overwhelms.

For an understanding of this great wall, the archaeologists can provide valuable information. The façade was begun about the year 1200. By 1208 sculptors were surely working on the portals. The entire base of the wall, to the Gallery of Kings, which defines it with a magnificent horizontal line, was finished by 1220. The rose and its flanking bays date from 1220-1225. The southern tower seems to have been finished about 1240; the northern, slightly later, in 1245, or at the latest 1250.

Approximately fifty years, then, were required to construct this wall and equip it with sculpture and glass. Five bishops and three kings, and the greatest queen in French history, Blanche of Castile, supervised the work. Perhaps as many as four or five master builders directed the actual construction. Several hundred master artists devised the decoration. At a conservative estimate, five thousand laborers, over the five decades, provided the manual toil. From the agricultural wealth of the nation, and from flourishing trade and manufacture, came the money to finance the tremendous cost. The façade was the result of a supreme community effort to produce a masterpiece; and few communities, even in Gothic France, have expressed themselves with such confidence and love and strength.

The strength came from the rich French earth. The love, as will be seen in the sculpture, was largely—not to say exclusively—inspired by the Virgin. The confidence grew from seventy-five years of experiment and discovery, from the start of the Transition at Sens and Saint-Denis, to its conclusion in the nave of Notre-Dame. As had every other construction technique, the use of the ribbed vault had grown refined and powerful along with France. The ogive had sharpened as it lifted, from the round arch of Saint-Denis to the pointed arch of Notre-Dame, and was ready, in 1200, to perform any task demanded.

Dates are deceptive and exist largely for the convenience of historians. The Middle Age had moved into its classical phase, but when, exactly, the medieval man would have been the last to say. The date 1200 in itself meant as much or as little as the date 1900, although pessimists were afraid that both would mean Domesday. Paris lived through one as Chicago lived through the other, as simply another twelve months, not much different from the twelve preceding or those to come, in spite of profound changes that were taking place in art and society. Several dates might serve as well as 1200. In international politics the election of Pope Innocent III in 1198, or the sack of the Christian city of Constantinople by an army of French and Venetian Crusaders in 1204, had extraordinary significance for the West. The death of Coeur-de-Lion in 1199 was also an event of first importance. But if any date was remembered and cherished by Frenchmen during the first years of the century, it was March 6, 1204, when Philip Augustus took the great Norman fortress of Château-Gaillard. After the fall of the castle, which had been Richard's supreme accomplishment in art as well as war, Philip was able to seize the whole of Normandy in just two months from a John Lackland whom Petit-Dutailis has described as a "semi-madman" pathologically unable to resist the most rational of the Capets. With the acquisition of the duchy, the French national state was formed in its essentials.

In the history of Notre-Dame the start of the classical age can be dated from 1197, when a new Bishop of Paris was enthroned in the Cathedral to replace Maurice de Sully. By coincidence, he too came from the town of Sully-sur-Loire. But he came from the château of Sully rather than a peasant hut.

The seventy-fourth Bishop of Paris, Eudes de Sully, was born into one of the princely families of Europe. Philip Augustus, Richard the Lion-Hearted, and Count Thibaut of Champagne were his cousins. He had exceptionally powerful relations within the Church: the Archbishop of Reims was his cousin; the Archbishop of Bourges his brother; the Abbot of Cluny his uncle. As a bishop himself, he was doubly a great lord—a prince of the Church and a leading noble of France. Significantly he was one of the few French prelates with the courage to enforce the interdict pronounced against Philip Augustus in 1200, when, because of the monarch's singular antipathy for his second wife, Ingaborg of Denmark, and his bigamous attachment to his third, Agnes of Meran, the doors of Notre-Dame were locked. In retaliation a band of royal sergeants, without Philip's knowledge or approval, sacked the episcopal palace, and Eudes was forced to flee the city. Philip was conscience-stricken by this act of brutality, however, and indemnified his cousin by releasing him from the obligation of military service to the Crown. In return, Eudes tried to arrange a settlement of the affair: he is thought to have urged Ingaborg to become a nun, and he also used his influence to reconcile the King and the Pope.

Yet in spite of Eudes's high station in European society, it may be remarked that his feudal status both as a prelate and nobleman was less than it would have been fifty or even twenty years earlier, before the reign of Philip Augustus. Philip was the first Capet to proclaim that the Crown was vassal to no one, including the Church; and, accordingly, he refused to render personal homage when the Bishop made his triumphal entry into the capital. To be sure, he sent a knight as a substitute to carry Eudes's litter, but a precedent had been established nevertheless. In Eudes's home fief, the Sires de Sully were no longer virtually independent rulers, as they had been when Maurice was born on their lands in 1120. The Sullias had been caught in the centralizing current of the times, and they now held their castle as chatelains of the King. Every serf along the Loire, between Orléans and Nevers, was aware of a new association with the kingdom of France; and although the Bishop of Orléans, as nominal suzerain of the area, protested the violation of his feudal right, Philip rebuilt the donjon at Sully, manned it with royal troops, and refused to vacate.

In spite of these incursions of the Crown, Eudes de Sully came to the episcopal throne of Paris with private means, including property as far away as England, which were to have a considerable effect on the splendor of the façade. Although he died in 1208, after a tenure of only eleven years, and four bishops followed him before the façade was completed in 1250, the western wall belongs to Eudes as the choir and nave belong to Maurice. It was Eudes who selected a new master builder—the third at Notre-Dame—and who permitted him to redesign and enlarge an already existing plan for the façade. To judge from the tympanum of the Virgin in Majesty, which had to be expanded to fit the thirteenth-century portal in which it was placed, the design drawn up by the First Master about 1163 called for arches that were almost round. It also anticipated a wall that was comparatively modest—two-thirds or three-fourths the size of the façade that was actually built. The Third Master, who may have been the grandson or grandnephew of the First, rejected this Transitional plan and designed a Gothic façade of his own.

And again, as construction progressed, the Cathedral grew in scale and deepened in conception. To guess how the Third Master grappled with the problems of a façade which, like the vessel behind it, was the largest on earth when it was undertaken, it is useful to leave Paris temporarily, as the Master did sometime in his career, and visit a few masterpieces from which he received direct stimulation. The study of façades is a joy. Even in the oldest standing monuments, which date from the close of the Dark Age, before 1000, there is an engaging combination of rugged strength and grace. One of the earliest ancestors of Notre-Dame, the abbey church of Tournus, has a most subtle façade of golden Burgundian stone, begun at the end of the tenth century, in which the twin-towered motive emerges from a windowless wall with a happy religious imagination that lives side by side with plain military force. Burgundy has many other beautiful and early façades—most of them built by monks of the Cluniac Order—as have Poitou, Touraine, and Auvergne. More fortunate than all is the Duchy of Normandy, the most inventive state in Europe until King John surrendered it to France.

There are scores of powerful Norman façades, from Jumièges in the eleventh century to Coutances in the thirteenth, when Normandy had become totally French in politics but only half-French in art. All possess the grandiose Norman ambition; all succeed because of Norman courage and perseverance; all are shaped by the unfailing Norman sense of monumentality; but none is more splendid than the virile creation of William the Conqueror: the Abbaye-aux-Hommes at Caen, the church of Saint-Etienne.

It is a shock to walk through the shabby faubourg of the abbey, which once stood alone in the fields, and come upon Saint-Etienne. The Norman impulse is here expressed ideally: direct to the point of open force, as unsentimental as the Conquest of England, which took place only two years after this church was begun in 1064, and as unmistakable in motive and execution. It was in such Norman churches that the master builders of the Ile de France—Suger's architect the first of them—discovered the basic French façade of four stalwart buttresses, three monumental doors, and a display of meaningful windows, the whole dominated by a pair of strong and sensitive towers. At Saint-Etienne the divisions of the wall reflect, with absolutely no compromise, the exact inner dispositions of the church. There is no melodic treatment; rather, four clear notes rising to a double crescendo.

The very simplicity of Saint-Etienne is deceptive. It holds the perfect proof of the theorem of Mies van der Rohe: "Less is More." Saint-Etienne has a splendor that requires no more than plain eyesight to see; but the master builders of France complained of one shortcoming in this and virtually every other Norman façade: the absence of figurative sculpture. There is much carving, true, some of it extremely rich; but in general the Norman was content with wide cuts in the rock, which simply gave scale to the wall. If he chose to express softer sensibility, the Norman preferred the interior of the church as the logical place for it, as in the almost feminine refinement which Henry Adams observantly noted behind the threatening masculine exterior of Coutances; or, behind another mighty façade, the exotic carvings of the nave of Bayeux, copied from oriental cloths the Crusaders carried home, for which the Norman unshackled his reserve utterly.

That the austere, non-figurative decoration of the Normans is superior to the hundreds of thousands of recognizable images in the rest of France is something the French, and the Parisians in particular, have never admitted, although the Rumanian sculptor Brancusi in modern times has argued the case as skillfully as any Norman of the Middle Age. Norman reticence troubled the French; but undisguised Norman power, like the Norman flèche which attacks the sky directly, jutting as a lance from the tough structure beneath, demoralized them completely, in art as on the battlefield. Throughout the twelfth century the French reaction in art followed the same pattern as French diplomacy, when arms failed. Force was answered with eloquence.

As the stern Norman impulse charged into France it was deflected and softened, like the Norman military assault. By the time it reached Paris it was transformed altogether, and no longer dangerous. The façade of Saint-Denis has an entirely different premise than the façade of Saint-Etienne of Caen. Suger's façade speaks with voluble French persuasion. The energy which is rigidly confined at Caen is here allowed to spread generously across the wall, beneath the defensive battlements. Saint-Denis has a profusion of line. Broad diagonal currents sweep across the uneven stories; but at the same time, in spite of the loss of the northern tower, the façade thrusts upward, with almost the force of the Norman church, from three portals, which originally were filled with sculpture. Saint-Denis, built before 1140, also has a rose window. The rose is only ten feet in diameter, and totally restored, but neither its date nor its importance should be overlooked. In 1140 the Capetian monarchy was weak but gaining in prestige. By 1200 it had flowered with the rose, as the compressed domain of Louis le Jeune became the powerful France of Philip Augustus.

After Saint-Denis, the next Transitional façades were undertaken at Sens, about 1160, and at Senlis some fifteen years later. Both have the rich French scheme of uneven stories, and led, at the end of the century, to the culmination of the style at Laon. In the opinion of no less an authority than Villard de Honnecourt, the beautiful towers of Laon are unequaled in Europe, although Villard may also have seen the towers of Notre-Dame, which followed Laon's by only a decade or so. But more than the towers, the whole of this enchanting façade carries the French system to remarkable richness and charm. The triple portal is emphasized by projecting rooflike gables, making the base of the church a tremendous open porch, some twenty feet deep, and is filled with a wealth of sculpture. Above, the rose is three times the size of the rose of Saint-Denis, and housed beneath a profound round arch that gives it a drama unique among the roses of France.

France and Normandy, in art as they were in political fact, were separate and hostile nations; and where the two met, in head-on clash, the result was stirring, as in the southern tower of Chartres. The main Norman thrust traveled through the valley of the Seine, past Rouen, like the raids of the Norse pirates three centuries before, in surge after surge that threatened to sweep the Capets from their throne. Invariably the attack was stopped by the doughty French town of Mantes. William the Bastard was killed at Mantes in 1087. The troops of Coeur-de-Lion were checked there a century afterward, almost to the year. Not without reason, the town is still called Mantes-la-Jolie, sitting as it does on a lovely reach of the Seine, high on the southern bank, forty miles from Paris.

In architecture Mantes may seem, as it did to Henry Adams, Paris itself. The façade of the Collegial Church of Notre-Dame rises to twin towers, greatly resembling the towers of Notre-Dame of Paris, that are connected by an open gallery which seems a copy of Notre-Dame's. The gallery *is* a copy—constructed by a nineteenth-century restorer who also rebuilt the towers. In truth, the Middle Age left Mantes unfinished. Old gravures show a façade which looked much less like Notre-Dame of Paris, and which, for study, need be considered only to the level of the rose.

The main resemblance vanishes, but there is some rapport nevertheless. Yet this wall preceded the façade of Paris by a good twenty years, and if either influenced the other, it was Mantes—bravely facing the Normans downriver—that affected the capital. The four buttresses rise straight as steel uprights, boldly marking the main divisions of the wall, which, as in no construction thus far, has been emptied of its stone to make room for a double line of windows and, dominating the façade, a rose that has blossomed to a diameter of twenty-six feet.

There seem to have been earlier large roses in France, but the rose of Mantes, dating from the end of the twelfth century or the first years of the thirteenth, is the earliest to survive. It is also one of the loveliest. The rose should be seen from the inside of the church, where its blue vision of Domesday is utterly charming and gentle, with Christ enthroned on a green and red rainbow. Not only the rose but the entire narthex should be examined from within, so that the audacity and quiet inner strength of the construction may be appreciated. The intelligence of a great master shows itself unmistakably: an intelligence as sure, as calm, as soundly based as the intelligence of the façade of Paris. Was it the same? There is no evidence for the assumption, which has been made frequently. In any case, it was at Mantes, for the first time in the Ile de France, that the uneven façade of the Transition gave way to the symmetry of the Gothic, with a visible increase of force.

The force, obviously, was Norman, or Norman-inspired; and the façade, as may be expected, dates from the moment when the French were taking all things Norman for their own. Confronting Mantes, twenty-five miles westward as the crow flies, forty miles on the twisting river, was Château-Gaillard, barring the route into the duchy. It is an indication of the Norman temper that this castle, whose ruins give only a partial impression of its immensity, was built in the single year of 1197. Its architect was Coeur-de-Lion himself, who risked excommunication by seizing the height of Les Andelys from the Archbishop of Rouen, and there erected a stronghold which, as long as he lived, was impregnable. With a capable prince directing the garrison, Château-Gaillard could do more than merely withstand a siege. It could serve as the main base of an offensive whose ultimate objective was Paris. John Lackland was hopelessly unequal to such an adventure, but he could at least expect to hold his fortress.

For nearly five years after the death of Richard, Château-Gaillard commanded its wide bend of the Seine, protecting Normandy. Then, in September 1203, Philip Augustus moved forward from Mantes and set up his engines before the castle's ingenious concave walls. Now, if ever, King John would have to make his move too. But he remained stubbornly hidden in England, oppressing his barons and the Church. Philip besieged the fortress until February, when he suddenly attacked the triple rampart. The first wall was sapped, broken, and stormed. The second wall, also protected by a moat and formidable towers, was penetrated through a latrine. It fell when a fire ignited by the defenders turned against them, and the Normans were compelled to retreat to the innermost circle. Philip, who, like Richard, had learned the art of warfare in the Holy Land, now brought up his catapults and bombarded. On March 6 the wall was breached, and the French charged through and killed the remaining one hundred and eighty Normans, who resisted to the end.

It required ten weeks to subdue the rest of the duchy. Avranches and Pontorson were sacked. The Mont-Saint-Michel was burned, so that Philip would help finance the Merveille in atonement. Caen, with Philip beneath the walls, surrendered without a battle. Rouen alone held out, partly in hope that John would counterattack, partly from fear of economic catastrophe at the hands of the bourgeoisie of Paris. On June 24, however, the city was Philip's; and Rouen, for the first time since Charlemagne, was again French.

On his return Philip stopped at Mantes to pray in the church and saw the rose under construction or completed. A few miles farther, and he was at Poissy, where his grandson Saint Louis would be baptized, in 1215, in a fascinating old church. Then, at the head of his army, he rode to Saint-Denis, to prostrate himself before the Patron of France; and at last he entered Paris, a city jubilant with triumph, and proceeded to Notre-Dame to thank the Virgin for his victory and to offer a *Te Deum* to the Lord.

Here too he saw a great façade rising—much greater in every dimension than the façade at Mantes, greater than any wall in

France. It was planned in broad and regular divisions, like a Norman wall, with Norman simplicity and strength, and four heroic Norman buttresses mounting from an enormous base. Yet it was also rich with French sculpture and the French rose. A national architecture had been formed with a national state, and it would be a total architecture: a home of all the other arts and meaningful for all the nation's people.

Chapter Twelve

*t*HE ROAD—every road—has led to this moment and this place. Paris in the thirteenth century was one of the main stopping points in history, like Athens in the fifth century before Christ, and Byzantium in the sixth century after. Each city had a social and political lesson for the world; each made the world a gift of architecture: the Parthenon, Sancta Sophia, the western façade of Notre-Dame. For the fifty years the façade was building, and a little longer, until the death of Saint Louis in 1270, Paris maintained its maximum strength in art and politics; and then history wandered out on the roads again, to the Florence of Dante and Giotto, and elsewhere, although neither the Cathedral of Paris nor the Capet Dynasty had reached completion.

They had attained the pinnacle of their Christian ideal, which was enough. At the summit of the façade the Church Militant is the Church Triumphant, and the sky, as the architect wished, is subject to Notre-Dame. Heaven drifts between the towers, governed by rock, mastered by idealism. The high air is fixed, fluid, alive. And here is the Cathedral's gift. Heaven comes rolling downward through the front of the church, charging richly through the stone, emitting a great circular flash of light in the rose, and collects in the solid base of the monument. In the chiaroscuro of the portals—the ceaseless exchange of light and shadow that is the religion of the Virgin—Heaven is brought to earth, waiting, quietly, for the people to see and understand its medieval traces of gold.

Christian architecture, in all the churches of the Renaissance, the Neo-Classic Age, and the Baroque, could do no more; and it is odd, is it not, that this culminating triumph of Christian art should be found in Paris rather than in Rome? If, at the heart of Bernini's colonnade, Saint Peter's could achieve the same effect of mystical grandeur, the Church Militant might still be the Church Triumphant. Although Saint Peter's is more than twice the size of Notre-Dame, an effort is required to appreciate its true dimensions. The Pope on the remote balcony has been reduced to a speck by the architecture, whereas at Paris he would be plainly visible as a human being on the terrace before the rose, yet Notre-Dame seems every bit as large a church. What happened between the construction of the two monuments is as clear as the recantation of Galileo: science lost its home within the Church; the Church lost its necessary human reference and sense of scale. Both churches suffer from the out-sized plazas which have been placed before them, but Notre-Dame nevertheless still accomplishes what Saint Peter's tries to do, and fails. The Cathedral of Paris conquers Heaven, stands victorious over earth, and crushes Satan beneath its weight of rock.

The theme of victory is written in every grand line of this wall, and in every monumental detail. To either side of the central portal stand two queens, restored after the lost original statues. On the right of the spectator, but on the vengeful left hand of the Christ of the Last Judgment, the Synagogue is posed in defeat, her crown pushed from her head, her eyes masked, her staff shattered. From her hand slips the overturned Tablet of the Jewish Law. Across the portal the Church Victorious proudly wears the crown she has taken from her enemy. She commands with her banner of Christian faith, and stands regally erect; the chalice she holds is the Holy Grail. The forward wall of Notre-Dame belongs to this indomitable queen, whom the Middle Age saw as the Virgin; and who, from 1200 to 1250, as the façade rose, ruled the West, took France for her nation, and Paris for her capital.

Rarely has triumph been so engaging. The façade is a happy thing to live with. For seven hundred years Parisians and strangers have taken pleasure and confidence from this work of art whose supply of both is inexhaustible. Merely to walk through its broad, living shadow, when the sun stands behind the towers at morning, is to share its optimism. As the afternoon sun reddens the stone and colors the rose, the façade laughs at the tension of the working day. At evening, when Paris goes home, the towers hold the last light of the sky. Finally the moonlight seeks the galleries and wanders among the white colonnettes. Only when the façade is floodlit, and artificial brilliance attacks the stone, does the wall show fatigue or age.

Many claims have been made for the façade, several of them worth repeating. Victor Hugo made the first modern appreciation of the "harmonious parts of a magnificent whole":

. . . crowding upward before the eye without disorder, their innumerable details of statuary, sculpture, and carving united powerfully with the tranquil grandeur of the ensemble; a vast symphony in stone . . . like divine creation whose two-fold character it seems to have appropriated: variety, eternity.

Speaking for the archaeologists, Marcel Aubert has written: "This façade, one of the most perfect built by the Middle Age, is a masterpiece of composition and execution." Nor did the medieval man stint his adjectives when speaking of Notre-Dame. In 1323, for example, when the age of construction was near its close and there were famous façades throughout Christendom to compare with the façade of Paris, a scholar named Jean de Jaudan looked at the western wall of Notre-Dame and asked, frankly, where else could be found "two towers of such magnificence, so lofty, large, and powerful, and with such variety of decoration?"

Few of the façade's elements, of course, were new to the thirteenth century. Some had been used since the Hittites built double-towered temples in the time of King David. Most of the others had been developed during the Romanesque and the Transition. Never before had they been combined with this strength, calm, and natural order. Out of the past, quite suddenly, came what Le Corbusier has called *"pure création de l'esprit,"* a unique and astonishing masterwork. An identical phenomenon occurred when Phidias gave his imagination to the Parthenon. All the elements of the Doric temple had been known and had occasionally been treated with remarkable beauty, as at Paestum, for two full centuries previously. Yet no temple, before or after, equaled the Parthenon.

To utilize past experience and obtain results that still seem modern, as did Phidias and the Paris Master of 1200, is to create truly classic architecture, which, once built, cannot be conceived as standing otherwise or in any other place. The site, climate, the amount of light in the air, the materials available, are all part of great construction; they were all deeply considered by the Master Builder and evaluated with such precision that it is impossible to imagine the Cathedral except on its island in the Seine. The same Master would have built a different church, as his contemporaries did, at Reims and Amiens.

In the broadest view of medieval society the façade is a product of centralization. France, as it absorbed Normandy and the other feudal provinces, also acquired what was most persuasive in their art. It is the Norman principle of regular divisions, for example, that gives the wall its great appearance of stability. There are only three major horizontal elements: the base, the story of the rose, and the towers. Each level is boldly marked, a Norman technique which here has become completely French by the use of galleries. The façade is also divided in three vertical elements, rising from the sculptured French portals, in a Norman mood of symmetry. Taken to the birth of the towers, the wall is virtually a perfect square of one hundred and forty feet (42 meters); and this is its fundamental source of calm. The towers convert the square to a rectangle, exactly one and a half times as high as it is broad: dimensions that preserve a sense of order as the wall lifts to more than two hundred feet. At the center of the entire composition is the French rose, grown to a diameter of thirty-two feet.

There can be little doubt that this design was first drawn on parchment. The regularity of the proportions alone is proof of an advance plan; but there is the supporting medieval evidence that, before work at Strasbourg began in 1275, a number of projects were sketched for the façade, which are conserved in the museum of the Cathedral.

Medieval use of the drawing board has given satisfaction to the Beaux-Arts, for drafting is a métier in which the French have long believed and excelled; and it is interesting to know that the façade of Notre-Dame was traced in advance, like the façade of Versailles and the court of the Invalides. But with what verve in execution! The façade rises with a broad display of force, sweeping upward through the Gallery of Kings, to the calculated circle of the rose. And from the rose the wall climbs easily again, gaining in lightness and speed and grace, without loss of vigor, as it flows through the open gallery to the towers. The rose, at the heart, gives its tone to the whole; and to appreciate the importance of Mary's mystical flower is to grasp the meaning of the virile wall. The rose is Beauty and Love—the ideal of the Virgin—framed in a great square of masculine strength. The façade is France.

It is medieval France depicted ideally, larger than life, as the nation expressed itself in all the arts. Here it might be best to recall that the kingdom of the Capets, like the city state of Athens, was after all a small place. Its population could not have been much more than a million; and although one-tenth of its people were already concentrated in or about the capital, Paris was a small city. Utica, New York, at 101,000, has approximately the same number of residents and occupies a larger area. Scranton and Tampa, Shreveport and Sacramento, are all larger; Minneapolis is five times as large.

How large, precisely, is this celebrated piece of architecture? Quite small indeed, if compared with the steel and glass surface of the UN Secretariat, which, like the Cathedral, is purportedly a monument to idealism. M. Aubert's measurements show that the façade of Notre-Dame is only one hundred and thirty-five feet wide (41 meters), and one hundred and forty-one feet high (43 meters) to the birth of the towers: not quite a perfect square, in the end, but an exceedingly adroit rectangle—a true square would have given the illusion of greater width than height. To the summits of the towers the façade is two hundred and seven feet (63 meters), which is equivalent to a twenty-odd-story modern construction. Countless office and apartment buildings surpass these modest dimensions; few appear to approach them.

The extraordinary scale of the façade has fascinated contemporary architects. "The determining surface of the Cathedral," remarks Le Corbusier in *Vers une Architecture,* "is governed by the square and the circle." To prove his point, he took ruler and compass and marked a photograph with straight lines and arcs. The result is impressive. Outlined in ink, the great square contained in the façade emerges vividly; a great circle, to which the sides of the square form tangents, emphasizes the wall's geometric purity. For, as Le Corbusier next demonstrated, the radius of the circle—roughly, sixty-nine feet—provides the module for the composition. Arcs drawn to the same radius from any number of critical points will fall strikingly across the various compartments of the wall and will indicate, among other things, how the module determined the height of the towers.

Regular proportions alone can give a building scale, but they do not guarantee an impression of size. Notre-Dame has more secrets than simple geometry, and there are more ways to study a photograph than Le Corbusier's. The easiest is to place your hand over a picture postcard and slowly move it upward, uncovering the wall's successive elements. The action of the two colossal side buttresses, outside the square of the façade, immediately becomes apparent. They recede as the wall rises, in movements at once persuasive and refined, like Mozartian music, speaking to each other across the width of the construction, allied to the main body of the façade, inseparable from it, in fact, for without them it would fall; yet with independent value of their own as voices in a symphony. To see how far French architecture had come in two generations, it is illuminating to return to Saint-Denis. Suger's façade has two side buttresses, which fill, as these do, with dramatic shadow on a summer day, and which frame the wall with staunch power. But they do not give it height—at least, not height like this; nor do they sing with this Jupiter music.

To uncover a photograph of Notre-Dame will also reveal how the façade opens as it rises and multiplies in vertical line. The solid base —an incomparable showplace for sculpture—can be seen as the supporting element, which provides assurance that the ambitious structure will hold; the eye wants such assurance, and gets it here, as it does not in every church. Above, the Gallery of Kings is a dense stripe of force: heavy, serious as the wall beneath, yet giving the façade a short, vigorous upward impulsion with its fifty-six sturdy colonnettes. Next, the pointed bays to either side of the rose should be noticed. They repeat the portals, but with a new feeling of lightness and humor; their small roses play like children near the maternal circle of the grand rose; their lancet windows, presumptuous as children, match their size against the belfries of the towers above, which stand open for sixty feet. And leading into the towers, with the graciousness of air, is the completely open upper gallery, which has twice the height, but only half the density, of the Gallery of Kings below. The lines of these two galleries, and their difference in mood, send the façade springing into the sky.

All these elements, and many more, some of which will never be understood except by architects, are at work in the façade, all active, asserting themselves, all to be seen, to be registered by the eye and evaluated by the mind; yet none clamoring for attention; none existing for its own sake—not even the rose; none disrupting the harmony of the whole; none which would not be missed if it were removed. What makes this the façade of all façades is the complexity of the composition and the resulting simplicity of over-all effect.

Both Shakespeare and the Master Builder borrowed materials from previous artists, only to transform and color them with unprecedented beauty; and it may be noted that Notre-Dame, after being conceived as pure geometric form on the drawing board, was constructed, like *The Tempest,* with the unpredictable poetry of ripe genius. The symmetrical wall is not symmetrical. Not one of the three portals has the same dimensions or outline as its partners. The central door is taller and wider than those on either side. The northern door is slightly smaller than the southern, but it has been given a gable, which intentionally disrupts the order of the wall. The three vertical divisions all differ in width, a peculiarity that may be detected by counting the figures in the Gallery of Kings. There are nine statues in the central arcade, but only eight on the north and seven on the south. The northern tower is larger and has greater abundance of detail than the southern. The decoration of the open gallery beneath, however, is more elegant on the south than the north.

The conception of the façade was large enough to admit human irregularity; and, like all things human, the wall lives. It is more than human: it is natural. The stone was not cut to an arbitrary size but removed in natural shelves and then laid in continuous seams, so that the courses of masonry, like strata, vary in height. The average runs about sixteen inches high (40 centimeters); some are eighteen inches, others fifteen. This results in an exceptional vivacity of surface texture; but at the same time the irregularity is just regular enough to contribute to the scale of the wall. Here the ingenuity of the Master is startling. It would seem that the hundreds of crockets that project from the towers are superficial ornament. Without them, however—and this is a fault of Amiens—the towers would appear badly weakened. For each crocket represents a course of masonry, and fifty such crockets, visible at a distance when the joints of the construction can no longer be seen, indicate fifty courses of masonry of the same height as those near the ground. From any angle, whichever way the spectator turns, he sees the crockets jutting from the profiles of the towers, and he credits the construction with its true dimensions.

Enemies of Gothic architecture have attacked this impression of size and called the Gothic "an architecture of fear." The Middle Age anticipated the objection. One chronicler, at least, confessed that the mass of Notre-Dame aroused "terror among the spectators" on the parvis. He said so by way of praise, like the Elizabethan frightened by Prospero's storm.

In truth, against the supernatural background of Notre-Dame, man appears surprisingly small, and surprisingly vivid. An individual on the high terrace between the towers is as tiny yet as conspicuous as a crouching gargoyle. On the lower terrace a human measurement is provided by the balustrade, which shows that if ordinary mortals still walked there, as they once did freely, they would be dwarfed by the rose window and by the statuary of the nearby gods, but they would not be obliterated, as at Saint Peter's of Rome. Even on the uppermost platform of each tower the human being, minute as he is, can be seen distinctly by those on the ground; and it is through this constant human reference that the Cathedral achieves its superhuman scale. Everyman—king or pope, merchant or serf—appears insignificant against the total image of the community, but this image was nothing more than his own idealism.

If to design this façade, to give it life and profound meaning and its effect of height, demanded the mind of a supreme master, to construct it required the skill of builders as accomplished as the world has known. Viollet-le-Duc, who also attempted to erect Gothic churches, can explain from experience:

Nothing is more simple in appearance, as construction, than the enormous façade of Notre-Dame of Paris, and this is one of its virtues. Looking at such a mass, one scarcely suspects that certain artifices had to be employed, and combinations carefully studied, to give it perfect stability.

It would appear that it sufficed merely to pile up courses of masonry from the base to the summit, and that this immense mass ought to maintain itself by its own weight.

Nothing, Viollet-le-Duc hastened to add, could be further from the truth; and in his article "Construction," one of the finest in his *Dictionary,* he explains in detail, with diagrams, the secrets of the façade's stability and strength. The structure, according to the man who knew its last details, is in every way "irreproachable." The masonry "lives, acts, fills a function; it is never a passive or inert mass." The main buttresses, for example, were devised with an ingenious system of filling that enabled them to stiffen as they settled, so that, the greater the pressure upon them, the greater their resistance. Up, up, these buttresses rise, hugging the wall with flexible strength, with the result that the wall section, apart from the buttresses, is the lightest in any cathedral of this class. The walls of Laon are nearly twice as heavy, and Laon is a smaller church.

Not everyone, Viollet-le-Duc remarked with regret, has been privileged to uncover the buttresses and examine their inner dynamism, but anyone standing on the parvis may see the façade's magnificent scheme of functional decoration. The galleries, arcades, friezes, columns, bases, capitals—all the visible adornments of the wall—are without exception active structural members, each serving to steady or strengthen the construction. Stone, like wood, has a live internal being. It has a natural grain, running in the same direction as the horizontal seams, along which the medieval stonecutter made his easy incision. If stone is set against the grain, the master builders knew, it cannot be compressed; and therefore most of the decorative wealth of the façade was used in this way, its grain set at right angles with the courses of ordinary masonry that make up the facings of the wall. In some cases this technique has been employed with such grace, as in the open gallery beneath the towers, whose slender colonnettes stand sixteen feet high, but less than a foot in diameter, that their functional purpose may be overlooked. Yet without the seemingly fragile and air-filled gallery the towers might have tumbled down.

These technicalities, if pursued, would be endless. Instead, it is worth while to observe the façade's assortment of stone, simply as an example of its complexity. By the thirteenth century the Parisians had already used so much rock for so many purposes that they were totally familiar with its properties. The Master Builder of 1200 had only to ride out to the quarries to select materials from a number of available seams, each of which he knew was suited for a specific role in the construction. For the facings he chose a limestone of exceptional homogeneity and suave strength. For the sculptures he preferred a more easily worked limestone, as its name, *liais tendre,* indicates, which he extracted in thick belts that enabled him to make large statuary from single blocks. Where maximum resistance was needed, as in the colonnettes of the galleries and the overhanging cornices, the Master preferred the hardest and most beautiful stone in the Cathedral: a silvery white calcareous rock called *cliquart*— a matchless material, adds Viollet-le-Duc, for the framework of the rose.

Viollet-le-Duc has dwelled on the excellence of the masonry of the façade. It ranks with the finest of the Middle Age. The stone was carefully dressed by removing its outer crust; the inner crust was retained for the sake of patina, which the Master, like every intelligent architect, anticipated. The sand mixed for mortar was of the highest quality to be found on the Seine; it seems to have been fastidiously selected or else passed through a sieve to remove pebbles. The white lime used for the joints was remarkably pure. The Master employed mortar, rather than laying stone to stone, as the Romans frequently did, because of the elasticity it gave the structure. The mortar was compressed to the utmost, and at Notre-Dame is only a few millimeters thick.

Now the façade began to rise, and, among other delightful eccentricities of the Cathedral, small holes may be seen here and there, which received the putlogs of the scaffolding. It is not difficult to visualize the scaffolds of Notre-Dame. Except in rare projects where a steel frame is used, the same scheme survives in France today. Light timbers were simply lashed with the putlogs to form boardwalks. While work remained close to the ground, the bottoms of the upright timbers were fixed in little mounds of mortar. As the construction lifted, the scaffolding lifted too, and was dismantled in the lower parts of the monument because it was no longer needed. When a medieval wall was built, it was finished: there was no repointing of masonry, and no reason to accumulate useless and expensive scaffolding. Nor did the masters see any reason to fill the putlog holes. They left them empty, and so provided the church with additional charm and vitality.

For half a century the façade rose—slowly by present standards; fast enough, if it is remembered that the construction was stone, and not steel or concrete. How large was the actual labor force? Although the stonecutter did not do so at Notre-Dame, he often left his mark, an anagram or an initial, on his finished block, as he does yet in rural Burgundy and Auvergne. At the Château of Coucy, the mightiest in France, Viollet-le-Duc counted one hundred such marks, indicating at least as many skilled workers on the job at one time, for Coucy, like most castles, was built quickly, and there was little labor turnover. Viollet-le-Duc estimated that seven hundred other workers assisted the stonecutters, including two hundred masons, their journeymen and apprentices, pattern-tracers, foremen, barrowmen, tongsmen, puddlers, furnacemen for the lime kilns, sand carriers, teamsters, quarrymen, and common laborers. He supposed an equal number of carpenters, roofers, metalsmiths, painters, and other craftsmen, making sixteen hundred in all.

Less than two thousand men would not seem many to construct Coucy, or Notre-Dame. Yet the force continually present at Paris may have been smaller, for the project was not executed under military pressure. Probably there were no more than a thousand workers at Notre-Dame at one time. When they grew old or died, moved to another city or quit or were fired, they were replaced—a few at a time; in all likelihood, it took a decade for a complete turnover. This is one reason for the continuously fine quality of the work; and it is hard to imagine getting the same results from a gang of one thousand in Paris today. They work with almost the same trowels and hods, fill their wine flasks at home from the same wicker-protected demijohns, climb identical handmade ladders, and sweep up with the same brooms of rough brown faggots. They simply have less stake in their job. What stake their ancestors had was expressed in the façade itself, and in the carven images which, between 1200 and 1220, were taken from the atelier of the sculptors and lifted into the three portals.

Chapter Thirteen

THE THREE PORTALS
1200 - 1220

a T SUNSET, when Paris grows silent, and the great square before the Cathedral is empty, the portals are alive. The sunlight finds traces of gold, and there was quick movements in the dark archways as the stone populace of Notre-Dame awakens. Long ranks of angels dance upward to the strange music of the Apocalypse, above the crowned figure of the Virgin. Mary is found at the center of the dark portal, as she is found at the center of the Trinity: the heart of the medieval religion. The pointed Gothic portal itself joins with the symbol. The two sides rising from a third suggest a triangle, and the number three. The three portals, taken together, again suggest a triad, or Trinity. There are three major divisions of the façade; and if the towers are seen in the context of the spire lifting behind them, three great impulses leaving the Cathedral for Heaven. This is not fancy. In the thirteenth century any boy theologian of the Sorbonne saw the Trinity everywhere.

Yet not even the finest analytic mind of the Middle Age, Aquinas, with the aid of Aristotle, could explain the Trinity to the world's— or the Church's—satisfaction. In general the medieval man accepted the Trinity without proofs, as the Church advised, by implication, as it were, in the triple and triangular forms of Gothic architecture. *"Trium una et gloriosa,"* Suger described a procession of three bishops passing the three principal doors of Saint-Denis: "a single and glorious Triad"; yet the Trinitarian association with the Gothic portal stops there. The Trinity is nowhere to be found in the triple portal of Notre-Dame. The places that theoretically belong to the Father and the Holy Ghost have been taken by the Virgin. Two of the three portals are Mary's; and her Son, except in the central Last Judgment, is scarcely more than her equal, and usually only her child.

To explain this is difficult. The cult of Mary is a dangerous subject, and likely, if pursued with enthusiasm, to result in heresies. Under the Inquisition excessive enthusiasm could lead to the stake. Power, wisdom, and love were the primal attributes of the Trinity. Together with purest humility, these attributes were also the Virgin's. From the twelfth to the fourteenth centuries, when her power was greatest, her wisdom infallible, and her love all-embracing, she was a Trinity in herself; or rather, in Coulton's phrase, virtually a fourth person of the orthodox Trinity.

The cult of Mary, then, was the concentrated ideal of an idealism. The foremost medieval authority on the subject, Dante, found the incarnation of the ideal in Saint Bernard. Once, in ecstasy before an image of the Virgin, Bernard was favored by a singular stroke of Grace. Mary pressed her breast so that three drops of milk—the divine number—fell upon his lips as he recited the *Ave Maris Stella.* The liquid left the saint intoxicated. He was drunk with Mary's essence, which he found everywhere in the Bible, in the Old Testament and the New. In his sermons Mary was the burning bush of Moses, which flamed but was not consumed; she was the all-containing ark of Noah, the fleece of Gideon, Jacob's ladder; she was the green tree that flowered from the loins of Jesse; she was the passionate sweetheart of the Song of Songs. The Virgin was the star, the garden, the door, the wedding chamber, the dawn. In all these metaphors the enchanted crowds, gathered by thousands to stare at the taut, wiry figure of the saint, saw a single triumphant goddess: Mary as queen. Not only queen, but, as Mâle demonstrated, thrice an empress, with three separate dominions. She was the Queen of Heaven whose brilliance dazzled and healed the eyes of Dante; Queen of the Earth whose miracles, like news items, were each day recorded with vivid truth by the chroniclers; and also Queen—although this may be startling—of the Underworld, where, like a suddenly strong Proserpine, she wrested sinners from the cruel Prince of Darkness.

It is as Queen of Heaven that Mary reigns high overhead, before the western rose of Notre-Dame. To either side of the Virgin and her Child, barred from proximity by the escorting angels but mounted on the same balustrade, are restored statues of Adam and Eve. The progenitors are depicted after the Fall: naked and mortal, shivering when the January wind blows from the Seine, burned by the August sun, at their great height above the nonchalant city. Yet Adam prefigures Christ, and Eve is Mary's other self. "Blest Marie," John Milton could write in the Puritan age, "second Eve." Medieval poets were more ingenious. To them the name Eva, reversed, spelled Ave; therefore Mary both preceded and followed Eve and contained Eve's lesser figure in her greater one. Therefore, too, the Genesis of the Virgin's Bible may be found not only on the lofty level of the rose but also far below in the southern portal, the earliest door of the façade, where the Virgin is enthroned in Majesty which dates from before the Garden of Eden. *"Ab initio et ante saecula creata sum,"* repeated the celebrant during Mary's service each day within the Cathedral—"I have been created from the beginning and before the centuries."

For the Virgin herself is the Church. Here, seated upon a throne, she herself is a throne—the "Throne of Solomon" so dear to the theologians, the "Seat of Wisdom" upon whom her Son is in turn enthroned as king. Christ is king, but the Virgin bears the scepter and rules. The commands of the little prince Jesus, who does not yet wear a crown, may be taken no more seriously than his boy's haircut or his tiny book. This scene of palace life, so luxurious and dignified, surpassed by any dreaming the rough and ready existence of the Capets and Plantagenets. Nevertheless, like all royalty, the Virgin and Son ruled because of fortune in birth. Much—sometimes all— depended on genealogy in a feudal age; and therefore the medieval man took pride, as the Greek took amusement, in the pedigree of his gods. He was happy to note that Mary and Jesus were regally de- scended—in fact, ideally descended—through the Houses of Israel and Judah; and that they could with certainty trace their line many more generations than a Philip or Louis Capet. The name of Solo- mon recurs in this façade, and King David, together with twenty-six other princely ancestors mentioned by Saint Matthew, who stand as colossi in the Gallery of Kings.

The branches of this incomparable family tree spread as freely through the bright air of the New Testament as the roots plunged deeply in the strong earth of the Old. The Holy Family, like the

Capets, had many connections, all peers of Christianity. No less than six great saints, including three apostles, were descended from the same grandmother as Christ, Saint Anne. For in addition to her marriage with Saint Joachim, the union that produced the Virgin, Anne was said to have had two other husbands, and as dowager grandmother of a household that included not only the Savior but Saint James of Compostela and Saint John the Evangelist, she commanded remarkable devotion.

Consequently, when it was found that there was not enough twelfth-century sculpture to fill the portal of the Virgin in Majesty, Bishop Eudes de Sully consecrated the remaining space to the history of Anne and Joachim and to the supernatural birth of their child, Mary. The story proved so fascinating that it has given Anne's name to the portal—the Portail Sainte-Anne—although properly it is the Portail de la Vierge.

You will look in vain in either the King James or the Douai Bible for this tale of grace. Saint Matthew and the other Evangelists are reticent when they speak of the Virgin, and they say nothing of her mother. The Middle Age read not only Saint Matthew, however, but the pseudo-Saint Matthew as well, and other apocryphal authors; and their accounts of Mary's birth, childhood, marriage, death, and resurrection were considered fully as important as the biblical saga of Christ; certainly it occupies a much larger place in Notre-Dame.

The Conception of the Virgin is staged as a play or *mystère,* in modern dress of the thirteenth century, against the backdrop of a Gothic Jerusalem, on the lower lintel. Since the action takes place before the birth of Jesus, when the Holy Family were of course orthodox Jews, the *personae* are appropriately dressed as Jews—French Jews of the Middle Age. For twenty years, according to the Apocrypha, Joachim had been married to Anne, and they were childless. For this reason they are seen, at the right, entering the Temple with offerings for the Lord. The Temple is signified by a double arcade, whose little arches and capitals make it seem a most sumptuous doll's house. Actually it is a French synagogue of the year 1200: the Scroll of the Law is unrolled upon a simple stone altar; above is the Eternal Lamp. With one hand the high priest, a bearded rabbi, rejects the offerings of the sober couple; with the other he points to a text of the Law: anathema to barren marriages.

Joachim, overwhelmed by sorrow, departs for the wilderness with a young friend. The old man's few necessities are tied in a kerchief and hang from his staff; his long cloak is hitched about his waist. His hat, which resembles a circular, overturned cake mold, is a Jewish fashion, as is his companion's, a jaunty conical headpiece. Next, at the base of the voussoirs to the right, Joachim is seen tending his sheep in a desert pasture. He has passed five months in prayer, and now an angel flies from a cloud and informs him that God has heard his supplications and will grant him a child. To show the speed of the angel, who spoke simultaneously to Anne and Joachim although they were leagues apart, the sculptor repeated this annunciation in the center of the lintel: Anne stands in a touchingly serious attitude of prayer, while Joachim listens intently, miles away, to the same heavenly messenger. The story then returns to the voussoirs, where Joachim is seen hurrying through the wilderness, with his dogs and lambs, to Jerusalem. In the last voussoir he meets Anne, who has expected his arrival and come to greet him. They embrace reverently beneath the Golden Gate; and this, to the Middle Age, was the precise moment of the Immaculate Conception.

Fourteen years pass before the second act of the drama takes place at the left of the lintel: the tale of Joseph's blossoming rod. The Virgin has been reared in the Temple, where she is shown praying on the steps of the *bima,* the raised platform of the tabernacle. Although she is no more than a child, the high priest has already suggested that she take a husband, since, like Juliet Capulet, she has reached the age for marriage. The Virgin has submitted to this request only when it was agreed to leave the choice to Heaven. Accordingly, each of the eligible men of the tribe of Judah has offered a leafless branch to be stored overnight in the Temple; no less than fifteen branches may be seen stacked on the altar. The suitors look on hopefully from the voussoirs at the left, but, handsome as they are, none will be successful. For Joseph has arrived on horseback: an elderly and altogether unsatisfactory-looking bridegroom. It is his rod, naturally, which blossoms. Saint Anne thereupon embraces him, or rather touches him on the brow with a delicate gesture, while two disappointed suitors look on. Finally, hands joined, Joseph, the high priest, Mary, Joachim, and Anne celebrate the marriage. The Virgin, still a girl whose hair flows over her shoulders, wears the coronet of a princess; and although she inclines her head to the priest, her hand reaches backward for the hand of her father. This extraordinary group, at once earnestly serious and utterly charming, is a Jewish wedding of the thirteenth century.

After the marriage the story touches the Evangel for the first time. Joseph doubts the Virgin, but an angel informs him that her approaching maternity is divine, and he drops to his knees to beg forgiveness. The Virgin, in an exquisite movement, lifts him to his feet, and they go off, hand in hand, to Bethlehem.

The action now rises to the full glory of the Evangel and to the brilliance of twelfth-century sculpture. Delightful as the thirteenth-century carving is, it cannot compete with the wizardry of the atelier of Maurice de Sully. The actors here do not wear realistic modern dress, but the abstract robes of Heaven. The haloed old man on the left of the upper lintel, with a beard grown in the Semitic desert, is the Prophet Isaiah. Here he has been moved from the Old Testament to the New so that he can witness his prediction of the birth of the Messiah come to life in the Annunciation. The Archangel Gabriel, facing the audience with one naked foot extended, pronounces the will of the Lord in a voice of gold. If there has ever been a messenger from Heaven, it is this wingèd prince. The Virgin inclines her head, and lifts a hand to signify that she understands and, of course, accepts, her divine mission. Next is a Visitation in which Mary and Elizabeth embrace, as goddesses do, with the light touch of immortals. All five of these figures have a powerful celestial hauteur, which is not at all disdain but simply the distance the artist has placed them from the spectator. They are not three feet high. They seem thirty.

Now, in the central tableau, comes the superb instant of the Nativity. Mary lies beneath a silken coverlet on the bed of a queen, whose posts have been turned on the lathe of a master. Jesus sleeps in a cradle that is simple but luxurious, the sort that royalty prefer. It might be made of rosewood or cedar, which profits from clean line. The baby is wrapped in swaddling clothes so expensive that only the Lord could afford them. There is nothing of the manger, no hint of straw, dung, or any common touch of realism that would soil this magnificent chamber. The farm beasts themselves—the ox and the ass who warm the baby with their breath—have never seen a stable. They are urban creatures so sensitive and fine that men are visible behind their masks. Joseph, a turbaned potentate, sits with hand on chin, nodding. This late at night he feels his age, and does not look at his young wife's startling beauty. Does he dream that the irreverent French, laughing at his gravity, call him the King of Cuckolds? He does not even peek over the edge of the cradle, like the inquisitive angels, to admire the handsome child. Outside, harking to the strange music in the clouds, are the old and the young Shepherds. Beside them are the three sceptered Oriental Kings, scornful Herod, and his sly doctors.

In this portal, so frankly the work of two different ateliers, working fifty years apart, the two periods blend with perfect felicity, as the round and the pointed arch blend. The thirteenth-century sculptor, whose art was not at all the art of the twelfth, made a special effort to match the mood of the earlier carvings. That he succeeded may be seen in the beautiful portraits of Joachim as shepherd, in the voussoirs to the right. How well he could carve on his own terms will be seen in all the remaining doors of the Cathedral.

Whether, on occasion, he surpassed the sculptor of the twelfth century, you may decide for yourself, keeping in mind the head of Barbedor, the gown of Louis VII, and above all the dominating Virgin in Majesty. The major figures count most heavily because, it would seem, they were carved by the major sculptors. In fact, the sculpture of Notre-Dame can be studied only at extreme disadvantage because its most valuable portion has been lost. *All* the freestanding statues of the façade, without exception, were destroyed either by the Revolution or through the vandalism and neglect of the Ancien Régime. Some wreckage has been salvaged for museums, but the harm done is irreparable. Viollet-le-Duc did more harm still, replacing the lost figures with imitations. The new work is a travesty of what must have been one of the finest ensembles of statuary ever carved.

In particular the nine statues which the twelfth century created for this portal were superb. Viollet-le-Duc has restored the original iconography: to either side of the Saint Marcel on the central pier were Saint Peter with his keys, the Gentile; and Saint Paul, representing the Jewish tradition in the Church; beside them were Solomon and the Queen of Sheba, David with his harp, a queen who may have been Bathsheba; and two unidentified kings. They were tall "statue columns" whose pleated robes joined mystically with the vertical architecture, similar to those which survive at Chartres, as the Paris Virgin is similar to the Chartres Virgin, but not identical. Of the nine figures only the Saint Marcel has been recovered, and may be examined in the lapidary room of the northern tower. Mended though it is, the battered original—so superior to the copy that stands in its place—reveals the epic twelfth-century beauty. With his crosier Bishop Marcel is seen driving the vampire from the tomb it had ravished in the Gallo-Roman Paris of the fifth century. Marcel, like his Bishop's staff, is tense and slender as a lance, indomitable as the early Church, in the days when there were giants and dragons upon the earth.

Overhead, in the voussoirs, is more twelfth-century sculpture. Around the Virgin in Majesty, in tiers of glory, is her Court of Heaven. Closest to her is a corps of fourteen angels; then fourteen patriarchs and sixteen prophets; and, outermost, sixteen old men of the Apocalypse, with their musical instruments and vials, as they were seen by Saint John the Divine. In truth, these splendid old men, singing their mysterious music, were not originally intended for Mary's court. They were meant for a central portal, taken from the vision of Saint John, which was never installed and was discarded by the thirteenth century for the Last Judgment of Saint Matthew. The old men were considered too beautiful to be thrown away and were employed here for their loveliness alone. Singing, dancing, their rich beards tossing in winds from the corners of the earth, they sail upward, as if mounted on a wheel of air, to the Lamb of God and, at the apex of the triangle, to the Christ of the Apocalypse—alpha and omega, the beginning and the end, the first and the last, whose terrible two-bladed sword, after seven centuries, has shattered in his teeth.

II

The four great buttresses of the façade rise up, like the Books of the Evangel, defining the three doors. Yet, except for the single episode of the Nativity and the terrifying souvenirs of the Crucifixion displayed in the Last Judgment, the life of Jesus Christ on earth is absent from these portals. Not a scene from the Passion appears, nor do any of the miracles reported by the apostles. In the façade of the Marian Cathedral, Christ is God. The Word alone inhabits the rock, and the Word is the giant abstract face of the Lord. But as the façade comes to an end at the northern portal, the Evangel ends too, with a verse of Saint John the Middle Age took to heart: "And there were also many other things which Jesus did, the which, if they were written every one, I suppose that even the world itself could not contain the books that should be written."

The world did, of course, find room for them in the portals of the cathedrals. The stories were first recorded by the primitive Christian communities of Asia Minor, which retained a strong feeling for Hellenistic, and even Persian, mythology. As they traveled westward, the apocryphal books were embroidered by Coptic priests in Egypt and by churchmen in Rome, so that by the fourth century Saint Jerome had already protested against *deliramenta apocryphorum*—they wandered at such distance from probability. Yet the tales had not attained their full dimensions. Pope Gregory the Great in the sixth century enlarged them further; Bede added what he could in Anglo-Saxon Britain; and naïf French monks of the eighth and ninth centuries, Abbot Hilduin of Saint-Denis among them, in the fortified monasteries of the Dark Age, expanded them most of all. These private and often anonymous works of art, like their intricate manuscript illuminations, waited centuries, in some cases a thousand years, to find public expression in the portals and windows of the Romanesque and the Gothic. And at the moment they made their monumental appearance in stone and glass they were collected, for a rapidly increasing number of readers, in a wonderful anthology, the *Golden Legend* of James of Voragio, who was born in 1230 in the town now called Virazze, near Savona on the Gulf of Genoa.

The term "legend" is meaningful. The good Bishop James felt that his main duty as anthologist was to collect all relevant material; and that the reader's responsibility was to determine if it was valid. Occasionally James distrusted a source and mentioned his doubts, but he did not omit the text. This method of scholarship proved remarkably successful. From the moment the *Legenda Aurea* appeared in Latin in the second half of the thirteenth century until such men as Francis Bacon dismissed it as superstition, it was the most popular book in Europe. After the invention of printing, when it could be had cheaply and in the common language, it became a bestseller from London to Prague. No less than thirty translations in several European languages appeared before 1500, including two English editions by Caxton. The price of these books today passes imagination. But happily a better text—the thirteenth-century original—may be read without charge in the portals of Notre-Dame.

Indeed, without the *Legenda Aurea,* which summarizes all the Apocrypha, the northern door of the façade is inexplicable. This portal too is consecrated to the Virgin, and has always been called the Portail de la Vierge; but there is not a verse in the Bible to justify its great scene of Mary's Coronation in Heaven. James of Voragio, however, knew the story from "a certain apocryphal book which is attributed to Saint John the Evangelist." After the Crucifixion, he relates, the Virgin remained in her house near Mount Zion, praying, fasting, and making pilgrimages to the scenes of the Baptism, Passion, Resurrection, and Ascension of her Son. Since the Virgin had given birth to the Savior at the age of fifteen, and since she survived by twenty-four years His death when He was thirty-three, James calculated that Mary was seventy-two when she died. "But it is more probable, for thus it is read elsewhere, that she was sixty at the time of her Assumption."

Quite suddenly Mary was taken with "an uncontrollable desire" to see her Son again. Whereupon an angel appeared in great brilliance, and with great respect informed her: "Thy Son awaits thee." The Virgin had two requests: first, that she die in the presence of the apostles, who were at that moment scattered among the nations of the earth; and, second, that her soul, when it parted from her body, should "encounter none of the powers of Satan." The angel was puzzled by this last demand. "Why dost thou fear to see those evil spirits whom thou hast crushed?" he asked. But he granted the request nevertheless.

And having said this, the angel remounted to Heaven in glory. . . . And it happened that, Saint John being at Ephesus to preach, the sky suddenly thundered, and a white cloud enveloped the apostle, and carried him to Mary's door. He knocked on the door and entered. . . .

The eleven other apostles arrived immediately afterward, transported in the same manner. When the Virgin saw that all of them had come she blessed the Lord; and then she had her bed placed in their center, lamps were lighted, and they waited.

And, at the third hour of the night, Jesus came accompanied by a multitude of angels and martyrs, patriarchs, confessors, and virgins; and the choirs of virgins arranged themselves before the bed in which Mary lay, and began to sing hymns in beautiful harmonies. . . .

Jesus spoke first, and said: "Come, thou whom I have chosen, and I shall place thee on my throne, for I have yearned for thy beauty."

And she replied: "My heart is ready, Lord, my heart is ready."

. . . And Jesus answered: "Come from Lebanon, my wife, come receive the crown."

And she said: "I come, for it is written that I shall do Thy wish, and my spirit rejoices in Thee, O Lord, Who art my Savior."

And thus the soul of Mary left her body, and flew upward into the arms of her Son.

The death of Mary was unique for the Middle Age: free from pain, anguish, or suffering of any kind. The Virgin was spared even a disagreeable meeting with her old enemy, Satan, who, unless angels stood guard, was sure to appear. Her body suffered no decomposition, her face no sign of illness, age, or sorrow. Three virgins, relates the *Legenda Aurea,* came to wash her corpse, "which shone with such radiance . . . that the human eye could not look upon it." Then the apostles, following instructions they had received from the Savior, carried her body to the Valley of Jehoshaphat, and placed it in a jeweled tomb they found waiting there, and kept vigil for three days.

This sepulcher, hung with golden lamps, was seen in Palestine by the Crusaders; and from their descriptions the sculptor was able to carve the magnificent coffin that occupies the center of the northern portal of Notre-Dame. No Capet ever won a tomb such as this, with its seven remarkable rosettes, each different from the other, and which was once covered with gold and studded with colored stones. Beside the coffin the twelve apostles are still keeping their vigil, looking out over Paris with expressions of such intelligence and sadness, and such profound meditation, that they do not notice that Christ, accompanied by angels, is already in their midst.

Jesus came the third day, with a multitude of angels; and He greeted them, saying: "Peace be with you."

And they replied: "Glory to You, O Lord, Who alone have accomplished great marvels."

And the Lord said to the apostles: "What honor and what glory ought I confer on her who bore me?"

And they replied: "It seems fitting to Your servants, Lord, that You, Who have triumphed over death for all of the centuries, should resurrect the body of Your Mother, and place it on Your right hand for eternity."

The Lord approved, and the Archangel Michael arrived instantly with the soul of Mary, and gave it to Jesus. And the Savior said: "Arise, my dove, tabernacle of glory, vase of life, celestial temple. . . ."

And immediately the soul of Mary returned to her body, which rose up glorious from the tomb, and mounted to the sky, followed by a host of angels.

This is all the story that need be known; the sculpture tells the rest.

From isolated phrases in the legend, such as "come receive the crown" and "I shall place thee on my throne," the Master Sculptor of Paris created what Emile Mâle called "the chef d'oeuvre of the school of the Ile de France." In the highest register of the tympanum Christ and Mary are seated side by side, on the same broad throne, in equal majesty, both gowned in the flowing golden robes of Paradise, while angels kneel to either side with burning candles. Christ is crowned as king, and with His right hand blesses His Mother. With the other He gives her the flowering scepter, which is a symbol of the royal power she shares with Him. The Virgin joins her hands and bows her head in adoration, while at the summit of the triangle an angel flies from a cloud and places the crown of precious gems upon her head.

This is idealized beauty at as high a point as the Phidian Greek. Christ is already the Beau-Christ of Amiens, which would not be carved for two decades, until 1230, and which would not be more beautiful. The portrait of Mary is the most lovely of the thirteenth century. Compare it with the Virgin in Majesty of the southern portal and decide—if a decision is necessary—which you prefer. The Virgin, in 1210 as in 1160, was still Queen of Heaven and Earth. She was still radiantly young, with long, golden hair, and unmarked by sorrow. But an obvious change has taken place.

The Virgin in Majesty has been transformed from the Mother Empress to the Queen and Bride of Christ. How hesitantly she made the change can be seen in a series of portals at Senlis, Mantes, Laon, and Chartres, in which she first allowed her Son to take His adult place on a throne beside her and then slowly bowed her head to Him. At Paris, for the first time, her submission is complete. It is Christ who bestows the crown, and the Virgin is curiously dependent on His royal will. She seems younger than the Son, and her worship of Him is absolute. Make of this what you will, remembering that this stone was carved seven hundred years before the theorizing of Sigmund Freud, and perhaps seven thousand after the first story of Oedipus the King was related. The mystery is Christian, so chastely treated that only a great Christian artist could have depicted it; the Sermon on the Mount is not more pure. Its purity is Christian; its essence is universal. Primitive legend has become the sophisticated legend of Sophocles; primitive art has become the classical art of Phidias.

The Woman—the mother goddess—has become more human, less remote, softer in expression, female to a degree never before revealed in the West. In previous representations of this scene, all of which—if we accept Mâle's theory—developed from the "Triomphe de la Très Sainte Vierge," the last blue window which Suger gave Notre-Dame in 1150, Mary had been crowned in advance and wore her royal insignia, like the Virgin in Majesty, as if they had been hers since the beginning of time. The first actual coronation takes place in this portal. The thirteenth century would crown the Virgin again and again, almost as it did a terrestrial queen, to emphasize a royalty that earlier periods seem to have taken for granted. Each coronation would show a further step toward realism, or even naturalism, so that by 1500, in the choir screen of Chartres Cathedral, Mary would take needle and thread and, with an uncanny resemblance to Queen Victoria, sew. Later, as *Mater dolorosa,* she would give way to hysterics.

This humanizing—and eventual cheapening—of the goddess proceeded so gradually, as one world became another, that the changes were scarcely perceptible to those who lived through them. In 1200 the change had not truly set in, or at least must not be exaggerated. The Byzantine empress had become a French queen, but she was not yet recognizably an earthly queen of France. Saint Louis, the incarnation on earth of a divine king, was not yet born. Reims and Amiens, the Virgin's two largest temples, remained to be built. Yet Mary, and the physical beauty of the sculpture shows this, had been depicted in her first classical posture; and however slowly it follows, decline alone may succeed classicism. Men in 1200 had become more civilized or refined. Their art had become more considered.

All has been simplified for monumental effect, all is massively calm and strong. At no other church is the Triumph of the Virgin treated with such absence of petty detail. Rather than a tympanum and supporting lintels, as in the other portals, this is a single enormous tympanum, whose source of power is the key Gothic symbol at its base: the Ark of the Covenant. The Ark, of course, is Mary: the vessel of the Lord, which contained the promised Messiah. The unrolled phylacteries of the three splendid Prophets and the three Kings seated to either side were inscribed, probably, with Old Testament verses that elaborated the mystery.

Thus based solidly on the Old Law, the mystery branches upward, like the shrubs of the Valley of Jehoshaphat, to the great Christian scene of Resurrection. The apostles guarding Mary's tomb possess such beauty that Christ may be distinguished among them only by his cruciform halo. Saint Paul and Saint John, the old intellectual and the young, are seated to either side on low thrones, and balance the symmetry of the whole portal by the deliberate movement of their hands. The jeweled coffin, the Virgin's shroud, the profile of her sanctified body, the angels bending above her, have been studied with the same awareness. A rich touch of asymmetry is provided by the keys of Saint Peter, whose portrait is perhaps the most beautiful in the frieze.

But none of these figures can match the Christ and the Virgin above. The Coronation, as it should, dominates, not only in the pure intelligent beauty of the god and goddess, but in the broad folds of their robes, the display of their hands, the kneeling pair of angels with their tall candlesticks. This is the Virgin's spacious golden Paradise; and in the surrounding voussoirs she is attended by the celestial court that accompanied Christ in the legend: angels, kings, prophets, saints—sixty figures in all, giving an impression of sixty thousand.

Beneath this limitless Heaven, spreading through the lower half of the portal, is a limitless earth. The Virgin's green medieval world crowds about her restored central statue in the doorway, where dozens of small bas-reliefs, on the frames and jambs of the entrance, depict nothing less than the whole natural universe as it was known at the start of the thirteenth century.

At the lower left a woman bestrides a bridled whale, or a porpoise, riding the huge fish as a horse, and holding a ship in her hand. She is the Ocean; and across the portal is her counterpart, the Earth— Mother Ceres—whose pagan effigies were still standing everywhere along the roads of France. She holds a pair of growing plants, while Humanity, a maiden, kneels and nurses at her breast. All Nature moves in a heavenly arc between these two symbols, rising from the Ocean on the left to a hot summer solstice and passing downward on the right, like autumn leaves, to Earth.

Perched on the tail of the Ocean's great fish sits Aquarius, an easy god of water, who formerly held an urn that poured forth a double torrent. Beside him is January, the cold month of feasts, who sits like a prince at table, waited upon by a servant. Above are the Fishes, and with them February, a traveler who warms himself at a roaring fire, so chilled that he holds his foot to the hearth; from the ceiling hang a ham and sausages, a good Frenchman's provision for winter. Next, the Ram, accompanied by the earliest sweetbriar; and March, a peasant pruning his vine, for the indoor life is over. Now the Bull skips in a meadow, beneath plum trees; and April watches his young wheat at the happiest time of year, Easter, when the earth softens, and yields.

Tere de France, mult estes dulz païs!

How sweet a land this is, Roland knew. The Twins are friendly brothers, one holding a flowered twig, the other's arm thrown affectionately about his shoulder; May, a young nobleman with a falcon on his wrist, has picked a branch of wild roses. At the top of the door the Lion plays in a rather comical tree—he is out of place and should be exchanged with the Crab on the other side, to whom the beginning of summer belongs. June has made his first cutting of hay and carries a heavy bale on his back, barefoot, across the warm fields.

Across the door, July prepares for the wheat harvest, honing a scythe that farmers still use in the Ile de France.

Now the year, as it must, descends. Beside the sign of Virgo (restored), August reaps his grain with a sickle that has been lost. The scales of Libra have also been broken; and September is missing his head, but he tramples his grapes energetically—dances them —in a stout wooden tub. Scorpio is a simple abstraction; but October is one of the great figures of the Cathedral: he sows his wheat as his autumn cloak flies behind him. Below, Sagittarius shoots an arrow, while November chases his hogs through the forest of ancient oaks, where the Druids lay hidden; the first winter winds have shaken down acorns, and the hogs gobble them. Finally, a restored sign of Capricorn means the end of the year; and the fattened hog is killed by December for the banquets of Christmas and the New Year.

All revolve about the central figure of the Virgin. She controls not only the Months but the broader cycle of the Seasons, which are within touch of her right hand, on the jamb of the pier. Winter, Autumn, Spring, and Summer are men who successively shed their clothes and grow younger as the year grows warmer, so that Winter, at the base, closest to the freezing pit of Hell, is a shivering old man; while Summer, at the summit, is a naked healthy lad, warmed by the golden heat of Heaven. On the other side of the pier a companion set of reliefs also demonstrates the Virgin's irresistible attraction. These panels show the Ages of Man, six rather than seven, and described with none of Shakespeare's sarcasm. From the delicate infant to the venerable patriarch, the sculptor has portrayed human wisdom and refinement, increasing as they ascend, guided by Mary, to Paradise.

The Virgin, like the Saint Marcel on the pier of the southern portal, was placed here, in the midst of the symbols of her force, to rule the entrance of the church, her image available to common touch and common examination, larger than life but in the center of life. As Patroness of the Cathedral she is a divinity of Earth rather than an abstract deity of Heaven. Surrounding her are other major Patrons of the Cathedral, also restored. On her left are three of the powerful saints of Paris: John the Baptist, Stephen, and Geneviève. On Mary's right, between two angels, the Patron of

France, Saint Denis, holds his severed head in his hands. The restoration is incorrect—Denis should hold the top of his scalp only, as at Reims.

The less said of this restored statuary the better; but beneath the saints are a series of bas-reliefs that show how the thirteenth century, in less than a square foot of space, achieved epic effect. Each panel contains an episode from the lives of the patrons. Beneath John the Baptist the executioner serves the saint's head to Salome; and the dancer takes it in her hand and stands tall and astonished as she studies the face. Beneath Saint Stephen a member of the stoning mob lifts his arms to gather force as he launches his rock at the Protomartyr. Beneath Geneviève an angel lights the Saint's candle each time a demon tries to blow it out—one of the best stories in the *Golden Legend;* until the Revolution the candle was a treasure of Notre-Dame and one of the most effective relics in Christendom. Across the portal, Saint Denis dies in the same mood as Stephen, kneeling to pray among pretty plants. Beneath the angels there is war in Heaven: Michael crushes the dragon, and a second angel knocks an imp sidewise through eternity, so that he tumbles among stars.

These bas-reliefs provided sure clues for the restoration of the statues destroyed by the Revolution, but the two outermost panels are ambiguous, and it would seem that Viollet-le-Duc misunderstood them. On the right, where a pope is called for, he placed Saint Sylvester; the pontiff was more likely Alexander III, in Paris when Notre-Dame was begun. Facing the Pope, Viollet-le-Duc installed Constantine. But look at the panel beneath the Emperor. A young person, crowned, kneels and offers a scroll to an enthroned figure, who wears a halo as well as a crown. Who are they? Late in the Middle Age, in 1410, an official document of the Cathedral spoke of the statue above as *"l'ymage du roy Philippe le Conquérant, figuré en jeune aage pour ce qu'il fut couronné ou xiiij*e *an de son aage";* that is Philip Augustus, whom the Middle Age called the Conqueror, depicted as a young man because he was crowned at fourteen. If it was Philip, there was another reason to show him as a youth. In 1186, when he was twenty-one, the King made a valuable gift of relics to Notre-Dame, including mementoes of the saints in this portal; and the bas-relief would seem to have him making precisely this offering to the Virgin in Majesty. Very likely the portrait is his, the only one to survive in all the cathedrals that went up during his reign.

Men gave, as Philip did, and the Virgin accepted. No intelligent woman has ever refused flowers, and the Middle Age covered Mary's church with them. For not only had the Annunciation taken place in a flowering springtime, but the name Nazareth itself meant "flower." *"Nazareth interpretatur flos,"* the *Legenda Aurea* quoted Saint Bernard—"the flower had wished to be born of a flower, in a flower, at the time of flowers." "Consider the lilies of the field," said Jesus, "how they grow." The Virgin herself, some said, was born not after the embrace at the Golden Gate but when Saint Anne inhaled a rose.

All was green and flowering as the sculptor sang in his chains of time and as he gathered blossoms for Mary. The Virgin walked beside him in the Parisian fields and helped him pick the superb bouquet in the outer frame of the door: wild sage and ivy, sprigs of walnut and eglantine as dainty as Chaucer's Prioress; and grape vines, oak leaves, and pear and olive branches with their fruit, growing sweetly through the stone and curling outward to the façade. And above, climbing on the edge of the voussoirs, are unrecognizable blossoms and vines in which odd birds hop, with little monster heads, or heads of monks, nibbling on cress or hiding in the foliage. The birds, who have flown straight from the Romanesque, mean nothing but delight. They are toys for the Virgin's amusement, year-round companions for real birds who make their nests in the portal and sing cheerfully through the June morning.

III

"I know that my Redeemer liveth," Maurice de Sully spoke out on his deathbed in 1196, "and that He shall stand at the latter day upon the earth." But when, precisely? When would the trumpet sound and the graves fly open? "Ye know neither the day nor the hour," replied the Lord through Saint Matthew. Not even the angels of heaven knew, but the Middle Age thought the day might come very soon. Predictions varied. Saint Hildegarde foresaw Domesday as imminent after 1180; the year 1200 seemed more likely to the

Abbot Joachim of Calabria, a Cistercian monk whose prophecies elevated him to Dante's *Paradiso*. When the Day of Wrath failed to arrive at the turn of the thirteenth century, new prophecies fixed the end in 1300.

There were signs. The four horsemen of the Apocalypse were riding in the West. Kingdom had risen against kingdom, and there was bloody war on the earth as Philip the Conqueror battled first with Coeur-de-Lion and then with King John. Plague erupted, and was called "sacred fire"—*ignis sacer,* or, more properly, *ignis infernalis.* Famine struck France repeatedly at the end of the twelfth century: the starvation of 1195-1199 was hideous. Men ate wine dregs for bread and devoured beasts dead of disease. They chewed on roots; there were cases of cannibalism. In 1197, according to the Chronicle of Reims, innumerable persons died of hunger: *"innumeri fame perempti sunt."* Hungry nobles rode out of their donjons, like minions of the Anti-Christ, and sacked such rich abbeys as Saint-Loup of Troyes in 1184. Such men did not spare the barns of the poor.

All this provides a correction for the idyl of agricultural plenty depicted in the portals of the cathedrals. The twelve Months of Notre-Dame are pictures of *ideal* conditions and must be understood as such. Often, they were irresponsibly wrong. The Church itself could be a cruel exploiter of its serfs; and during Saint Louis' first Crusade, when Queen Blanche governed the kingdom, she personally came with soldiers and liberated a crowd of prisoners from a jail of the Cathedral of Paris; the serfs and villeins of several suburban villages had refused to pay a tithe, whereupon the Chapter of Notre-Dame had arrested men, women, and children and jammed them in cells, where "several died of heat."

Beyond widespread human misery, there were other warnings of Apocalypse. Heresy had grown out of hand during the twelfth century, especially in the charming and articulate South. The whole of Languedoc lay in the passionate error of Catharism, and would soon be put to the sword by Simon de Montfort, in the name of the Church Militant, but to the profit of the Capets. The Albigensian Crusade destroyed more than the fine cities Béziers and Narbonne; it eradicated an independent civilization that had produced the troubadours and such churches as Saint-Sernin of Toulouse. Never again would the Midi construct a monument as friendly as Saint-Sernin, although it built the red fortress-church at Albi.

There were false prophets even in Paris. In 1210 there was a heretic hunt in the capital, and the body of Amaury of Chartres, an intellectual who during his lifetime had the bad judgment to read Averroës, was ejected from the cemetery of the Holy Innocents. Some ten of Amaury's students were burned at the stake; others were sentenced to life imprisonment. The writings of Amaury's disciple, David of Dinant, who had the good fortune to flee, were publicly consumed by fire. The Church Council responsible for these condemnations also decreed that to study the natural philosophy of Aristotle, or Averroës's commentary on it, was an offense punishable by burning. A generation later Aquinas and Albert the Great would make Aristotle the foundation of their theology—Amaury, like Abélard, had simply been ahead of his time. Finally the Council declared a heretic any man in whose home either the *Credo* or the *Pater Noster* was found translated into French. These prohibitions were renewed five years later in Paris by the papal legate; at the same time the Lateran Council of 1215 was establishing the Inquisition at Rome.

In this atmosphere of heresy, sin, and disaster upon the earth there were natural calamities and accidents that added to the general fear of the unknown. Fire was a constant danger. From 1200 to 1225 the city of Rouen burned five times. In the single year of 1188, not only Rouen, but Troyes, Beauvais, Provins, Arras, Poitiers, and Moissac were virtually destroyed by flame. There were also floods, shakings of the earth, and landslides, like that which inspired Dante's steep descent between the sixth and seventh circles of Hell.

Every sign indicated that Judgment was near; and the Church insisted—by force, if necessary—that the world be ready. This urgency was intensified by phenomena in the heavens. Comets passed overhead in irregular flight; there were showers of stars and eclipses of the sun and the moon—any of which could have meant that the Day of Wrath was at hand. Heavy bursts of thunder were signals that the Archangel Michael—who had replaced Mercury as the god of hilltops and storms and the guide of the dead—was about to begin his wide voyage over the earth. "For as lightning cometh out of the east," announced the Evangel, "and shineth even unto the west; so shall the coming of the Son of Man be." So, too, in every cathedral after 1200, the Last Judgment of Saint Matthew, rather than the astonishing vision of Saint John, appeared at the heart of the western façades.

Here, at Notre-Dame, about the year 1210, is the Son of Man come to judge! Meet His glance, if you are able. Against a background of golden glory, of which bright traces remain, Christ sits enthroned in His human image: a half-naked God of suffering, showing His wounded hands, and the wound in His side. Angels hold the instruments of torture that became symbols of triumph: the nails, the spear, the cross. As they did at Golgotha, the Virgin and Saint John have fallen to their knees at either side and pray.

"But behold," cried Saint Paul to the Corinthians, "I shall show you a mystery":

. . . and we shall all be changed, in a moment, in the twinkling of an eye: for the trumpet shall sound, and the dead shall be raised incorruptible. . . .

And the dead have awakened! blinded by the light of eternity, deafened by the ivory trumpets of the angels. On the lower lintel they rise startled from their tombs, fully dressed, distinguished from one another by sex and age and by social rank. In the upper lintel a little naked soul has already hopped into the scales of Saint Michael and outweighs his evil deeds, which take the form of an imp. In the wink of an eye (*"in ictu oculi,"* the theologians specified), the Elect have started off to Heaven, overcome with joy, crowned as queens and kings, attired in celestial robes; on the left hand of Christ, the Damned, weeping and swearing, pushed by devils, are led in chains to Hell.

This tremendous scene of Judgment, spilling over into the Heaven and Hell of the voussoirs, has ramifications throughout the central portal, which has suffered more than any other at Notre-Dame. Even before the Revolution, which destroyed the original statues of the apostles, the Ancien Régime, too, showed its gift for vandalism. In 1771 the Cathedral Chapter commissioned Soufflot, the architect of the Panthéon, to enlarge the portal so that the canopies of processions could pass more easily beneath judging Christ. Soufflot accordingly cut an arch through the lintels, removed the jambs of the doorway, and demolished the central Christ, which had served as model for the Beau-Christ of Amiens.

Viollet-le-Duc's restoration, for all its melodrama, is more or less correct, as may be seen in the fragments of the lower lintel that survive at the Cluny Museum. One piece, which Viollet-le-Duc copied, is made remarkable by the presence of a Negro among the resurrected dead. This touch is more than medieval racial toleration, although then, as now, the French were fascinated by the beauty of black skin; it shows the universal dominion of Christ over all the races and nations of the earth—a feeling expressed in arms by the Crusades. It also emphasizes a favorite dogma of Maurice de Sully: that the dead would be resurrected in their own bodies. This is the reason they rise fully dressed from their tombs, rather than naked, as was usual in medieval iconography. The restoration of the upper lintel, where the last four Elect and Damned on either side are original, is also accurate. The devil, attempting to tip the scales in his favor, does so at other churches; the indifference of the archangel, who knows the scales will be accurate, is also typical.

The scales, incidentally, go back further than the teachings of Saint Augustine and Saint John Chrysostom: they date at least from Bronze Age India and Egypt. So does the idea of Hell itself; and in the curious Egyptian principle of divine reward or punishment may be found all the difference between the pyramids and the cathedrals. "The lucky Egyptian," says Professor Gordon Childe, "could buy a magic passport through the dread tribunal"—with cash. No sum of gold, no terrestrial power, could assure the medieval Christian his entrance to Heaven. The priest could give absolution, but the priest himself might burn with the absolved. The only currency accepted by Saint Michael in his weighing stall was that of the Sermon on the Mount.

Those who could not pay went off sobbing or cursing, on the vindictive left hand of the Judge, and tumbled into the jaws of Leviathan, as a well-dressed woman is doing, while another lady and a prelate await their turn. This is the hell beast of Job:

. . . his teeth are terrible . . . out of his mouth go burning lamps, and sparks of fire leap out.
Out of his nostrils goeth smoke, as out of a seething pot or cauldron.

Leave all hope, ye that enter. The cauldron is directly beneath, and its flames have already mingled with the hair of the descending victim. Two devils stand ready with hooks and forks and drag and push another sinner into the frothing pot. The devils' skin is flame; the mouth of a beast opens on their lewd bellies; their faces are snouts or horrible masks. The fire rises hot about the cauldron, and monstrous toads bite at the hands of the Damned, which search even here for a grasp.

In the next voussoir a pale horse, with a pale blindfolded woman rider, her ghastly breasts flapping on her ribs, springs out of the Book of Revelation and rides over a fourth part of the earth. Death kills with the sharp daggers she holds in either hand; and Hell follows her: an eviscerated sinner with his entrails pouring out and bleeding, his arm lopped and falling behind, his hair spreading backward in the dust, his legs yanked forward by the momentum of the ride, crossing the vile legs of the old woman riding nakedly before him, her arms flying outward about the neck of the whinnying horse, her daggers striking.

More Hell follows. Bodies and parts of bodies twist and struggle but cannot escape. And another Horseman of the Apocalypse gallops past on a frantically neighing steed, whipping his mount savagely over the ears.

And more Hell: Carnal Pleasure is a satiric queen, sporting a shattered crown. Her inhuman mask would do credit to the corrupt judges of Georges Rouault. Her sharp claw-feet dig into the shoulders of a bishop, whose chest is crammed against the back of a king. Below are flames.

Hell, deeper and crueler. A horned demon points to the text of the Avenging Christ who had ordained these hot tortures. Below, other devils have a woman upside down and prepare to devour her loins. Toads and serpents bite away her breasts, while another devil hooks at her belly. This is the end: the Damned have begun to torture the Damned; and a male figure reaches up out of the lower flames and drags her downward with him.

Hell is an allegory, explained Saint Thomas; but the medieval man, when he was presented with this burning vision of the underworld, must have believed, like Shakespeare's Horatio, at least in part. Jesuits in Ireland could believe—with amazing visual imagination—as recently as the young manhood of James Joyce. Hell is easy to understand. The Middle Age knew as well as Sartre that "Hell is other people"; and knew better than any Existentialist that there is no exit once Hell is entered. For the medieval man was perhaps as aware as any Frenchman who endured the Occupation that Hell is possible on earth. The Gestapo did not invent torture chambers; the jailers of Philip Augustus were expert in chaining men to great timbers, blinding them, and cutting off their hands and ears; smearing their bodies with grease before a roasting fire; hanging them up by the hands; breaking their limbs with iron bars; immersing their heads in water. Eventually, when the Inquisition was in full force, the jailers of the Church, too, would accomplish so thorough a job on prisoners that there was nothing left for the secular arm to burn.

Heaven, as it seemed to the Fabian Bernard Shaw, may very possibly be boring. The author of *Aucassin and Nicolette* found Hell, like Shaw's underworld, made charming by good conversation and fashionable ladies. Yet Heaven has a subtle delight of its own, which is visible to him who will see and which may be heard by him who will listen. Dante's Heaven is music and golden space: the backdrop of a Giotto. And at Notre-Dame the same Heaven shows hundreds of varied attitudes and joys, such as the happy little winged cherubs who lean over their celestial balustrades to have a view of the Lord, smiling, sighing, closing their eyes, lifting their hands, touching their breasts, flying forward over the railing to Christ. Heaven takes all the room it can claim in the façade, lifting slowly in the air until the apex of its triangle touches the Gallery of Kings, almost to the rose. Neither of the other doors has this majestic field of sanctity, which in the thirteenth century was painted with gold.

On the benevolent right hand of Christ the Elect go to Paradise with quiet smiles, as a tall angel shows them to their places, like a celestial usher. They are crowned as queens and kings, since the only rank in Heaven is royal; and all seem uniformly young. From the battlements of the True Jerusalem they look down serenely at Paris, done with cares and filled with wordless joy at the thought of the future. One holds a sovereign's orb, as if it were a ball, in anticipation of a game.

In the midst of the Elect, Abraham, Isaac, and Jacob are

surrounded by flowers and haloed. Abraham holds three lately arrived souls in a scarf, cradling them to his bosom. Above, the circles of Paradise wheel upward, in liturgical precedence: Moses and the other patriarchs and prophets are nearest Christ; then a college of confessors, holding books opened to some illuminated page, or with the gemmed covers closed; next, a host of beardless martyrs, so mild that they scarcely gesture with their palms of triumph; and, finally, the great outer choir of virgins, also carrying palms, and chanting Dante's music.

Heaven, then, was attainable. The Church showed the Way, which was Christ—Christ Teacher—who holds the book at the Door and with his feet tramples the aspic and basilisk of ignorance. The original central Christ of this portal was not only the model for the Beau-Christ of Amiens, which was in turn copied in the restoration, but the very image of intellectual Christianity as it attained its encyclopedic triumph in the West. The Teacher was mounted on a pedestal of the liberal arts and surrounded by his teaching apostles, who may be imagined as the apostles of Amiens, but in a graver mood, which the Paris atelier gave all its creations. They composed the faculty of the University of Christ, whose one essential textbook was the Evangel. A single lesson, in fact, properly learned from Saint Matthew, would provide the whole education. The parable of the ten virgins has been restored on either side of the entrance: above the five who were wise, the door is open; above those who were foolish, the door is shut.

Formal instruction, classroom arguments, examinations—Robert de Sorbon compared final exams to the Last Judgment in a sermon to his students—all the wearisome apparatus of academism emerged in such simple and lively form in the medieval church that the curriculum could be understood by all. A favorite lesson, placed beneath the apostles so that it could be read even by children, was the old story of Vice and Virtue. Compared with Vice, which is as exciting as Hell, Virtue is rather dull. The twelve Virtues are women in heavy shawls, seated on thrones and carrying symbolistic shields: stately as Roman matrons but pretty much the same. Below, their corresponding Vices, personified as both men and women, and attired in medieval dress, riot in little scenes that are one-act plays. Patience and Gentleness, for example, are uniformly placid; but, beneath them, Anger is a lively lady who stabs a chiding monk, and Harshness kicks a servant head over heels, so that a cup flies from his hand. Yet, of all these figures, the Virtue Courage is perhaps the most interesting. Although a woman, she is cloaked in chain mail and armed with a sword and shield bearing a heraldic lion. Below, Cowardice drops his sword and runs from a hare.

The lesson was monumentally simple, but it could be carried as far as any intellectual wished, to the extremities of the portal, into the obscurities of four small bas-reliefs that modern Schoolmen find baffling. These panels are of superb quality, unrestored but badly mutilated, and M. Aubert sees them as symbols of patience, courage, submission, and pride—not quite a symmetrical combination. On one side, Job suffers painfully on his dungheap as his three friends attempt to comfort him, while his wife advises him to curse God and die. Below, a man leaning on a staff crosses a biblical land and comes to a swift stream on whose bank a tree rises. This may be David, en route to fight Goliath, choosing five smooth stones from the brook with which to arm his sling; or, conceivably, Joshua at the Jordan, selecting twelve stones to build an everlasting monument for Israel—if so, a remarkable signature for the artists of the façade. On the other side of the portal, Abraham—an extremely beautiful portrait—prepares to sacrifice Isaac, who has been lost. Below, Nimrod, a feudal warrior, stands on the fortified Tower of Babel and lances his spear at the sun. Perhaps M. Aubert's interpretation of these scenes is correct, yet they seem to contain more than allegorical significance. The torment of Job, David's mission against Goliath, and the sacrifice of Isaac all prefigure the Passion of Christ. Nimrod may be seen as a foil for the others, prefiguring the proud terrestrial kings in Hell.

To its final detail, the lesson did not vary. Man possessed intelligence—reason—and had free will to exercise it. But sooner or later he would confront his omnipotent God, who had suffered for him, and there would be an accounting. The lesson was there to be learned, as profoundly as intelligence permitted, whether or not it could be read in written words. Literacy did not matter; it might—and this was the unpardonable weakness of medieval society—even do harm. And although the theologians sometimes claimed that the number of the Elect was severely restricted—some calculations fixed the proportion as only two or three among a hundred Damned —the common man of the Middle Age had powerful hope of salvation. For, kneeling beside Christ, imploring forgiveness for unworthy humanity, is the same all-forgiving and all-understanding goddess as in the northern portal, the Virgin, perhaps by the same sculptor. Christ would seem to be the work of a later artist—at any rate, a different one.

And along with Mary, pleading as she does for mankind, is the beloved disciple Saint John, whom Christ on the Cross had confided to His mother as her new son. The world's pitiless reality was the business of the Avenging Christ; the world's potential of idealism was expressed in the Virgin and the boy poet Saint John. In spite of the pessimism of the theologians, the medieval man refused to believe that the door was completely closed. For had not Saint Bernard, the foremost intercessor before the Virgin, clung like the basest sinner to the hope of her intercession before the Lord? *"Ad quid tendam ut tremendam evadam sententiam?"* cried out the saint in the most anguished hymn of the Middle Age: "To whom shall I turn to escape the terrible sentence? O Mary . . . appease the formidable Judge in the name of your supplicants, so that, in His anger to punish our sins, He does not deliver us to flames."

Chapter Fourteen

THE FACADE AS FRANCE: THE KINGS, THE ROSE, AND THE TOWERS, 1220 - 1250

*t*HE SCAFFOLDING lifted. The workmen climbed to the stages by ladders, hoisting stone after them with winches and cranes, and prepared a grand surprise as the Parisians watched with delight. Through the scaffolds could be seen a gallery crossing the width of the façade, surmounting the base with a powerful line, which was unlike any gallery in France. About 1220 its niches were filled with twenty-eight heroic statues, each ten feet tall and crowned as a king, and carved ingeniously so there would be no effect of distortion when seen from the parvis sixty feet below. Yet distortion there was. The crowd guessed that they were Kings of France, placed in the façade to guard the Rose and the Church, as they had done from time immemorial: a mistake in identity that would cause a disaster for Notre-Dame in 1793. The kings were sovereigns not of France but of Judah, and their scepters were leafy branches of Jesse's Tree. The crowd missed the clue and instead took the first monarch for Childebert and the last for Philip Augustus.

To expect the multitude to have distinguished nicely between the Houses of France and of Judah would be asking a great deal. The distinction was based on a text of Saint Matthew, which the ordinary man, if he could read, was denied in his own language. Moreover, with unerring social perception, the people guessed one of the truths of the façade. To them, as to the historian, the sons of Clovis were as closely related to Notre-Dame as the sons of Jesse. The adornments of the Cathedral supported the assumption. The names of thirty-nine French monarchs, implying a continuous dynasty from Clovis to Saint Louis, were inscribed on the central doors. Louis VII kneeled beside the Virgin in Majesty; Philip Augustus stood witness to the Virgin's Coronation. But more than in its sculpture and bronze inscription, the entire façade is a mirror of the palace that faced it. The wall speaks not only for fifty years of French society but also for half a century of the French political state.

Notre-Dame speaks for the nation; it was a national church constructed simultaneously with a national state, at a time when neither could have existed without the other. Kings and queens were the makers of national manners, in art as in politics; and the Capets of the thirteenth century exercised the prerogative as no royalty on earth. The wall speaks for itself. The dark and massive base is the military kingdom of Philip Augustus and his son Louis VIII, the Lion. The upper part of the façade, lifting whitely from the rose, is the interregnum of Blanche of Castile, Louis VIII's widow, who dominated the kingdom even after their son, Louis IX—Saint Louis—reached his majority in 1236. The towers, joining Heaven, are Saint Louis himself, a divine creature, who through pure moral grandeur and irresistible political strength at last brought medieval Christian government to its ideal.

Taken only to the rose, the façade is as uncompromising, stubborn, and determined as Philip Augustus alone could be. The statue which was his in the northern portal dated from the conquest of Normandy; the sculptor's wages, in fact, may have come from the twenty silver marks his mother, Alix of Champagne, bequeathed to the Cathedral in 1206. The statue could not have been lifted to its pedestal later than 1215: the year of the signing of the Magna Carta, when King John met his barons at Runnymede, ceded to their ultimatum, and then chewed wood and grass.

But what occurred in England in 1215 resulted largely from a storybook battle fought at Bouvines, in Flanders, the previous summer. In 1214 a pincers movement was organized against France by John and his nephew Otto of Brunswick, the Holy Roman Emperor who had been excommunicated by the Pope in 1210. John was to strike at Paris from his remaining territory below the Loire. Otto, together with the rebellious Counts of Flanders and Boulogne, whose economic connections with England and Hanseatic Germany were stronger than their feudal allegiance to France, were to attack from the north at the same time. John's part of the movement, as might be expected, failed miserably. He fled when challenged by a smaller force led by the crown prince, Louis the Lion. In the north, confronted by a coalition army of eighty thousand men, the situation was somewhat different for King Philip himself.

The Battle of Bouvines, the most crucial of the Middle Age, was fought on a low, cultivated plateau, between Tournai and Lille, rising from marshy, half-deserted country which was largely underwater. Philip had no more than twenty-five thousand men, but he had a superb corps of five hundred knights, led by Guillaume des Barres, who will be remembered making a gift of fifty livres to Notre-Dame; these horsemen constituted the best fighting men in the world. After considerable maneuvering, Philip had retreated across the marshes to find dry land where his cavalry could deploy. It was July 27, 1214, a Sunday, which ordinarily would be free from fighting. The heat was extreme. The French were marching slowly toward Lens, in good order. The foot sergeants, carrying the Oriflamme of Saint Denis, were already beyond Bouvines and had crossed the Marcq on a bridge which Philip ordered enlarged, so that the remainder of the army could pass over the little river more quickly. While he was waiting for this operation to be completed the King received word that his rearguard was in a sharp engagement.

Whereupon Philip did an about-face and, with cool reasoning, arranged his forces on the plain of Bouvines with the sun behind them. The army of the Emperor drew up in a parallel line, and briefly the two hosts faced each other in silence. In the center of the French was their armed King, the conqueror of Normandy, forty-nine years old, and in the most difficult action of his life. The scarlet Capetian banner, blazoned with golden fleurs-de-lis, was held beside the monarch; surrounding him were the knights who had been at Château-Gaillard. Opposing them were the Emperor Otto, in golden armor, and his Saxon guard, above whom lifted the banner of the Holy Roman Empire: a great dragon surmounted by a golden eagle.

Although Philip's right flank went quickly into action, he waited for the commons of France to arrive on foot from across the Marcq before joining the central engagement. They hurried over the plateau, the Oriflamme before them, and took up their traditional place before the King. Then, as Julius Caesar had, Philip spoke to his troops:

In God is all our hope, all our trust. King Otto and his army have been excommunicated by the Pope, for they are enemies and persecutors of Holy Church. The payroll for his soldiers comes from the tears of the poor, from the pillage of lands belonging to God and to the clergy. As for us, we are Christians, in peace and communion with Holy Church. Sinners though we are, we are in accord with the servants of God. . . . Thus may we count on divine mercy. The Lord will give us means of triumphing over our enemies, who are ours!

A strange speech, perhaps, for a man who himself had been excommunicated a short time before, and who, after standing at odds with Rome for a decade, settled his major differences with the Holy See only so this battle might be fought with the blessing of Innocent III. Nevertheless Philip seems to have spoken in this tone if not precisely in these words; his chaplain, William the Breton, stood behind him as he spoke, and later recorded the language as a clerk remembered best. After the address the knights begged the sovereign to bless them, and Philip raised his gauntlets and implored divine benediction. Then trumpets sounded, and the struggle began.

The German infantry immediately penetrated the French lines, cutting through the outnumbered opposition, who had just arrived and were out of breath. Otto and his cavalry charged through the breach and came in sight of Philip. Instantly the household guard went into action. The French knights headed straight for the Emperor. Philip followed, but somehow he was enmeshed in the shouting crowd of Germans on foot, who, with hooks and pikes, pulled him from the saddle. Luckily his armor was perfect. It was impossible to find a chink through which to stab him. A knight arrived and shielded Philip with his own body. The standard bearer signaled frantically. Guillaume des Barres, who had reached Otto, turned and went back to his King. The French knights thereupon slaughtered the infantry, which they customarily overlooked. Philip mounted again and resumed the fight, this time with a guard that stayed close to him.

Guillaume des Barres, Gérard la Truie—"the Sow"—and Pierre Mauvoisin—"Bad Neighbor"—rode back to find Otto. After a furious charge, they had him. Pierre grabbed the Emperor's bridle. La

Truie stabbed him full in the chest, but the dagger slipped on the rounded breastplate. A second blow, badly directed, struck the eye of Otto's mount. The horse reared, galloped off a short distance, and fell dead. Now the Emperor was dismounted and in peril. But one of his barons lifted him onto his own horse, and Otto was fighting again, with his gauntleted hands, against Guillaume des Barres. Guillaume had ridden flush against him, seized him by the throat, and was choking him by pressing the flexible neck armor. To make him let go, the Germans killed his horse. The French knight stood alone, on foot, surrounded by mounted enemies. None dared approach for single combat, but remained at a distance, and threw maces at his head. Suddenly he was saved by a troop of French horsemen. In the melee Otto escaped, threw off his royal insignia, and rode without stopping to Valenciennes.

"We won't see his face again today," remarked Philip.

The day, indeed, was soon over. The Dukes of Lorraine, Brabant, and Limburg had fled with the Emperor. Four renowned German barons were prisoners. So were the Counts of Flanders and of Boulogne. Everywhere the enemy was retreating across the marshes.

After Bouvines, Philip never again personally took the field. He sent deputies instead: Simon de Montfort to subdue Languedoc on the pretext of a holy war; and Louis the Lion to carry the battle across the Channel, claiming the English throne by marriage to Blanche of Castile, who was granddaughter to Henry II and Eleanor of Aquitaine. In 1200 old Eleanor had brought the thirteen-year-old Spanish princess to marry in the French court, perhaps in the hope that Blanche might help the fortunes of her uncle John, now that her uncle Coeur-de-Lion was dead. But no one could help John, last of all himself. After the death of Eleanor, virtually no one wished to.

The Plantagenets were beaten, driven from all but the southwest corner of France by the intelligence and resolution of a single man. And as he saw his statue placed in the façade of Notre-Dame, Philip Augustus must have smiled wryly at his portrait as a youth. No trace remained, now that he was in his fifties, of the "badly combed" and emotional boy of fifteen who had taken the throne in 1180. Philip was as bald and sinewy as Caesar, and the foremost king in Christendom. Joinville speaks respectfully of him as *"li grans roys Phelippes,"* the great King Philip. He was known to all the West as the Conqueror and the master of Popes of the stature of Innocent III and Honorius III.

As he grew old he was still as hard as ever, as rapid and sure in his thought, as considered in his actions, as ruthless as the occasion required. He systematically fortified the major cities of the realm, as he had Paris, and assured the royal house of the loyalty of the bourgeoisie. To the end, he was tight-fisted in money matters, but occasionally debonaire, as only a great king can be. He did not read, at least not in Latin; perhaps he never had time to learn. After dinner, like any feudal prince, he listened to the songs of minstrels. His temperament, wrote a thirteenth-century biographer, "ran to wine, good living, and women." He was personally courageous, as Bouvines proved, but, in Gibbon's phrase, "the statesman predominated in his character." He was pious, and from time to time fiercely persecuted the Jews, burning them in groups; he burned Christian heretics as willingly. He trusted no one, and supervised Louis the Lion closely, to the point of making his ambitious son swear oaths of fidelity. At last, on July 14, 1223, after a year's illness, he relinquished his tenacious hold on life, at Mantes, less than a day's journey from Paris, where he had wished to die. He was nearly fifty-eight.

Louis VIII immediately showed his determination to rule as energetically as his father and to continue his policies. The Lion was short in stature, thin, pallid, and weakened by childhood illness; in manner he was reserved, almost cold; his religious devotion was extreme. Yet it was on the battlefield that he had earned his formidable nickname, and at the age of thirty-six he was as confident and decisive as Philip had ever been. For three years he consolidated and extended his father's conquests, carrying the battle to the Midi, where, in 1226, at Montpensier in Auvergne, he fell mysteriously ill and died—probably of dysentery—after a reign of only three years. The barons, respecting his wishes, accepted his thirty-nine-year-old widow, Blanche of Castile, as regent for his eleven-year-old heir, Louis IX.

Had the Lion lived, it is likely that Queen Blanche's role in the French monarchy would have been minor. But events compelled her to act with the force and resolution of a man. It soon became evident that the barons had agreed to her regency only because they had hoped to rule her. For Blanche "had neither friends nor relatives in all the kingdom of France"; furthermore, she was suspected of foreign allegiances, and she intensified suspicion by surrounding herself with Spanish retainers. Her position was weak, but when the barons demanded, as the price of their support, that she cede them "great lands," they found to their surprise that she would "do nothing of the kind." This refusal placed the Crown in peril. Since diplomacy had failed, the nobility decided to recoup by violence a century of losses to the Capets.

Now a voice enters the history of France—and of Notre-Dame, for nation and church are inseparable—which will be heard again and again as the thirteenth century proceeds. This is Joinville, writing of the start of the reign of Saint Louis, when the barons trapped the King and the Queen Mother in 1227 at the castle of Montlhéri, which the Crown held in fief from the Cathedral of Paris, and which, on its great crag, still thrusts its ruined tower five hundred and fifty-six feet (170 meters) above the fields of the Ile de France, twenty miles south of the capital:

And the saintly King told me that neither he nor his mother, who were at Montlhéri, dared return to Paris until the people of Paris came to deliver them with arms. And he told me that from Montlhéri to Paris the whole way was filled with people, armed and without arms, and that they all cried to Our Lord to give him a good and long life, and to defend him and keep him from his enemies. And God did so, as you shall hear later.

The way to Paris is familiar: the Roman road has been traveled for centuries, but never before has it been lined with the people joyously cheering a child king because of so great a stake in his future. The moment belongs to the completion of the western rose of Notre-Dame; and to Queen Blanche of Castile, whom courteous poets saw as a rose; and to the exquisite child, exquisitely dressed by his mother in royal velvet and fur, blond and already tall, whom the Virgin, the Rose of Roses, saw as her own.

The Virgin had saved them. And as a sign of salvation, when they arrived in Paris, Louis and Blanche saw the rose of Notre-Dame extending across the central compartment of the façade. In 1227 the rose had been completed for two years and already showed its mastery of the wall. Possibly it was already painted a royal blue and blazoned with golden stars, as a halo for Mary. If the Virgin were *"cele qui la rose est des roses,"* and Blanche of Castile the rose of earthly queens, this immense window too is a rose of roses. Ever since then it has been copied and recopied, and it is still imitated in pseudo-Gothic structures; yet no copy has surpassed the original. Men have built larger roses, although not many, including the roses of the north and south transepts here at Paris, after 1250; none has this supreme openness and audacity, none this faultless equilibrium, which will be seen to full effect when the three great roses of the Cathedral are compared from within the church.

Blanche of Castile governed France as the rose governs the façade, with intelligence, logic, strength, and the charm and grace of a flower. *"Sexu femina, consilio mascula, Semirami merito comparanda"* was a contemporary appreciation of her loveliness and ability. Semiramis! with an unexpectedly masculine frame of thought. For a quarter-century longer, until her death in 1252, masculine thought and feminine sex enabled her to dominate not only Saint Louis but every man about her. The gift she possessed was Spanish. She was a mixture of Castilian piety and pride, warm affection and unrelenting hatred, imaginative courage and striking personal beauty. Her temperament, like her son's, was to a certain extent mystical, or ecstatic. Her Christian devotion was considered extraordinary, and she transmitted it early to the baby prince. Louis attended a daily Mass and a service at vespers; he recited prayers on the hour; he did not learn children's songs but such anthems as *Ave Maris Stella.* He acquired a habit of reading, and with it one of the best classical educations of the Middle Age. His charity became famous while he was still a small child, as did his exemplary behavior and precocious self-privation. In all matters he obeyed his mother implicitly. She told him that she would rather see him dead than have him commit a mortal sin, and he remembered this injunction the rest of his life; identical training also made a saint of his sister, Isabelle of France. And by the same methods, at the same time, Blanche's sister, Berengaria of León, was making a king and a saint of his cousin Ferdinand III of Castile.

After the coup de main failed at Montlhéri, the barons appointed the most formidable man in France to deal with Queen Blanche: the Count of Brittany, Pierre de Dreux. Pierre may have earned his nickname of Mauclerc—"Bad Clerk": he was said to have buried a priest alive and to have walled up living fugitives in their place of asylum within a church. Yet there is much evidence that Pierre was a man of cultivation and taste, as well as a redoubtable warrior and prince. He wrote poetry, and also endowed the southern porch and rose window at Chartres; and, except for his cousins the Capets, seems to have been admired by the high society of his time. If he could handle, or mishandle, priests, the barons were confident that he could handle a young widow. Joinville reveals their mentality:

And they did this to see if the Count of Brittany could master the Queen, who was a foreign woman, as you have heard; and many people say that the Count would have mastered the Queen and the King, if God had not helped the King in his need, as He never failed to do. The aid which God provided him was such that Count Thibaut of Champagne, who was later King of Navarre, came to serve the King with three hundred knights; and through the help that the Count gave the King, the Count of Brittany was obliged to submit to the King's mercy. . . .

What return Queen Blanche made Thibaut—and some return was invariably expected—chivalrous Joinville does not say. His contemporaries were not so reticent. The couple were talked about, says one chronicler, as much as Tristan and Iseult; and at one point the indignant populace of Paris compelled her to appear publicly in her chemise, to prove she was not with child. For Thibaut was not only a prince but a poet—one of the best France has produced; and the public demanded a romance that would draw crowds on the boulevards.

The plot was traditional. The young nobleman was in love with the beautiful queen. Like Tristan or Lancelot, he seems to have been considerably more attractive than her husband; and so the queen permitted him to sing her love songs. But there is the tincture of violence here—murder—which caused a sensation: Thibaut, like other famous lovers, was reputed to be conversant with philters; not only did he sing to Queen Blanche, goes the legend, but he poisoned King Louis—*"ob amorem reginae ejus, quam carnaliter amabat"*—out of carnal love for her.

The fable was believed longer than most and, as romance, should be accepted still. Yet it might never have been concocted if medical diagnosis had been in vogue or if a Syrian physician could have attended Louis VIII during his final illness in 1226. Suspicion fell on Thibaut because he had committed, only four months before the death of the King, what was considered treason. After serving the obligatory forty days in the field, the Count had withdrawn from Louis' army during the siege of Avignon. Significantly, too, this was the first time he had shown the Capets anything but loyalty. He had been at Bouvines with Philip Augustus when he was only fourteen; he had accompanied Louis the Lion to England. For Louis' last campaign, however, which was a resumption of the Albigensian Crusade, Thibaut was unenthusiastic. He had reasons. Champagne and Languedoc were united by temperament and friendship: Troyes and Toulouse were the most brilliant centers of poetry in Europe; Raymond VII of Toulouse was the sort of man Thibaut liked. Furthermore, Thibaut was heir to Navarre and saw no advantage in giving the Capets a foothold in the Pyrenees. Whatever his motive, he went home, taking the green-clad knights of Champagne with him. Louis was furious and threatened reprisals, which he never had time to execute.

Blanche seems to have shared her husband's anger. She denied Thibaut permission to enter his own city of Reims for the coronation of Saint Louis. For a time thereafter, although he appears not to have been in earnest, the Count was actually in the field against her. How, then, can his turnabout be explained?

The facts here are more interesting than fantasy. In 1227 Blanche was almost as old as Queen Gertrude in *Hamlet.* She was forty and the mother of a sizable family. Although she was of *"grant biauté,"* she was also a *dilecta matrona,* an excellent matron known for unusual piety. Thibaut was thirteen years younger. He was married, but that made no difference; marriage was rarely a matter of love for a feudal prince. Blanche had known him since he was brought to the court of France as an infant. Probably, during the years she waited for the birth of her own children, she loved him as a child. Conceivably, now that he was a man and she a widow, he hoped for a different love. Yet Blanche was a *"si haute dame, de si bonne vie et de si nete"*—"so fine a lady, of such good and spotless life"—that he could not hope for more than the privilege of addressing songs to her.

Love—or feudal self-interest? The question will never be answered to everyone's satisfaction. Love is the more pleasing motive;

politics the more sound. Thibaut had worries of his own. Only three years later he would need military aid from Blanche to fight off a new coalition of barons, again led by Pierre Mauclerc, who were trying to take Champagne from him. The mere presence of the Queen Mother and the King on the battlefield in 1230, with the army of France to be sure, was enough to scare them off. This is one indication of the speed with which she consolidated her hold on the kingdom after her early troubles. Then, in 1232, she had a most unexpected opportunity to show her strength. Thibaut, finding himself a widower, inexplicably decided to marry Yolanda of Brittany —Mauclerc's daughter. With the bride at the altar, Thibaut received a stern warning from the Crown:

"Lord Count of Champagne, the King has heard that you have covenanted with Count Peter of Brittany that you will take his daughter in marriage. Consequently the King warns you that unless you wish to lose all that you have in the kingdom of France, you will not do it; for you know that the Count of Brittany has done worse to the King than any man who lives." The Count of Champagne, on the advice of those he had with him, returned to Château-Thierry.

Joinville is surprised by none of this. He shows no puzzlement whatever as the Capets put together the jigsawed provinces of France. Motives shifted and interests varied with the slightest change in the balance of power; and Joinville was too familiar with what was at stake, and with the personalities involved, to feel astonishment. It was easy, if one were born well, to be on close terms with the entire ruling class of Western Europe. Joinville, as Seneschal of Champagne, knew most of them. They formed only a small family of two or three hundred cousins, all related by blood or marriage, all connected by the complex, interlocking system of real estate. Such a peer as Mauclerc, with an imposing list of titles, owned property everywhere; he held important fiefs of the Cathedral of Paris and was a vassal of Notre-Dame.

France, as it gathered into a nation, was a crazy-quilt, a puzzle, but it did not seem so at all to its vivid men and women. They fought and, under the continual pressure of the Crown and Church, were reconciled or forced to make peace. They hated and, with illogical haste, loved. Sometimes the brutal fortunes of the Middle Age thrust them violently together, as when Mauclerc and Joinville were taken prisoner by the Saracens in 1250 and thrown into the hold of a galley: ". . . we were so crowded together, that my feet were against the good Count Peter of Brittany, and his were against my face." The *good* Count Peter! There is no trace of recrimination, although Joinville was a liegeman of Thibaut and attached by family, tradition, and personal love to the House of Champagne, for which his father, old Simon of Joinville, had fought against Mauclerc.

The fighting subsided gradually. Raymond of Toulouse, exhausted by an interminable war with the Capets and the Roman Curia, surrendered at last in 1229; his friend Thibaut of Champagne helped negotiate the capitulation but could not obtain very good terms from Blanche and the papal legate, who assisted her even more than the Count in her moment of peril and was popularly thought to have received even greater favors. The place of surrender was Notre-Dame of Paris, on the vigil of Easter, April 12, 1229. Raymond was stripped of his magnificent clothing and led by the priests into the Cathedral. He was not scourged; that humiliation had already been applied by the monks of Saint-Gilles. What he suffered in the capital was not loss of pride, but loss of the lands of his ancestors, as he knelt in the church of the triumphant Virgin of the Capets, and made apology to the Church Militant, which, personally, he had never wronged. "And it was a great pity," wrote one chronicler, "to see so great a man, who for so long a time had been able to resist so many strong nations, to be led naked, in his shirt, his arms and feet bare, to the altar."

The surrender of the nobility also ended independent provincial art; or rather, transformed it. The victors imposed their artistic style on the conquered, as they imposed their economy, and neither suited the warmer South. As Raymond left Notre-Dame he saw the western rose rising before him; and it is no accident that the rose was immediately copied at the Cathedral of Toulouse. The circular window, designed for the North, where light is scarce, was placed beneath a deep arch to protect it from the southern sun. The result is poignant but, like most of the southern Gothic, a failure.

Time passed, while the façade of Notre-Dame rose victoriously to the towers. By 1241 there was general peace, and the Capets held a firmer grip on the kingdom than ever before. Soon they would turn east, to the Crusade of Saint Louis, but for a perfect instant the King and his brothers and their mother Blanche sat with their barons to a delicious dinner beside the Loire, in what had been the home province of the Plantagenets—Anjou. Joinville was present:

The King held a great court at Saumur in Anjou; and I was there, and testify to you that it was the best-ordered court I ever saw. . . . Before the King, his brother the Count of Artois served the food, and the good Count John of Soissons carved with the knife.

At the King's table, among the great peers, were "the good Count Peter of Brittany"—Mauclerc; and "my lord the King of Navarre" —Thibaut—"in a cloak and mantle of samite, well adorned with a belt and clasp, and a cap of gold." Guarding the table were three barons and "a good thirty of their knights, in tunics of silken cloth":

. . . and behind these knights were a great number of sergeants, their clothing embroidered with the arms of the Count of Poitiers in taffeta. The King was dressed in a mantle of blue samite, and a surcoat and mantle of ruby samite lined with ermine; and a cotton cap on his head, which suited him very badly, for he was then a young man. . . . There was yet a table where twenty bishops and archbishops dined; and . . . near their table dined Queen Blanche, his mother, at the head of the cloister. . . .

There they dined in the summer evening, for once at peace with one another, united by their better instincts of courtesy and honor, enjoying the wines and sauces for which France was already famous. Perhaps they called for dice; or, more likely, with the Queen Mother present, for song. And Thibaut IV, King of Navarre, Count of Champagne and of the Brie, in his golden cap, called for an instrument and offered his melody, not to Blanche, but to the Queen of Queens: "To the Lady who surpasses all good things. Go, little song! If she will hear thee, nowhere wilt thou find blessings so great."

> A la Dame qui touz les biens avance
> T'en va, chançon! s'el te veut escouter,
> Onques ne fus nus de meillor cheance.

The ideal had triumphed. Saint Louis and Blanche of Castile ruled a nation that was invincible in Europe; and at the heart of the realm the white towers of Notre-Dame lifted above a Paris that was one of the wealthiest cities on earth and the new center of Christendom. Rome, like Washington, was an artificially located capital, set apart from the strong realities of medieval industry, trade, and finance, and, above all, from social innovation. Christian society had two more natural centers—Paris and Constantinople— both of which, after the Fourth Crusade, were French. Yet the Franks were overextended in the Orient. In 1238 the Emperor Baldwin II was in such financial difficulty that he offered to sell to the King of France the supreme Christian symbol of Byzantine prestige: the Crown of Thorns.

Louis immediately dispatched two Franciscans to make the purchase, but when they arrived at the Bosporus the monks found the relic in pawn to a Venetian businessman, Nicola Quirino, for 177,300 livres—about five million dollars. A heavy down payment disengaged the sacred treasure, as well as the pawn ticket—a parchment that is still in the French National Archives. Then the monks made their way back to France with the Crown. In August 1239 they were received in the Burgundian town of Villeneuve-l'Archevêque by the king in person, accompanied by his brother Robert of Artois. On August 11 the Crown was welcomed at the Cathedral of Sens by the archbishop, in the name of the Gallican Church. Eight days later the Crown arrived in Paris. The King and the Count of Artois, both clad in simple tunics and barefoot, carried the reliquary on their shoulders; and with a brilliant procession following them through the city they at last deposited the emblem of Christ's Triumph at Notre-Dame.

In the next decade treasure after treasure was transported from Sancta Sophia to the Church of Paris. The Crown of Thorns was joined by the True Cross, the tip of the Holy Spear, the Holy Sponge, and a number of other instruments of the Passion, all purchased by Saint Louis' emissaries with little or no regard for price. As each shipment arrived the King repeated his pious trip to Burgundy and with his own hands carried the relics into the capital. Notre-Dame did not keep these mementoes of the Savior, for, as can be imagined, they were not long in exciting an architectural miracle—the Sainte-Chapelle—in which they were stored until the Revolution.

If there can be any doubt that medieval idealism was real, the mere cost of these relics and of the unique structure built to contain them is proof of how true an idealism it was. The Sainte-Chapelle, built in the court of the Palace in five short years, from 1243 to 1248, is a reliquary in itself, a shrine of blue and ruby glass held together by an open frame, which logically could have been in gold rather than stone. Five hundred and fifty years later, when the ideal was no longer even a memory to the French, the chapel, like the Cathedral a few hundred feet away, was desecrated by a mob. The reliquaries were melted for currency by the embattled Republic; many of the relics vanished, but the Crown of Thorns was saved. Today it is back in the Treasure of Notre-Dame.

The fragile Crown of Thorns perhaps goes further than the stone Cathedral to explain the central Gothic enigma of why an able and intelligent king, acting neither from pride nor cynicism, spent a fortune for a materially valueless object, and more still for beauty to surround it. Possibly his purpose was more utilitarian than is generally thought. France, argued Henry Adams, invested in religious art as the industrial age invests in a railway system. But it was not quite that. All kinds of useful ventures—bridges, roads, barns, workshops, mills, enormous public hospitals—were undertaken at the same time as churches. The vital difference is that medieval accounting did not keep separate books for utility and art, which is one reason that the bridge at Avignon, the kitchen of twenty chimneys at Fontevrault, and the hospice at Beaune may compete in loveliness with the Sainte-Chapelle and Notre-Dame.

Virtually everything man touched for practical use, from the eleventh to fifteenth centuries, became lovely, which is a test of a civilization. There was almost no medieval bad taste, as there was, say, under the Second Empire. What the medieval artisan never considered fine art is prized as such in museums: chairs, tables, coffers, locks and their keys, dishes and flagons, pots and knives, hot-water urns, chess sets and other games, children's toys, inexpensive religious medals, coins of low value, seals for ordinary business. All were in continual use, all handsome, and the man who used them knew it. On every page, Joinville is aware of this usual beauty, but no more so that Saint Louis or Blanche of Castile, or Thibaut, or Mauclerc. They were all connoisseurs.

In the best sense, these men and women liked to live well; and as the year 1250 approached it was possible to live better, in every way, than at any previous time in French history. The Occident was calm at last. Louis made a generous peace with his brother-in-law, Henry III of England—too generous, protested hard-headed courtiers, for Louis went so far as to return lands that Philip Augustus had taken from John Lackland. Yet Louis replied, and this was perhaps the only time the idea occurred to a French monarch, that it was a Christian peace. It was also, he felt, a correct feudal peace, since the King of England had become his man, "which he was not before." The unreal abstraction—homage in itself no longer had value by the thirteenth century—became real because Louis himself was the abstraction come to life. The House of Capet had grown so mighty that it could afford to live up to its ideal. And so the King sent emissaries to restore peace wherever he could in Europe, within and without the boundaries of France. Again the Royal Council protested, pointing out that it was good strategy to allow neighboring countries to battle among one another, and so grow poor and weak. But Louis answered:

. . . if the neighboring princes saw that I let them fight, they might consult among them, and say: "The King lets us fight out of malice." Thus it might happen that from the hatred they would have for me, they would fall upon me, which might well cause me loss, not to speak of the hatred of God I would incur, Who said: Blessed are the peacemakers.

What this sort of royal mentality meant to the plain people of France can be imagined. "For truly," Saint Louis once remarked to his son, the future Philip the Bold, "I would rather a Scot should come out of Scotland, and govern the people of the kingdom well and loyally, than that you should govern them ill." Injustice remained, of course—medieval society could not be changed by a single dedicated individual; nor did Saint Louis have any desire to change it, except to make it operate in practice as in theory. After his death, conditions quickly grew worse than ever. But for a remarkable moment, brief as it was, the ordinary man, if he had a cause to plead, could walk out to the Bois de Vincennes and there, beneath an oak tree, find his King. Seated on a scarlet blanket, dressed in a simple coat of wool but with a cap of peacock feathers, Louis delivered decisions without concern for wealth or social rank. "Hold firm to justice," the King instructed his son, "and be faithful to the rights of your subjects, turning neither right nor left, but always to what is just; and support the cause of the poor until the truth is made clear."

From this unique court of justice, modeled after Solomon's, the man of the thirteenth century walked back from Vincennes to Paris, moving with the crowds that converged on the parvis of Notre-Dame. Above him lifted the façade, in its final stage of construction, and he could not help associating its majesty with that of the King. Both displayed idealism, refinement, and strength. Both had the appearance of simplicity and were limitlessly complex. Both acted solidly from a foundation of mysticism.

Up, up, the façade lifted masterfully to the summit. The workmen, when they reached the uppermost stages, no longer mounted to the scaffolds by ladders but by the broad stairways in the side buttresses. They crossed the façade by the circulation passages behind the Gallery of Kings and the upper arcade; they probably had a tool house and a pattern room on the terrace before the rose. To hoist rock they had cranes with iron pulleys, like the derrick that remained at Cologne until the last century, which lifted heavy loads to the height of the main vault. To increase mechanical advantage they used wheels six and seven yards in diameter, which were turned by teams of men inside. Such wheels were operated by prisoners until a short time ago in England and France: one is on show at Madame Tussaud's—ostensibly as a medieval horror. Despite their formidable aspect, these wheels are not at all difficult to turn for short periods of time; in fact, they are rather hard to stop. The cog wheel, powered by a winch, was more easily controlled, and possibly already in use. Most medieval engineering devices are visible in such structural fantasies as Brueghel's "Tower of Babel" and Fouquet's "Temple of Jerusalem," which shows a fifteenth-century façade under construction.

The last stones were hoisted to the towers of Notre-Dame between 1240 and 1245, at the latest 1250. M. Aubert has called attention to the less ornate carving on the southern tower, and since decoration was growing increasingly richer, it is assumed to be the earlier; it may have preceded the northern tower by five or ten years. Both towers were capped with powerful cornices, which contribute to their stability, as even a house of cards will be steadied by two or three cards placed flat across the top. These cornices, each ten feet high, are quite unlike any others in medieval architecture. They give the towers an emphatic note of completion; and it is worth noticing their conquest of the air between them. The eye guesses that a final line has been drawn between the towers, and here is another mystery of the Cathedral.

Was the great forward wall complete? Notre-Dame has often been reproached for its absence of spires; and, in truth, the upper composition of the towers; the size of the cornices; the assemblage of pinnacles, crockets, and other ornaments; the lines of the buttresses, which seem to be preparing a transition from a four-sided figure to an octagon and then, presumably, to a cone—all indicate that spires were anticipated. Certainly the façade could easily have carried the additional weight, for thirteenth-century flèches, like that at Senlis, are hollowed out with such audacity that they scarcely tax their supporting construction. Viollet-le-Duc was fascinated by the missing spires of Paris, and he once drew the façade with twin spires of the Senlis type. A look at this drawing, however, shows that the Master Builder would never have adapted the Senlis spire, lovely as it is, to Notre-Dame; nor the Norman spires of Caen and Bayeux; nor the lost French spires of Laon and Saint-Denis. None would have been equal to his façade.

Perhaps, it has been suggested, this is why he built no spires at all —he could not find a design to satisfy him. Yet he found designs for the other elements of the façade—the Gallery of Kings, the rose, the upper arcade—which are among the most accomplished of the Middle Age. Nor did he lack money. The quality of the materials and the workmanship is perhaps finer at the top of the façade than at its base; the decoration is more rich. Furthermore the Cathedral had resources enough to keep adding to Notre-Dame, and rebuilding, at great expense, for seventy-five years after 1250.

All of which leads one to believe that the Master stopped where he did because he thought it would be a mistake to go higher. Spires would have given his façade a new effect of aspiration, and perhaps of added mystery, but he had an entire church, and not just his façade, to consider. Study from the Left Bank, if you will, the relation of the forward wall to the rest of Notre-Dame. The towers could not have gone ten feet higher without harming the total proportions. Nor, if spires had been added, could the façade itself have retained its present effect of calm. A feeling of pride might have resulted instead, something the architects of Notre-Dame had avoided for nearly a century.

Thus, like the modest giant Saint Christopher, the façade uses its strength only for the sake of the whole Church. This is one of the major texts of the bible of architecture, and one that the designers of the United Nations might have learned. The UN Secretariat is a façade with nothing behind it; "a knife," Frank Lloyd Wright has called it, adding that he does not like knives. This wall is not a knife but a display of the principles of Christ and the Virgin and Saint Louis: goodness and lordliness, mystery and intelligence. For fifty years the Master Builders and their workmen labored to give Paris as great an architectural gift as any city has ever been given. They painted their creation with precious colors and plated it with gold, as the Parthenon was adorned by Phidias. Here and there, on sheltered pieces of carving, traces remain of the medieval color; and from them Viollet-le-Duc was able to see it as the Masters intended:

. . . the artists of the Middle Age never had the idea of covering entirely with color a façade 70 yards high and 50 broad, like that of Notre-Dame of Paris. But on these immense surfaces they adopted a *parti* of decoration. Thus at Notre-Dame the three portals, with their voussoirs and tympanums, were entirely painted and gilded; the four niches connecting the doors, containing four colossal statues, were also painted. Above, the Gallery of Kings formed a broad heraldic bar completely colored and gilded. Above this line, no painting was applied, except to the great windowed bays, under the towers; and to the central rose which sparkled with gold. The upper portion [of the façade], lost in the atmosphere, was left the color of stone.

This coloring was renewed at intervals during the Middle Age, for the last time in 1486; and six years later an Armenian bishop, named Martiros, or Martyr, traveled from the Euphrates to the nation of "Frantza" and the city of "Pharez." En route he visited the "opulent" monuments of Constantinople, the golden church of San Marco in Venice, the "indescribably magnificent" churches of Rome, the "tall and superb" Cathedral of Cologne. None affected him as did the Cathedral of Paris. This was in 1492, at the moment the voyage of Columbus was relegating the medieval world, like the

Roman world and the Greek world before it, forever to antiquity; but when Notre-Dame still produced this impression:

> The great church . . . is spacious, beautiful, and so admirable that it is impossible for the tongue of man to describe it. It has three great portals facing west. The pier of the central door represents Christ erect. Above this door, Christ presides over the Judgment. He is placed on a golden throne and surrounded by adornments of plated gold. . . .
>
> An angel holds a scale, with which he weighs the sins and the good deeds of men. On the left, slightly lower, are Satan and all his demons; they lead enchained sinners, and drag them into Hell. Their faces are so horrible that they cause spectators to tremble and shudder. Surrounding Christ are the holy apostles, the prophets, the holy patriarchs, and all the saints, painted in various colors and decked with gold. This scene represents Paradise, which enchants all those who look upon it. Above are the images of twenty-eight kings, with crowns on their heads; they stand the whole width of the façade. Higher still is the Holy Virgin, Mother of God, adorned with gold, and painted with diverse colors.

No expense, either of gold or of the imagination, was spared to make the façade as splendid as men could conceive a work of art. Yet Bishop Martiros saw the front of Notre-Dame at virtually the last instant that men gave it their total love. The façade was never painted or gilded again. In its fortunate moments during the next centuries the Cathedral was simply allowed to decay. At worst, it was savagely attacked and mutilated. As time passed, men forgot how to build, and even to quarry, so that stone would be imported to Paris from Sens; and Lescot, when he built the Louvre, would use tombstones from the cemetery of the Holy Innocents for the steps of his staircases. All the high medieval skills degenerated— stonecutting, glassmaking, carpentry, metalwork. By the Neo-Classic Age men could not imagine how the marvelous straphinges of the northern and southern portals had been devised. It was as if Daedalus had made them, but Daedalus had flown away, never to return. The Parisians came to consider the great artificer a devil and gave him the ugly name Biscornet—Twin Horns—because they had noticed little horned imps hiding among the arabesques of the hinges. And they invented the tale that "a young metalsmith, pre-senting himself for the grade of master, was ordered to forge the ironwork of the portals as his chef d'oeuvre." The task was beyond him, but Biscornet offered his services in exchange for the young man's soul. The smith agreed, "and the very next day the doors of Notre-Dame were hinged, with the exception of the central doors," where the demon could not work because the Holy Sacrament passed through the portal during processions. The smith therefore was freed of his engagement and elevated to the rank of master.

It is amusing to think of the façade as a Faustian labor, but the Middle Age knew the truth, which was more entertaining by far. The central doors, engraved with the names of the Kings of France, originally had the most elaborate metalwork of the Cathedral, which was probably ruined when the Huguenots battered Notre-Dame in the sixteenth century. The hinges were hammered to shape in the forge of Notre-Dame, not by an evil jinni, but by a master who accomplished his task as part of the day's work, in the same way that the sculptors carved their statues and the masons laid their stones.

From foundations to the towers, the façade was built with absolute logic and integrity. In spirit and structure, it is joined indissolubly with the rest of the monument. Enter the church for a moment to examine its juncture with the nave. The last two bays of the inner vessel were visibly reinforced to receive the thrust of the forward wall. In the second bay from the façade, the pillars of the grand colonnade are each assisted with a stout engaged column that is a pillar in itself. In the first bay, where the strain is heavier, four such columns are banded about each main pillar. Where the nave and the façade meet, two tremendous piles—stronger even than the piles at the corners of the transept—soar without a break to the main vault. The façade has nevertheless pushed inward upon them and, over seven centuries, has driven the adjacent stonework of the nave a foot or two out of line. The nave has not yielded but rather has adjusted to this pressure; its masonry is still alive and intact.

Upward, resisting visible strain with visible force, rising in utter confidence within the embrace of the great surrounding buttresses, mounting above the formidable vaults of the narthex to the spacious rooms of the towers, the façade was built to its last millimeter with the same sincerity. These upper rooms, closed from the rest of the church, might have been plain as a barracks. They were intended only for the bellringers and for the unfortunates who sought a night's lodging or refuge from authority, yet they are treated as elegantly as chambers in a palace. Still higher, the interiors of the belfries, whose only residents were the bells, received the same fastidious care.

At last, in 1250, the job was done; and the thirteenth-century pilgrim, like today's tourist, climbed the northern or the southern tower to survey Paris from the summit of the church. In each of the central side buttresses are lodged winding staircases broad enough to be mounted on horseback, as indeed a skillful rider did in the eighteenth century. Step upon step, each supporting the one above, comprising more than three hundred and eighty steps in all, these spirals twist upward within the construction, turning and turning, high above the portals and the rose, the way ahead revealed only by slits of lights, until at last the climber reaches the terrace between the towers, where he is confronted by the play of sunlight on golden stone, with Notre-Dame rising mightily on every side and Paris spread beneath as on a chart.

And perched on the balustrades, staring over the city, crouching, grimacing, ready to spring into space and pounce downward, are hundreds of grotesques—the gargoyles of Notre-Dame—inhuman birds with half-human faces who have sprouted like myths from the rock. They have flown out of the construction, chased from the interior of the church by the Virgin, who from the middle of the twelfth century onward banished monsters from her sanctuary but kept them as terrifying guardians of the outer walls and towers. Of the thousands of carvings within the Cathedral, all show flowers and plants, signs of innocence, except for a pair of Harpies who hover at the turn of the ambulatory, the earliest part of the monument, howling with the fantastic voice of the Romanesque after a long flight from antiquity.

To please the Virgin, or not to displease her, the master builders placed their wildest beasts on the uppermost portions of the church. Their exact medieval appearance cannot be described, for the gargoyles seen today are the work of Viollet-le-Duc; the originals gradually weathered away, and when, during the Enlightenment, they commenced to fall from time to time, with a frightening crash on the parvis two hundred feet below, those that remained were destroyed.

A twentieth-century enlightenment, however, led by the intrepid exploration of C. G. Jung, has again begun to appreciate the value and necessity of the monstrous in art. The gargoyles belonged to the furthermost range of the human soul, deeper than the cave of Lascaux, overgrown by thirty, or fifty, or one hundred thousand years of progress from savagery, like the moss-grown oaks of the Druid forest. They underlie all the religions of the earth, as the Virgin Mother does, and the Hero Son who must endure torment, allegorical or real, in order to triumph.

Saint Bernard, the puritan, hated and feared the gargoyles. In a famous denunciation of the monsters which so enlivened the Romanesque, he denied that they had any significance but un-Christian enchantment. Erwin Panofsky's admirable translation:

. . . what business has there that ridiculous monstrosity, that amazing mis-shapen shapeliness and shapely mis-shapenness (*deformis formositas ac formosa deformitas*)? Those unclean monkeys? Those fierce lions? Those monstrous centaurs? Those semi-human beings? Those spotted tigers? . . . Here you behold several bodies beneath one head; there again several heads upon one body. Here you see a quadruped with the tail of a serpent; there a fish with the head of a quadruped. There an animal suggests a horse in front and half a goat behind; here a horned beast exhibits the rear part of a horse. In fine, on all sides there appears so rich and amazing a variety of forms that it is more delightful . . . to spend the whole day in admiring these things, piece by piece, rather than in meditating on the Law Divine.

The great bell Emmanuel, sounding in the southern tower, breaks the spell. This *gros bourdon,* weighing thirty thousand pounds, was rung, until the installation of the present electrical system, by teams of eight men, who rocked its clapper to and fro in a wooden swing. It is the only survivor of the renowned bells which were seized by the Revolution to be recast as cannon; and it was also the last to be presented to the Cathedral, by Louis XIV and Maria Theresa in 1681. The first of the bells was Guillaume, named for its donor Bishop Guillaume d'Auvergne, who endowed it sometime before his death in 1248, which gives a terminal date for the northern tower, originally the only one to contain bells. By 1283 Guillaume had been joined by Pugnaise, Chambellan, and Pasquier. Later came John "the big sparrow," and Nicolas his little brother, and Gabriel and Claude; and the ladies Marie and Jacqueline and Françoise, and Barbara, who, like her saintly namesake, drove off lightning.

Struck one after the other, the bells sent a scale of heavy notes ringing over Paris; and they were answered by the bells of the Cloister, and of Saint-Denis-du-Pas, and the episcopal palace; and the bell of Saint-Christophe on the parvis, and the Hôtel-Dieu, so that the Cathedral was surrounded by music. And from all the churches of the city more bells joined, ringing in towers that may still be seen, lifting above the smoking chimneypots and twisting streets of the medieval Paris which lies cramped behind the boulevards of the Second Empire: the "Tour Clovis" of the Abbey of Sainte-Geneviève high on the Left Bank; Saint-Séverin in the Latin Quarter, and Saint-Julien-le-Pauvre huddled nearby, beneath a row of Gothic houses; and off in the fields, beyond the wall of Philip Augustus, the Abbey Tower of Saint-Germain-des-Prés; and on the island, in the courtyard of the Palace, the gilded steeple of the Sainte-Chapelle; and off on the Right Bank, behind the Louvre, the *clocher* of Saint-Germain-l'Auxerrois; and the rich carillon of the Tour Saint-Jacques; Saint-Martin-des-Champs, outside the northern gates; and on distant Montmartre the bell of the little church of Saint-Pierre sounding faintly.

And directly behind the façade of Notre-Dame the transept bell of the Cathedral adds its bronze music, lifting toward Heaven with the narrowing spire over the crossing, at whose tip, three hundred and twenty-five feet above the earth, crows a golden cock. The spire is new, restored by Viollet-le-Duc, and its fretted outline lacks the austere dignity, although it preserves the proportions, of the thirteenth-century flèche, destroyed in 1792 after it began to lean dangerously. The covering of the roof is also new, and one must go to Mantes to visualize the medieval roof of colored tiles, black and golden and red and green, which captured the sun in geometric patterns. But beneath, perfectly equilibrated upon the upper walls rather than on the vaults which it does not charge, the dense oaken frame of the Middle Age is largely intact, its beams so thick and heavy that they have always been called the *forêt*. From the four points of the compass—from the tall crucifix surmounting the apse on the east, from the pinnacles of the transept façades on the north and south, from the massive towers on the west—the four arms of the roof rush inward to the socket of the central spire, defining, high above the island in the Seine, the shape of the Cross.

the completion of notre-dame

And Jacob vowed a vow, saying, If God will be with me, and will keep me in this way that I go, . . . this stone, which I have set for a pillar, shall be God's house.

GENESIS 28:20-22

Chapter Fifteen

THE BUILDERS OF ROSES

BOUT THE year 1250 a middle-aged gentleman, mounted on a good horse, and wearing a fine cloak and gloves, rode into the Bishop's courtyard on the southern side of Notre-Dame. At the gate he was saluted respectfully by the episcopal guard; and as he passed he himself looked up with respect at the great façade of the Cathedral, and possibly with a trace of satisfaction, for he may have been the man who directed the final stage of its construction. He was Mestre Jehan de Chelles, Master of the Work of Notre-Dame; and in an age of famous architects —Robert de Luzarches at Amiens, Jehan d'Orbais at Reims—he was as famous as any. His foremost rival was his friend Pierre de Montreuil, the Master of Saint-Denis and perhaps also of the Sainte-Chapelle.

Not much more is known of Master John than that he was surely in charge of Notre-Dame in 1257 and that he was dead by 1265. His name indicates that he was born in the ancient town of Chelles, fifteen miles west of Paris, on the Marne, whose church he may have built as a minor project. His family—relatives if not himself—are said to have been country squires, for the surname "de Chelles" occurs often in the cartulary of Notre-Dame with reference to property holdings in and about Paris. Conceivably Jehan was a poor relation who went into architecture and masonry as, a century earlier, an indigent gentleman would have taken orders in the Church. But it is equally possible that he had as little connection with the noble de Chelles family as Maurice de Sully had with the lords of Sully-sur-Loire.

Whatever his origin, the Master was comfortably off by this time of his career. To be the major architect of Notre-Dame meant at least owning a house in Paris and probably a garden and vineyard to go with it. For the master builders had gained new status, together with the whole rising middle class; and their period of anonymity was at an end. Henceforth the names of the Masters of Notre-Dame appeared on dozens of documents and on inscriptions within and without the church. In the fourteenth century, Master Jehan Ravi's portrait was carved on the screen of the choir, of which a drawing survives. Unfortunately there is no image of any of the Cathedral's great thirteenth-century Masters, but by happiest chance a portrait of one of their most gifted contemporaries, Hugues Libergier, remains clear as a photograph on his tombstone in the Cathedral of Reims.

Hugues is represented in a Gothic portal of Heaven, the empty universe stretching behind him, two protective angels hovering above. He stands beneath the pointed arch like a saint with attributes. In his right hand he holds one of his most beautiful churches, the now lost Saint-Nicaise of Reims. In his left hand is the baton of his métier, a long, graduated measuring staff, which he holds as if it were an easy scepter. Floating on either side are his compass and square—instruments of sanctity to a building age. The intellectual face of Master Hugues is young, lean, and rather cold. He is in his forties but looks less. In truth, he is a northern French ideal of masculine beauty, blond and blue-eyed, and fastidiously groomed in his pleated cloak and tall, thrusting collar. His hair falls in virile waves; and he wears a flat heavy beret which must have been velvet. His pointed slippers rest on a cloud.

Such a man, too, was Jehan de Chelles; and he was almost certainly honored with a similar gravestone in Notre-Dame or some other church in which he worked.

Now, after 1250, he addressed himself to the completion of the Cathedral. The church planned by Maurice de Sully, ninety years before, had been built. But the project was not yet finished—the thirteenth century could not rest until it had rectified the failings of the twelfth-century portions of the church. And so, about 1230, workmen had returned to the nave and done their best to transform the experimental vessel of the Transition into an accomplished structure of the age of Saint Louis. They did not quite succeed, for to be a church such as Amiens, Notre-Dame would have had to be rebuilt from the ground up. But the campaign of 1230-1250 nevertheless improved the stability and lighting of the nave, as has been seen within the church, and left it fundamentally changed in appearance. The clerestory was enlarged—an expansion that can be detected easily in the molding of the high windows. The double flights of flying buttresses were replaced by the single arches, which leap forty feet, in narrow flight, from the outer piles to the upper wall (Fig. E). At ground level seven chapels were tucked between the buttresses on either side of the nave.

Although he himself may have had a part in the construction of the chapels, Jehan de Chelles must have looked at them with regret. One didn't have to be a master architect to see that although the clerestory was providing additional light at the top of the church, the chapels were withholding an almost equivalent amount at the base. Moreover the chapels spoiled the Cathedral's exterior lines. Their low roofs crossed the vertical buttresses with a horizontal line at the very point no horizontal was wanted, so that the great uprights seem to rise only half their true height of seventy feet. In the bay nearest the façade, where a chapel was never built, the unimpaired original effect of the buttresses may be appreciated. They soar upward with uninterrupted strength, taking the eye quickly above the level of the tribune, and then diagonally with the flying buttress to the roof of the church.

Although the chapels detract from the beauty of Notre-Dame they cannot destroy it; and that they have not done more harm, thanks may be given to Jehan de Chelles. He could not fail to notice that the twelfth-century transept façades had been thrown out of line by the reconstruction of the nave. They now stood a yard or two back from the perimeter of the church, where formerly they had projected a yard or two in advance. If these walls, dating from 1180-1200, and now so plain-looking compared with the changed appearance of the nave, could be demolished, the Master told the Bishop, now Renaud de Corbeil, he could erect façades in their place which would be surfaces of glass.

The offer of more light was irresistible. All over France at this time, monuments as precious as Suger's Saint-Denis were being rebuilt, simply for the sake of more illumination. During the middle third of the century Pierre de Montreuil erected a new nave and transept and a new upper choir at the abbey church, keeping only Suger's façade and ambulatory. Glass, glass, glass, was Pierre's single concern. He emptied the walls of stone, even the walls of the triforium gallery, and kept them erect by a slender system of pillars and flying buttresses, beautifully calibrated and daringly conceived. All the rest, except for these fragile supports, was colored light.

It was with this revolutionary construction of Pierre's in mind that Jehan de Chelles undertook the rebuilding of the transept of Notre-Dame. Yet he could not help realizing that the façades he would demolish were beautiful. The northern transept of Laon shows what was lost at Paris: a composition so ruggedly sober and masculine, yet so sensitive, that there is a temptation to match it with Saint-Etienne of Caen and the Romanesque art of William the Conqueror. The first transept façades of Paris were as impressive. To judge from the side buttresses, which Jehan de Chelles left standing as reinforcements for his own, they lingered in the powerful mood of the Romanesque.

To replace such architecture would alone have provided the challenge of Jehan's life, but he was less interested in his dead rival of the twelfth century than in a very much alive competitor of the thirteenth. Pierre de Montreuil was enjoying a success unprecedented for a French architect. Archaeologists, in fact, attribute so many monuments to Pierre that he may have been two men, for it has been argued that his real name was Pierre de Montereau, after a town in Champagne, rather than Montreuil, in the Parisian suburbs on the edge of the Bois de Vincennes. More likely Montreuil is correct; and in any case it is sure that Pierre made his career in the Paris area. He served not only as Master of Saint-Denis from 1231 to 1265, but also as a private architect for the Capets, who commissioned him to build their delightful chapel at the castle of Saint-Germain-en-Laye (1230-1238); and a very old tradition has him as the Master of the Sainte-Chapelle (1243-1248). He was also hired by Saint-Germain-des-Prés, ever jealous of Saint-Denis, to construct a new refectory for the monks (1239-1244) and, immediately afterward, a chapel dedicated to the Virgin, which was perhaps his very finest creation. The wreckage of this chapel, stupidly destroyed in 1802, stands in the little park across from the Café des Deux Magots.

A single rib from its frame speaks as eloquently as the architecture of whole cities. You can hammer the Gothic to pieces, as you can hammer the Greek, remarked Henry Adams, but you cannot hammer the Gothic out of it.

Yet the Gothic was now turning to style as an end in itself. Every structural problem was solved, and refinement alone presented a challenge to the masters. The thirteenth-century architects studied one another's art with keenest interest. They kept notebooks, as Villard de Honnecourt did, and sketched their rivals' masterpieces. Gradually their favorite details drifted into one another's work, so that there are fewer real differences among twenty churches of the thirteenth century than between two of the twelfth.

It was from the lost transept façades of Notre-Dame, as well as from the flying buttresses of the nave, that the new classic Gothic got its start. During Viollet-le-Duc's restoration he found hidden in the masonry of the southern façade "fragments . . . of a rose of great diameter," some eighteen feet across. What is fascinating about this discovery is that the Paris atelier had already, in 1180, developed a full-sized rose with an open living framework rather than the carved-out slabs of stone that are found elsewhere, at Laon and Chartres, as late as twenty years after. This rose led to the rose of Mantes, about 1200, which in turn led to the western rose of Paris, in 1220, when for the first time a wall was opened to a truly tremendous diameter—more than thirty feet—and held open by a delicate frame that would not give even under the pressure of heavy towers.

It is possible that an uncle common to both Pierre de Montreuil and Jehan de Chelles constructed this rose and transmitted its secret to both of them, for its strength came from a radically new theory of structure. At Mantes the rose was built from the circumference to the center: the colonnettes and arches point inward to the central eye. In the western rose of Paris the system was reversed. The Master of 1220 logically built his arcades outward, with twice as many divisions in the outer ring as the inner, shooting out petal after petal, ray after ray of light, so that this Gothic is properly called *rayonnant*.

Pierre de Montreuil immediately put the new system to work in his beautiful chapels at Saint-Germain-en-Laye and Saint-Germain-des-Prés, erecting stone skeletons of exceptional lightness and grace, not only in the roses, but, in these small structures, from foundations to spire. His chance to use the rayonnant on a grand scale, however, came in the reconstruction of Saint-Denis. At the abbey church, Pierre employed the open frame on a universal basis, raising the vaults to ninety-five feet (29 meters), or nearly as high as Notre-Dame's, displaying a virtuoso's familiarity with statics and equilibrium, and expanding the transept roses to a diameter of about thirty-six feet (11 meters), against thirty-one and a half feet (9.6 meters) for the western rose of Paris, and twenty-six feet (8 meters) for the rose at Mantes.

It was the Saint-Denis transept, finished in 1245, which Jehan de Chelles frankly adapted at Notre-Dame five years later. Happily there seem to have been unlimited funds remaining in the Cathedral treasury, for costs ran high. From the architect down to the manual laborer, workmen were now better paid; stone was more expensive than formerly because the quarries ran deeper. The Bishop, Renaud de Corbeil, contributed at least one hundred livres; a canon of the Chapter, Raymond de Clermont, gave "one thousand livres parisis and more"; an archdeacon named Stephen also made large gifts. It was a formidable project. Merely to dismantle the old transept façades took courage. The transept vessel of Notre-Dame, forty-five feet wide and one hundred and fifty feet long, is larger than the central vessels of many cathedrals. A false move could have sent the heart of the church crashing. But Master John knew his job. He threw up a tough shoring of ash and fir and, with the vaults thus propped solidly, razed the northern and southern façades. He extended the transept a bay at either end, vaulting these additions with ogives, and commenced to build the walls of glass, which, once again, enabled Notre-Dame to cause a sensation throughout Europe.

The northern is the less opulent of these façades and therefore is earlier than the southern, which was begun on February 12, 1258; but their mood is the same, and they may be examined together. What Jehan did first was to establish powerful piles that, on the east and west of the transept wings, hold the structure erect with their one-hundred-and-thirty-foot perpendiculars. Lancing each façade into the air is an ornate portal, bristling with gables, pinnacles, fleurons, crockets, spurs—any number of pointed and triangular forms which send the wall rocketing upward like pyrotechnics. Above the portal is a narrow walk whose low balustrade, only three feet high, crosses from buttress to buttress, to give a human measure of scale. And suddenly the wall turns to glass—twenty-five hundred square feet of glass, held in a tense rectangle of forty-three by fifty-seven feet (13 by 18 meters). The stone frame is a net—a fillet—fine as hair, its thinnest strands scarcely visible. The immense window is composed of two elements, separated only by a ribbon of stone: below is a *clairevoie* or clearway, a glassed-in arcature of almost painful fineness, some sixteen feet (5 meters) high; resting on this intangible support, both in the northern and in the southern façade, is a rose window forty-three feet (13 meters) in diameter. Only the magnificent western rose of Chartres, a foot wider (13.36 meters), and composed of carved-out slabs rather than a tensed framework, surpasses these dimensions. The transept roses of Paris are the largest open roses ever constructed.

The first meeting with these roses of the transept, like a first reading of Dante, leads the modern man into a tapestry of light and space. For an instant the metaphysics is forgotten, but it is always there, the substance of the hot golden distances. Critics enough have discussed the architecture of Dante; Henri Focillon is one of the few who have grappled with the metaphysics of the Cathedral of Paris:

The vanished wall has made way for wheels of fire . . . which recall the wheels of the most ancient folklore, emblems of the sun. Yet they are the expression of an idea which seeks equilibrium in the active relations of its parts: all is at work here, all is combined to satisfy the eye and the mind at the same time. All is tensed in order to act. If they are compared with the perforated slabs which surmount the high windows of Chartres, or, better still, with roses of the twelfth century, still prudent and massive, which by their very economy respect the wall, it will be felt that the last step has been passed and that architecture as an organization of forces, in bewitching form, has finally replaced an architecture of heavy matter. But it is precisely in this triumph that the danger resides. Architecture should have weight, and even impose evidence of its weight upon us, without crushing us with it. The correct limit of solids and voids has been broken through. Wherever glass can empty the wall and color the light, the wall disappears. The corners between the circle and the square in which it is inscribed are pierced in their turn. This is the last phase of the evolution. It began with a modest oculus, enlarged little by little, and, spreading even beyond its circumference, ended by taking all the space available between the piles.

Three hundred years of continually developing art—the Romanesque, the Transition, the Gothic—have led to this final lesson. The rose, if nothing else, unites the unknown monkish architect of the tenth and eleventh centuries with Pierre de Montreuil and Jehan de Chelles. The rose opened slowly, as worship of Mary opened, like a flower whose seasons were centuries. It budded at the end of the Carolingian winter, in the oculi of Jumièges. By 1100, or shortly after, its petals unfolded in a primitive framework, in a *roue de fortune* at Saint-Etienne of Beauvais, in which a series of figures mount as on a ferris wheel and then tumble over, carried downward by luck as soon as luck brings them to the top of the circle. The last great roses of France are those of the transept of Amiens, after 1300, and their exteriors are still decorated by the rising and falling figures of the fortunate and the unfortunate. After Amiens the rose petals slowly drop, in the triste autumn of the Middle Age, and the flower vanishes.

Soon churches would shrink in size as they had once expanded; soon a barbarous taste for surface glitter would replace monumental solidity. But Notre-Dame of Paris in 1270 was at the apogee; and from the croisée of the transept, where a turn of the head will bring the southern, western, and northern roses in sight, one after the other, the Cathedral can be seen in maximum glory: the three currents of colored light descending through the long vessels, down through the perspectives of tall pointed arches, to the heart of the cross.

Which of the three roses is most lovely?

The question is not fair, for although the roses have all suffered, they have not suffered equally. Many tourists are taken with the purplish fire of the southern rose, and it is a pity to inform them that both its stained glass and stone frame are almost entirely the work of the last century. It is the masterpiece—and this is said without irony—of Viollet-le-Duc. He who laughs at this rose should try to build one for himself. The trick is more difficult than it looks, as the eighteenth century found out. The Neo-Classic Age tried to remake the original rose in 1730, with the result that the whole southern façade immediately fell into ruin. To avert a general catastrophe Viollet-le-Duc had to reconstruct the wall from the foundations upward. He gave the rose a heavier frame than the medieval original, of which traces remained; and he also rotated its axis fifteen degrees, so that the radii do not give quite the same effect.

Otherwise the southern rose is an amazing copy of a medieval chef d'oeuvre. The stained glass—for nineteenth-century glass—does not offend. The iconography, consecrated to the New Testament, is correct. Christ the Redeemer stands at the center, surrounded by the apostles and, radiating outward, a heavenly choir of confessors and martyrs. But it is in the outermost circle of the rose that are hidden eleven tiny medallions, telling the story of Saint Matthew, which are the most precious glass in the Cathedral. They are pure twelfth-century blue and are supposed to have been salvaged from the transept rose of 1180, which preceded the rose of Jehan de Chelles. Somehow they survived both the eighteenth- and nineteenth-century reconstructions, to provide Notre-Dame with a trace of the exquisite blue light which once filled most of its windows and which was quite impossible to duplicate after 1200.

But turn! At the end of the nave, shining with the golden light of the west, is the great rose of the façade, dating from 1220-1225. The indignities to which the western rose has been subjected, over seven hundred years, are unspeakable. Not only was it left to the weather, without care or maintenance, from the sixteenth to the nineteenth centuries, but in 1730 the organ of the Cathedral was attached to its frame by iron clamps. The organ continues to hide a third of the rose. although it no longer threatens to pull it apart, and so the full brilliance of the window cannot be seen. But it passes light into the church through a frame whose strength and weightlessness have never been equaled. Eighty-six per cent of its surface is glass; and yet the flowerlike frame, locked beneath a powerful round arch, has not budged. When Viollet-le-Duc came to repair this rose in 1850 he found only three colonnettes cracked and two sections of arcature altered by the strain of the organ. Nevertheless he saw fit to restore it heavily.

What effect the rose achieved with thirteenth-century glass may be imagined from the windows of the Sainte-Chapelle, which could have been painted by the same atelier. But by the sixteenth century many of the medallions had been replaced, more were gone by the eighteenth, and none remained at all by the nineteenth. The original iconography appears to have been retained through all the restorations, however, and it amusingly places the window apart from the other western roses of France. Since the west signified the afterlife, the western roses of Chartres and Mantes are typically given to the Christ of Domesday. At Paris the place of the Son is taken by the Mother as Queen of Eternity. Surrounding her are a ring of royal ancestors, who may be taken from a sixteenth-century Tree of Jesse. Filling the rest of the circle are the Virgin's most entertaining symbols, exactly as they were found in sculpture in the western portals. The Virtues and Vices, the Signs of the Zodiac and the laboring Months, move slowly around the perpetual arc of life to a red and blue Heaven.

The vanished original glass of Notre-Dame! The poignancy of the windows of the nave, filled with nineteenth-century *grisailles,* as the eye travels back to the transept, is heartbreaking. The blue and ruby windows were not simply dismantled but smashed by the eighteenth century, which was so seriously devoted to enlightenment. Only after a visit to the Sainte-Chapelle, where great pages of colored light unfold one after the other, can some idea be had of Notre-Dame when it was illumined by jeweled glass, predominantly blue, but with red and green and brown and yellow employed astonishingly —morsels of green and blue placed boldly side by side—to increase the intensity of the blue field, which was the Marian Paradise. But look above! in the northern transept blue medieval Heaven fills the wall.

Of all the miracles of the Virgin of Paris, the salvation of her northern rose is perhaps the one for which men ought be most grateful. This sheet of northern blue contains eighty subjects from the Old Testament, almost all in original glass of the year 1250. In the center (one of the few restored panels) the Virgin holds Jesus on her knee. About her are enthroned the sixteen prophets, who foretold the coming of the Savior, in brown and green and golden robes, and holding scrolls on which the Latin names of Ezekiel, Zephaniah, and Micah may still be read with opera glasses. Directly below the Virgin is a medallion saved from a twelfth-century rose: Pharaoh asleep in the bed of a Capet king, dreaming. In the second circle are thirty-two kings, royal ancestors who surround Mary everywhere in her church, including Abiah and Joram and mighty Saul, whose inscription is Samuel's prophecy: "Saul, thou shalt reign over the whole people"—*"Reges super totum populum Saul."* In the outermost circle are thirty-two patriarchs and high priests (*summi sacerdotes*). The names of Aaron and Joachim are among the few that are legible.

Fully as impressive as the survival of the glass is the integrity of the stone chassis, which has just passed its seven-hundredth anniversary. Over the centuries it has buckled in places and been repaired, but it remains the largest circular framework of the Middle Age, and should last seven hundred years more. When its cliquart stone is struck it rings like steel, so absolute is its tension and strength. "The effects of pressure," Viollet-le-Duc wrote with admiration of this great window, "are calculated with rare *adresse*"; and, indeed, the problems of equilibrium, which here confronted the Master Builder and which he solved with the appearance of ease, must be appreciated as part of the pure beauty of his accomplishment. In his professional language Jehan de Chelles tersely called the rose an "O"—an ideal circle. But the challenge of the round surface increases drastically with the slightest increase in dimensions. The western rose covers six hundred and fifty square feet; the northern, its radius extended scarcely six feet farther, occupies no less than thirteen hundred. To hold the frame intact Jehan increased the ratio of stone to glass to thirty-eight per cent, nearly three times more than the western rose. Does it seem that much heavier? Binoculars will reveal the countless stems and tendrils of this flower, many of which are hardly visible from the floor of the church.

It is pleasant to think that Jehan de Chelles saw this rose completed; the archaeologists assume that he did. But he certainly did not finish the southern rose facing it, for he died before 1265, when the southern façade had been building only seven years. To complete the masterpiece, Pierre de Montreuil—Jehan's rival, his friend, possibly his cousin—put aside his other projects and became the Master of the Cathedral. And that Jehan de Chelles might never be forgotten, Pierre inscribed across the base of the southern portal: ANNO D[OMI]NI MCCLVII MENSE FEBRUARIO IDUS SECUNDO [H]OC FUIT INCEPTUM CHRISTI GENIT[RI]CIS HONORE KALLENSI LATHOMO

VIVENTE JOHANNE MAGISTRO—"In the year of Our Lord 1257 [Gregorian Calendar, 1258], on Tuesday, February 12th, this work was begun in honor of the Mother of Christ, during the lifetime of Jehan de Chelles, Master Mason."

With the courtesy of the makers of roses, Pierre did not add his own name, although he probably built the entire upper half of the façade, taking it to the happy open turrets one hundred and thirty feet above the ground. But a few years after Jehan, Pierre died too, either in his town house in the faubourg Saint-Germain, on the rue du Four, or else at his country place in Cachan, on the south of Paris, near the quarries. The monks of Saint-Germain-des-Prés buried him before the altar of the chapel of the Virgin, and had carved above his grave: "Here lies Pierre, born at Montreuil, a flower overflowing with the perfume of virtue, in his lifetime the Doctor of Masons. May the King of Heaven place this flower on eternal heights. He died in the year of Christ 1267."

Chapter Sixteen

THE BISHOP'S COURTYARD AND THE CLOISTER

f LANKED ON the north by a dull street and on the south by the locked presbytery garden, the sides of Notre-Dame are silent and austere. The transept portals are always deserted, but once the northern and southern doors were as busy as those of the western façade. Crowds moved beneath their sculptures. Pilgrims knelt before the famous statues of the Virgin and Saint Stephen, and through the open portals saw the immense transept roses. Processions, winding out of the aisles, left the Cathedral by the southern transept and made a circuit of the nave, the cross held before the multitude, then returned through the northern transept to the altar.

The entire populace, not just the clergy, used to rush along the sides of Notre-Dame, enjoying the Cathedral from close, exciting vantage, as the buttresses jumped and flew, one after the other, one hundred and ten feet from the ground to the roof. Whoever had official business with the diocese, or unofficial business, came to the episcopal palace on the south; whoever had dealings with the Chapter conducted them in the cloister to the north, in the residences of the canons along the river, in the mansions of the archdeacons, in the Cathedral's warehouse, at the river port of Saint-Landry, or in the series of arcaded courts that spread through the northeastern corner of the island. The people were not shut off from the episcopal community. They were necessary to it, and welcome. Women were invited as well as men.

South and north, then, Notre-Dame was surrounded by its own city of the Virgin; but, like the city of Paris around it, the episcopal community was not quite rationally divided. Within and without the

Cathedral, the territory of the Church was marked by curious feudal boundaries. The Bishop held only the sanctuary and portions of the aisles as his own fief; the Chapter governed the rest of the structure. The Chapter's jurisdiction wandered south of the Cathedral, through the Bishop's gate to the entrance of his palace; the Bishop's traveled north, following certain streets, to little isles of authority within the cloister. In theory the organization of the Church was symmetrical, but, like the symmetry of Notre-Dame, it was never absolute. The Cathedral is superbly equilibrated, but it is not the same on either side. A flexible balance of forces keeps it erect.

On the south the Bishop's palace had some resemblance to a modern prefecture. Sergeants lounged in its hallways and stood guard at the gates. Ordinary Parisians came there for any number of reasons: to enroll a son in the Church, to register deeds, to pay taxes, to ask for relief, to stand before the law. Sometimes they were attracted merely by arrivals and departures of the great: the King or the Bishop; or archdeacons of Notre-Dame galloping with suites of horsemen through the long, cobbled courtyard between the palace and the Cathedral; or barons with troops of knights. In the courtyard hundreds of priests, clerks, and lay officials walked about, gesturing, talking, taking the air, then returned to their paper work like typical bureaucrats, on the ground floor of the palace. With them burghers discussed commercial affairs, such as the sale of a wine-press. Lawyers hustled about, arguing cases at the Bishop's court of justice, over which deputized judges now presided instead of the busy prelate. In the exchequer bailiffs reported the collection of tithes, tolls, and other taxes; accounts were settled, and coins stacked on the ruled table. Archivists entered all these transactions in the records; and somewhere in the palace Dominican and Franciscan monks also kept the files of the Inquisition. Outside the office of the chancellor, students waited to inquire after their bourses or to answer for breaches in discipline. To pass time they shot dice on the Bishop's stairway; and this, too, when they were caught by the sergeants, found its way into the cartulary of Notre-Dame.

Regularly, year after year, powerful guilds came marching in ranks—masters, journeymen, and apprentices, accompanied by their wives, carrying banners and singing, across the parvis and into the Bishop's courtyard, to make a gift to Notre-Dame. There were one hundred and twenty-eight corporations in Paris at the end of the thirteenth century, each competing with the others in generosity to the Cathedral. They endowed chapels, windows, statuary, altar vessels, ornaments of every kind. In 1258 the cloth merchants and tailors outdid all by underwriting the expense of the portal of the southern transept. Bishop Renaud de Corbeil dedicated the new door to Saint Stephen the Protomartyr, the patron of the first Cathedral; and after receiving instructions from the priestly iconographers, the sculptors of Jehan de Chelles went to work.

How differently they saw their art from their fathers and grandfathers who created the western façade! The very composition of the portal is new: an elaborate gable, like a fancy headdress, stands free above the doorway. To show that it is independent the gable is perforated with roses, through which the real wall may be seen rising parallel. The effect is startling. The portal asks for admiration, and gets it, but this is the first time that the Cathedral has made the request.

Despite the almost feminine mood here, as compared with the virility of the western doors, it may be noticed that for the first time Mary is excluded from a portal of her church! Even in the Last Judgment, so utterly Christ's, the Virgin was given a central place. But in the southern transept Saint Stephen has assumed his ancient privileges in Paris: the Protomartyr is the antique male divinity who preceded the Norse invasions; and neither Mary nor Saint Geneviève, nor any other female figure is allowed the smallest statuette. Indeed, the portal is almost exclusively Stephen's and Christ's, as was the whole Church before Mary came to France from Byzantium. The central tympanum carries the passion of the Protomartyr; the tympanum-like niches in the smaller gables to either side show Jesus, without the Mother, adored by angels; and Saint Martin of Tours sharing his cloak with the beggar. But it is Stephen who dominates the entrance of the Cathedral, in a restored statue, holding his book as a teacher. Its text remains the brief anecdote which entranced the Merovingians. When men could not carve, during the Dark Age, they scratched on the wall of a crypt a bloody head bashed by a stone. But under Saint Louis men knew too well how to carve—sculpture had become easy—and they had again learned to read. And so, after all the centuries, the martyrdom of Stephen was given a treatment neither savage nor monumental but literary.

The sculpture is meant to be *read* instead of *seen*. There is no single blinding God in the center of the tympanum, no Virgin in Majesty, no Judging Christ. The beginning action is hidden in the lower left corner, where Stephen is discovered as a youthful and very intellectual deacon of the age of Aquinas, matching wits with Jews. This was a favorite thirteenth-century diversion. Stephen's theological contest with the Jews might have taken place in any castle hall or abbey refectory, or, for that matter, on any street intersection. The Jews were baited, and because they could lose little more by resistance than submission, they argued back. "I tell you that no one should dispute with them," remarked Saint Louis to Joinville, "unless he be a well-trained clerk; but that the layman, where he hears Christian Law mis-said, should not defend it except with his sword, with which he should pierce the mis-sayer in the midriff, as far as it can enter." Stephen obviously is one of the leading graduates of the University of Paris. He quotes from a volume in his lap and makes a telling point; but a shrewd, bearded rabbi refutes him, striking his palm as he speaks. Five other sophists from the Synagogue smile and jeer, clutch their beards in derision, and bring up new texts to debate.

In the next scene Stephen has quit the rabbis and preaches to the common people. Unlike his intellectual adversaries, they listen intently, placing their hands pensively to forehead or chin. A bareheaded man takes down the saint's words on a tablet; a woman gives her breast to her child, but at the same time fervently turns her head to Stephen. Soon, however, the saint is haled before the magistrate at the right, who sits with legs crossed in the conventional medieval attitude of pride. Two of Stephen's jailers are ordinary ruffians, but the third is one of the most unusual figures in the Gothic: a cruel Negro in authentic Roman armor. Probably he was copied from a classical monument still standing in Paris.

Above, Stephen is murdered by the hard-faced mob. Stones are showered on the innocent victim, who, as part of the new realism conspicuous in all these carvings, raises his arm involuntarily. In the western façade Stephen dies in prayer, kneeling with hands joined, as before an altar, without a glance at the stoners. The detachment of the earlier work and the grandeur of its premise are gone. Moreover, in a touch that even realism does not call for, a hideous street child lances his small stone at the saint. To depict such a child in the church of the Virgin would have been inconceivable to the artists of the western façade. In a corner of the scene Saul—who has not yet had his weird experience on the road to Damascus—encourages the stoners.

Stephen's burial follows, the first of hundreds of funerals which would typify the macabre later Gothic. The corpse, cleverly carved in its winding sheet, is lowered by two old men into a stone coffin; the dirt heaped from the open grave is not omitted. A young priest reads the service, while a woman weeps, and a clerk stands by with the aspergillum and the cross. Above a bank of clouds Christ waits with angels to receive the soul of the Protomartyr; and this too is a new Christ, who shows characteristics of delicacy, and even weakness.

All has changed since the western portals were carved. Stephen, to be sure, has "the face of an angel"; he is handsome, intelligent, slightly ingenuous. Yet his eye—the pointed oval beneath a slanted brow—is already the aristocratic Florentine eye of the fourteenth century, which Giotto would paint as no one else. It is not hard to see a fresco here, or a mosaic, but a vast stone force has vanished. The gods have weakened in mood and shrunk in scale. The central statue of Stephen and those of his twelve accompanying martyrs were torn from the portal by the Revolution and replaced with imitations by Viollet-le-Duc; but the originals were found serving as posts in a coalyard and are again at Notre-Dame—minus heads, hands, feet, and other attributes—in the lapidary room of the northern tower. What is surprising in these mutilated figures is their small stature. The legendary saints of France are human-sized, and their supple robes contain human bodies.

This new realism would lead to a general artistic catastrophe before another century passed. Notre-Dame, fortunately, would escape serious damage, although other cathedrals were not so lucky. Yet is there not something to be said for realism at its best and working on its own terms? If realism is incapable of divinity, it can be as divertingly human as *La Comédie Humaine;* success depends largely on choice of material. Happily, when it was decided to include eight scenes of contemporary Parisian life at the base of this portal, the artists were given a free hand. The Church's motive in choosing profane subject matter in a divine context has puzzled scholars as learned as Emile Mâle, who warned that some unknown sacred meaning may be concealed.

Each of these panels is a picture within a picture. Between the outer and inner frames runs the Paris of 1258, its population hurrying through streets and squares; playing with pet dogs or fighting with gryphons and other mythical beasts of whom the street-singing jongléors sang; digging deep in purses to find coins for beggars with outstretched hands; taking the staff of Saint James and setting off barefoot for Compostela; accosting women, or being accosted; chatting, bargaining, borrowing; greeting acquaintances or, like all city dwellers, passing strangers without recognition. Within the square outer frame is a quatrefoil, or four-leaf clover, containing events of more particular significance.

The first, starting from the left, shows a woman fettered to the Bishop's "ladder of justice," which stood on the parvis until the seventeenth century, when it was replaced by the iron collar, for episcopal law remained in force until the Revolution. What crime the woman has committed is not sure. Because she is chained to a high rung, it is possible that she is an adulteress; and the punishment she is receiving may sober those who think of the Middle Age as invariably gay. The crowd on the parvis is pelting her with stones and filth, so that she may be seriously injured before her hours on the ladder are over. At the base of the ladder two of the Bishop's hefty policemen, armed with swords, turn their backs to the mob violence. From a garret window two men spit down on the helpless prisoner; in another garret two more men are fighting.

The panel below, by contrast, is tranquil. A distinguished visitor, wearing pontifical robes and followed by a secretarial-looking clerk, has arrived at the episcopal palace and embraces a personage, headless like himself, with the kiss of peace. A groom holds the bridles of two horses, while a man, woman, and child look on. The next scene is divided into two groups. On one side four clerks are bickering over an open book at a lectern in the Cathedral library. The other half, however, is in no way intellectual. It is a corner of a tailor's shop, where a man and woman are discussing cloth—yanking it, to test its strength; the proprietor sews with head down, so they are probably making a complaint. Both this and the scene below, in which another tailor sews for three impatient customers and a skillful salesman drapes a gown on a lady, may be signatures of the gift of the tailors and cloth merchants.

In the first panel on the right of the doorway students form a disorderly queue, arguing dialectics, comparing enthusiasms, sitting carelessly on the Bishop's staircase. A scroll is tacked on a wall, which can be taken as one of the Bishop's edicts in favor of the Dominicans and Franciscans, who were utterly transforming the old mood of intellectual freedom at the university. The students valiantly resisted the intrusion, and therefore M. Aubert interprets the scene as part of the Bishop's campaign to master them. Perhaps the same is true of the next panel, in which a young professor lectures to his absorbed class.

But now, although it is morning or early afternoon, these Parisians are going to drop what they are doing and hurry to the cloister of Notre-Dame, to see a miracle performed by the Blessed Virgin!

II

The crowd, as it turned to the northern side of the Cathedral, knew that fine entertainment was in store, this day about 1260, since the miracle play to be staged in the Cloister had been written by the most amusing trouvère in Paris—Rutebeuf, or Rustebeuf—he spelled the name whichever way happened to suit him at the moment: "Rough-Ox." No one knew his right name, no one cared; but everyone had seen him about town, either in noble hôtels or taverns, singing to his viol. He was a character—Elizabethans might have called him a "fantastic"—a dyed-in-the-wool Parisian who had spent most of his life in the capital, although he may have been born in Burgundy. And the marriage he made in 1261! To believe him, his wife *"cinquante anz a,"* and at fifty she was *"maigre et seche,"* dried up and lean. She nagged until he was thin as a willow, and he dared not enter his door empty-handed, she shouted so. Their kid yelled. The house was *"deserte et povre."* Often there was no bread, not a noodle to eat: *"Sovent n'i a ne pain ne paste";* and this was doubly painful because Rutebeuf loved *"bele chiere"*—good cheer. So he went raggedly dressed about Paris, carrying his beaten-up stringed instrument, and the north wind blew straight up his arse: *"Et droit au cul, quand bise vente."*

It was not all in earnest, but serious enough. Paris was fun if one had money; depressing if one was broke. But, when he did have a denier in his purse, Rutebeuf admitted he wagered it as soon as possible in the dicing game of *griesca,* or *griesche:*

Li dé que li detier ont fait	Dice, dice, those debtor makers,
M'ont de ma robe tout desfait;	Dice have stripped me naked;
Li dé m'ocient;	Dice do murder me;
Li dé m'aguetent et espient,	Dice watch for me, and spy.
Li dé m'assaillent et desfient.	Dice challenge, assault me, and I die.

Never, to such deft and intricate music, had songs seemed so drôle! To be murdered by blackguard dice in the dark streets of the Cité! This was no courteous poetry, like that of Count Thibaut, although it was as fastidiously composed. This was as bewitchingly discourteous as the poet could make it. He attacked hypocrites everywhere, especially smug monks. With the right of a former student, he freely —rashly—denounced the interference of the mendicant Orders at the university. And the nuns of Montmartre! they were up to mischief which he explained in detail to the laughing company. He lampooned the quacks who hawked patent medicines on the parvis of Notre-Dame.

On one matter Rutebeuf was serious to the point of gravity: his belief in Mary. Again and again the satirist abandoned the bawdy wit of the taverns and in a series of utterly sincere and moving lyrics addressed himself to the Queen of Heaven. Consequently Paris hurried to the première of his miracle play, to see how he would treat the ancient story of Theophilus. The plot, like the plots of Shakespeare, had been popular for nearly a thousand years; the intellectuals in the crowd knew its full bibliography. A real Theophilus apparently existed in the sixth century, at Ardana in Cilicia, near the shore of Asia Minor. This makes the legend older than that of Faust, which it resembles to an uncanny degree. After the death of the Syrian Theophilus about the year 538, at least eleven Greek accounts were written of his adventure with the Devil, one by an author who claimed to be an eyewitness of the events. In the ninth century a Greek manuscript was translated into Latin by a deacon named Paul in the polyglot, half-Byzantine city of Naples. Thereafter dozens of Latin versions appeared, and by the twelfth century the Virgin's salvation of Theophilus—now Théophile—began to be described in French. Curiously, of the thousands of miracles wrought by Mary, this was the one the Church singled out to depict repeatedly in glass and stone: at Souillac, Chartres, Laon, Beauvais, Le Mans, and, at the moment Rutebeuf's play was composed, in the northern portal of Notre-Dame. Emile Mâle discovered the reason for its predominance in Church art: in the eleventh century the miracle of Théophile was solemnly included in the liturgy of the French Church.

This, then, was the miracle of miracles, and the Parisians rushed to see it in the Romanesque court that fronted on the northern transept. It was as spacious as the cloister of Canterbury, and, like it, was dominated by the Cathedral and its bells, and surrounded by Chapter houses, dormitories, dining halls, and kitchens. There were covered staircases on which lucky spectators could find places, and galleries where they would also be protected if it began to rain. For this was the open-air theater of Notre-Dame, to which the drama had moved from the inside of the church during the twelfth century, at the same time that it had changed from Latin to the French language, and when paid professional actors and playwrights replaced clerical amateurs.

The stage was set before the northern portal. On the left of the audience, but on the right hand of the central Virgin, was Paradise: "a place of delight," as it was called in one medieval stage direction, decked with flowers and green plants, and with a golden throne for the Lord. At the opposite side was Hell: the gaping snout of Leviathan; in the monster's throat, behind a black cloth, prop-men were concealed with phosphorus pans and other smoke-and-flame devices. Between these extremities were four little houses, or *mansions,* in which the actors waited for their cues. Nearest Heaven was the chapel of the Virgin, surmounted by a spire and cross. Beside it, less imposing, was the palace of the Bishop, also Gothic in style. Next was the similar but still smaller house of Théophile. Nearest Hell was the exotic Moorish residence of villain Salatin, marked with an evil crescent. According to medieval color symbolism, the Virgin's chapel was hung with a blue curtain blazoned with gold stars, exactly as the rose was painted; the Bishop's palace with a scarlet cloth; the house of Théophile with a green hanging; and Salatin's with yellow silk.

Now a priest came from the interior of the Cathedral and called for silence. An invocation was spoken, and perhaps a short sermon. Then, by way of prologue, the priest recapitulated the legend, so that no one would be confused by the action, which, like good Elizabethan theater, begins not at the start but the middle. Théophile had been *vidame,* or seneschal, of a church in Cilicia. Because of exemplary character he was elected to the episcopal throne when his bishop died but refused to accept out of modesty. As might have occurred in the Chapter of Notre-Dame, the chancellor was thereupon elected in his place. A shock followed. In violation of Church custom, the new bishop dismissed Théophile from his post—a stroke of high-handedness that would have been virtually impossible during the Middle Age—and the poor fellow, in spite of his piety and virtue, found himself in disgrace and want.

This is where Rutebeuf began his play. Music sounded within the Cathedral, and God the Father, his white robe supported by a train of angels, walked slowly to his throne in Heaven. Théophile came from his house and, with the audience hushed, sang the opening recitative:

> Alas! alas! King of Glory,
> God so deep in my memory,
> That all I owned was expended,
> All to the poor I extended,
> Until nought remains in my sack.
> Well has the Bishop told me:
>   "Check!"
> And mated me in an angle,
> Deserting me to starve in need
> Unless I sell my clothes for bread.
> And who will meet my rent for me?
> I don't know if the Lord will pay.
> The Lord! How is it His affair?
> For help I'd better look elsewhere
> Since now He turns me a deaf ear.

My burdens are none of His care.
But I'll turn my worst face to Him:
Shame to the man who praises Him!

He is on high in happiness;
And I downtrodden in distress,
Weary of woe and suffering,
My viol has a broken string.

"Check!" The gamer, the thirteenth-century maker of songs, was speaking through his sixth-century personage. Rutebeuf, who in another poem described himself as "companion to Job," had transformed Théophile into himself. And now an old acquaintance of the poet—the Devil's agent—emerges from his bizarre lodgings, attired as an Oriental, but speaking more like a moneylender from a Right Bank Juiverie: Salatin the Jew, "who speaks with the Devil when he wishes." Salatin, showing instant concern, asks Théophile what is wrong: "*Qu'est ce? qu'avez vous, Théophile?*" Miserable Théophile enumerates his woes, and Salatin listens with sympathy. Théophile sees that he has found a friend in need, and asks the Jew if he does not possibly know some way to regain his former estate. Of course Salatin knows just the one who will help, but first he asks the crucial question: Would Théophile desert his Lord, like a disgruntled baron, and become another's man, hands joined between his hands, in an act of feudal rebellion? In his rage and despair Théophile says Yes.

It is settled! Salatin quickly goes to work for his client, but Théophile walks off a little distance and thinks the deal over. Suddenly he reflects that if he denies the Lord his soul will burn in blackest Hell—"*en la flame d'enfer le noir*"—for eternity, in Satan's "*hideus manoir.*" He knows what Hell is:

It's no fable.
For in those flames unquenchable
There is no one amiable,
Foul fiends only of the Devil:
Fierce their nature.
Their houses black and dark remain,
Gay, bright sunlight is never seen,
The pit flows over with ordure.
And there I'll go!

But it is too late. For with an incantation which the audience recognized as the foreign jargon of the Jews, Salatin has conjured up the Devil:

*

> Bagahi laca bachahe
> Lamac cahi achabahe
> Karrelyos
> Lamac lamec bachalyos
> Cabahagi sabalyos
> Baryolas
> Lagozatha cabyolas
> Samahac et famyolas
> Harrahya.

Fire! Smoke! The maws of Hell have opened and Satan has danced out in a lascivious blast of flame, his hairy legs writhing. Théophile is terrified, but the Prince of Darkness commands him to step forward. A simple Sign of the Cross could save Théophile, but his grief rankles, and he gives in.

Devil: Hast need of me?
Théophile: Yes.
Devil: Then join thy hands, and so become my man; I shall aid thee beyond reason.
Théophile: Thus do I render you homage.

In the tympanum of the northern portal, sculpture illustrates the harrowing scene of the play. Théophile kneels, trembling, his hands between those of the brawny demon. Salatin, in a turban, places a steadying hand on the vassal's shoulder; but with the other he holds the deed, already sealed and signed in blood, with which Théophile surrenders his soul. Next, Théophile is shown at his moment of Faustian supremacy, again the lord and master of his land, more powerful than his bishop, as occasionally a shrewd and unprincipled archdeacon of Notre-Dame stood more powerful in France than the Bishop of Paris. He has been restored to his post in the Church and misuses his authority with arrogance. Money buys all for him, and he has a limitless supply. While his right hand distributes gold pieces, a little imp surreptitiously slips more into the palm of his left. For seven years Théophile enjoys this haughty splendor—the play covers the long period with a few angry conversations between the proud seneschal and his friends.

But at last he comprehends the enormity of his sin; and the poetry bursts into a lamentation of twelve Alexandrine stanzas, one for each of the apostles, according to the sacred arithmetic which Dante also used; and the stanzas are quatrains for the four Evangelists, who, multiplied by the three of the Trinity, make twelve again. Does Rutebeuf's verse seem unsophisticated? Read it again, noting the rhyme schemes, the running measures, the complication of vowels. Then hear the tremendous music of his Alexandrine line:

> Maus chans m'ont fet chanter li vin de mon chantier.

> Bitter wines I distilled caused me sing bitter songs.

But all Rutebeuf's easy Alexandrine numbers, like the sum of the pillars and buttresses of Notre-Dame, add to the complex single figure of the Virgin:

> Je n'os Dieu ne ses saintes ne ses sainz reclamer,
> Ne la tresdouce Dame que chascuns doit amer.
> Mes por ce qu'en li n'a felonie n'amer,
> Se je li cri merci, nus ne m'en doit blasmer.

> Nor to the Lord, nor to his saints, may I appeal,
> But to the very sweet Lady all must love well,
> Since she has no quality bitter or evil,
> I'll cry out for mercy, I'll tell her my trouble!

And Théophile kneels before a charming Gothic chapel, in which an image of Mary may be seen on the altar, and implores her aid:

> Lovely and saintly Queen,
> Most glorious Virgin,
> O Lady filled with grace,
> In whom all good is seen,
> Who calls to you in pain
> Is saved from all disgrace,
> Who takes his heart's distress
> To you in Paradise,
> Will have new joy again.
> Fountain of happiness,
> Delightful with goodness,
> Commend me to thy Son!

On and on, in nine more verses, tenderly, but determined as only a Frenchman can be with a beautiful lady, Théophile beseeches

Mary's forgiveness and help. He enumerates the horrors he will suffer if she does not save him. He admits his infidelity but informs her tearfully that he again renders her total homage as his only right-ful sovereign: *"Or te faz hommage."*

The Virgin found the entire prayer adorable, but one verse, spoken beneath the blue northern rose, went to her heart:

> As does the sunlight pass
> Through stainèd window glass,
> God made thee mother, dame.
> His transit left no trace,
> As light in golden skies:
> Thou Virgin still, the same.
> Resplendent shining gem!
> Lady of gentle fame,
> Lift me from the morass.
> I know I am to blame,
> Yet save my soul from flame,
> Allow this sinner grace!

Suddenly the image on the altar comes to life! The Virgin speaks gravely: *"Qui es tu, va, qui vas par ci?"*—"Who art thou? who hast come to me?" Théophile cries out for mercy, telling her that he needs help urgently, for the dreaded hour is approaching. But the Virgin replies coldly: "I take no heed of your appeal. Go hence! take leave of my chapel!" Théophile refuses to budge. "I do not dare!" he answers, and implores Mary, the lily, rose, and eglantine flower —*"Flors d'aiglentier et lis et rose"*—to save him from an eternity in Hell *"avoec Cahu"*—with Cain. And the Virgin finds she can refuse him no longer:

Nostre Dame	*Our Lady*
Theophile, je t'ai seü	I recognize thee, Théophile,
Ça en arriere a moi eü.	In other days you loved me well.
Saches de voir,	Believe in me.
Ta chartre te ferai ravoir	Thy deed shall be returned to thee,
Que tu baillas par nonsavoir.	For it was signed unknowingly.
Ja la vois querre.	I'll bring it here.

After only token resistance, for she knew her aid was needed urgently, the Virgin gave in with a smile. In both the sculpture and the play, a happy denouement follows. All Mary's miracles were comedies. She detested the anguished cry of "Ah, Mephistophilus!" It is the Devil, and not the sinner, who must eat crow, since in the Virgin's code of justice there was no punishment but only pardon. Consequently she takes the great crucifix from her chapel and walks to the end of the stage, to the mouth of Hell, where she summons the Evil One: *"Sathan! Sathan! es tu en serre?"* The Prince of Darkness promptly pops out of his pit, strangely shrunken since he lorded it over poor Théophile. *"Rent la chartre que du clerc as!"*—The Virgin commands him to return the clerk's deed. But Satan attempts defiance: "Give it back to you! I'd rather be hanged!" Whereupon the Virgin, wearing her crown and handling the cross as a lance, yet with an exquisitely feminine grip, brings him to his knees. In a brief struggle she wrests the deed from him by force, answering him most informally: *"Et je te foulerai la pance!"*—"And I crush thy guts!"

That the Virgin knew such expressions, no one doubted. The Middle Age, although it could be exceptionally polite, was not prudish. Mary, however, resumes her courteous tone immediately and returns the sealed agreement to Théophile. Then she instructs him to carry the document to the bishop, so that it may be displayed to the people in front of Holy Church. Théophile answers: *"Volentiers, Dame!"* and rushes to a reconciliation with a paternal-looking prelate.

In the top of the tympanum, decorously arranged in the triangle, a crowd watches as the bishop holds up the deed, which is inscribed *"Carta Theophili."* An oval seal hangs from the parchment by a ribbon. Theophilus is seated on the bishop's right, perched on the edge of the throne, and holds a hand to his head, still marveling at his luck. The bishop addresses the throng:

> Hear, for sake of God, Mary's Son,
> Good people, the true-life lesson
>   Of Théophile
> Whom the Enemy tricked by guile.
> As clear as Blessed Evangel
>   Is this thing.
>
> Immaculate Virgin Mary
> Saved him from such a quandary.
> And now for this delivery,
>   Let us all rise,
> Singing: O Lord to Thee our praise!

With the anthem thundering in the Cloister, the rose window spreading across the transept overhead, the sculpture glowing gold and blue, and red and green and yellow; with Satan chased back to Hell, and Salatin locked in his house, afraid to venture on the hostile streets; and Théophile and the bishop standing in their open doorways; and the Virgin smiling in her chapel; as the players stood fixed in their colored costumes, and God the Father and His angels solemnly returned within the Cathedral, Notre-Dame echoed the triumphant music, taking it upward in buttress and arch, and through the transept spire to Heaven. The church became a great *Te Deum* in itself.

And in the center of the portal, dominating the stage, stood the new and beautiful statue of the Virgin that had been carved by the Master Sculptor of Jehan de Chelles, some time after 1250. This is the one piece of free-standing statuary that the Revolution spared Notre-Dame. No one can say why, except that possibly the French in 1793 did not see a goddess here but a woman. For this Mary, like Saint Stephen in the southern transept, was taken from life. She is not a divine abstraction of Majesty but a living portrait. Once this Virgin walked, breathed, smiled, like the actress in the Miracle. She was a proud and charming young mother, who held her Son high in her arms for the world to admire, who caressed Him, selected His clothes, amused Him with toys. Thousands of ordinary mothers and pregnant young wives saluted her as they entered the church through this door, which, like all northern portals, had special significance for women. Here Mary stood with an intimate court, not the peers of the western façade, but with her favorite ladies-in-waiting and gentlemen guards, whose statues have been lost. On her right were Faith, Hope, and Charity; on her left, the amusing Magi, with their gifts.

The frieze directly above the Virgin, if compared with the lintel that accompanies the Virgin in Majesty, shows that every Marian attribute had now become human rather than divine. Both lintels depict Nativities, but in the thirteenth-century carvings Mary's bed is no longer a rich Byzantine couch. It is a solid French bedstead, mounted on plain wooden posts. Christ has not been born in a palace but in what might be a maternity ward of the Hôtel-Dieu; a cloth partition, strung on a wire, alone seems to give the scene privacy. As a concession to the theologians, the Holy Ghost flies down in the form of a dove; and the Virgin does not recline as a goddess but leans up on a womanly elbow, looking into space, reflecting on the honor the Lord has bestowed on her. Jesus sleeps in a strong and simple cradle, which lacks the grace of his twelfth-century crèche. Joseph is no longer a dreamy and turbaned Easterner but a bushy-bearded and very concerned Frenchman.

The Shepherds and their flocks and little dogs are also gone, replaced by a Presentation in the Temple. Mary and the aged Simeon hold the Child above the altar, almost as a eucharistic offering, while Joseph and the Prophetess Anna look on. Next is Herod, a monarch of the John Lackland school, his leg crossed viciously. A knight in chain armor receives the command to massacre the Innocents; and the slaughter, absent from the western façade, is shown in pathetic detail. As the knights strike, and a sobbing woman clutches a sword with her bare hand in an effort to protect her babe, the Holy Family escapes by moonlight into Egypt.

All has been made personal, real; nothing is divine. Study these carvings as André Malraux has done, noticing eyes and cheekbones and elegant lips. You will not find the stark magic of the eye of Barbedor, nor the tall wonder of angels. The scale has been reduced; the intensity has been weakened. But the Virgin is still a queen who is all-powerful in France, who can still command resplendent gifts from her people and return more than she receives.

Chapter Seventeen

THE GIFT OF SAINT LOUIS

"*a* S THE SCRIBE makes his book, illuminating it with gold and azure," wrote Joinville, "so the King illuminated his realm with beautiful abbeys and . . . houses of God." France was covered with monuments of the pious generosity of Saint Louis. The Sainte-Chapelle, the new Saint-Denis, the Abbey of Royaumont, were his most celebrated endowments, but every major church benefited from royal gifts. The royal church of Notre-Dame of course was not excepted. King Louis and his Queen, Marguerite of Provence, together presented its last and smallest portal, and also the most charming: the little entrance on the north of the choir, through which the Chapter entered the church directly from the cloister. Because of its painted doors it has always been called the Portail Rouge, although it is consecrated to the Virgin and Saint Marcel.

An illumination it is: a gilded arabesque of fretted stone, traced in a corner of the great architectural page of Notre-Dame. The Red Door does not pretend to belong to the main structure of the Cathedral—it is painted on as an afterthought. Its Coronation of the Virgin is a miniature, taken from the immense Coronation of the western façade; the scenes from the life of Saint Marcel, including his eerie battle with the vampire, seem manuscript illustrations from the *Golden Legend*. The surmounting gable is completely hollowed out and stands above the pointed archway as an open triangle, from which roses and eglantine trail, as if the light frame were a trellis. The base of the portal is a menagerie of gryphons and eagles, arching centaurs and stags, tiny beasts which might have been put on with a brush. The style is unmistakable. Each detail shows the hand of Pierre de Montreuil; the door of his lost chapel at Saint-Germain-des-Prés was not much different. Pierre became Master of Notre-Dame in 1265, or shortly before. He died March 17, 1267, which fixes the dates of the Portail Rouge and of the portraits of its donors, who kneel to either side of the Coronation: King Louis on the right hand of the Virgin, Queen Marguerite on the left of Christ.

How gracious they are! The portraits are small, and worn by time, but it is easy to see that both were exceptionally handsome. And how young! Neither looks his age. Louis, in 1267, was fifty-two, weakened by the hardships of his crusade, illness, and the continual mortification to which he subjected his flesh. In three more years he would crusade again, and this time die almost as soon as he set foot on Saracen Africa. Marguerite was six years younger, the mother of twelve children, whose descendants would rule France, through the Capetian, Valois, and Bourbon lines, until the Revolution. She too had participated in the crusade in Egypt, and there had experienced terrors that would cause any twentieth-century queen to drop dead from fright. But, like Eleanor of Aquitaine and Blanche of Castile, she was one of the fearless and virile women of the Middle Age. She remained young and active, in body and mind, until her death in 1295, when she was seventy-four.

This, except in the first years of their marriage, is not a love story but a tale of greatness. Marguerite of Provence was brought to the French court in 1234 as a bride of thirteen, as Blanche had been brought, from a southern background of intrigue, easy manners, excitable men, and women with the habit of power. She and her three sisters made the best marriages of the thirteenth century: all were wed to kings. Eleanor of Provence was Queen of England and dominated Henry III as if he were an infant. Sancia married Richard, Earl of Cornwall, King of the Romans in title only, but a man to reckon with in England. Beatrice brought the inheritance of Provence to Count Charles of Anjou, Saint Louis' brother, and after him the strongest man in Europe. Charles also became a king when he was offered the crown of the Norman realm of Naples and Sicily.

Four sisters, four queens—it was a good record even for a house as famous for its women as Provence, and as strategically located in European politics, between France and the Holy Roman Empire.

Their mother, a princess of the House of Savoy, was as tough and canny as old Eleanor of Aquitaine had ever been, and she trained her daughters well. This was fortunate for Marguerite when she encountered her mother-in-law, Blanche of Castile. Joinville, like any other person with access to the court, knew of the young Queen's difficulties:

The harshness which Queen Blanche showed to Queen Marguerite was such that, as much as it was in her power, Queen Blanche would not suffer her son to be in his wife's company, except when he went to sleep with her at night. The residence where the King and Queen liked best to stay was Pontoise, for there the King's chamber was above, and the Queen's chamber directly below.

And they had thus solved their predicament: they communicated with each other by a spiral staircase which descended from one chamber to the other; and they so arranged matters that when the attendants saw Queen Blanche coming to her son's chamber, they beat on the door with their staffs, and the King would come running to his room in order that his mother find him there; and the attendants of Queen Marguerite's chamber did likewise when Queen Blanche approached, so that she would find Queen Marguerite there.

Once the King was at the bedside of his wife, who was in very great peril of death because she had been hurt during the birth of a child. There came Queen Blanche, who took her son by the hand, and said to him: "Come away, you are doing nothing here." When Queen Marguerite saw his mother leading the King away, she cried out: "Alas, dead or alive, you will not allow me to see my lord!" And then she fainted, and it was thought she was dead; and the King, who believed her dying, turned back; and with great difficulty she was brought round.

From the keystones of their chapel at Saint-Germain-en-Laye, carved when Louis and Marguerite had been married four years, in 1238, the King and Queen and the tyrannical Queen Mother look down through the space of seven centuries. The portraits were distorted to be seen from below, but nevertheless Louis' handsomeness is not that of a movie star. His nose is long and prominent, his chin strong, and his eyes, as the thirteenth century perceived, have the "candor of a dove." His hair is combed long and rests on his shoulders in rolled curls. He is twenty-three years old, and vigorous. Marguerite, at seventeen, appears singularly refined, her hair girlishly long, her lips sweet. She seems hardly a match for Blanche, whose face is pure force. Her chin and lips are set, her eyes piercing, her forehead severe beneath a crown more regal than her son's. She has just turned fifty.

Against Blanche, Marguerite could cry out in extremity, but she could say nothing against a larger force, which, as the years passed, utterly transformed her relations with her husband. Louis' pathological attachment to his mother was nothing compared with the systematic frenzy of his religious devotion. The extent of his mystical behavior was made clear only when his confessors and other priests made their depositions during the canonization proceedings after his death. During his lifetime his most extreme acts of penitence were kept secret, largely because there was reason to fear the effect such a revelation might have on the public. The King submitted regularly to flagellation. Either he himself or one of his clerks wielded a special whip made of five lengths of flexible chain. When the priests did not strike hard enough, he laughingly told them to increase their force. He lacerated his skin further with a hair shirt.

Beyond this, he prayed incessantly. He arose at midnight and heard matins at an altar. Then he returned to bed half-dressed, lit a candle stub, and ordered his valets to rouse him for the Prime Hour when it had burned down. Later in the morning he heard a Low Mass for the dead and a High Mass which was sung. He also attended services at the Third, Sixth, and Ninth Hours. If he were on horseback in the field the Hours were sung by mounted chaplains. If he passed a church he dismounted and heard services within, where he might remain half the day, his knees on the bare pavements, his elbows on a bench, until he awakened as if from a trance and asked his impatient knights: "Where am I?"

His acts of charity, unlike his mortifications, were impossible to conceal: their scale was too large. He not only fed the poor of Paris from his kitchens, he invited the beggars to the royal table! As many as two hundred at a time would be seated in the dining hall of the Palace. The King selected the most ragged and filthy and washed and kissed their feet. He carved their meat, cut their bread, and then, when they had their fill, ate what was left from plates they had held in their ulcered hands—*"manibus ulcerosis."* There was a particular monk at Royaumont whom he loved to wait on, a leper so disfigured that his lips and nose were gone and pus ran from his blind eyes. The King also volunteered for bed-pan duty at the hospitals, and seemed impervious to stenches that nauseated all around him. In the Holy Land, Joinville observed him help bury some Christians who had been massacred and left to rot by the Saracens: "He himself carried the putrid and stinking corpses, and never once held his nose, as the others did."

He was famous—notorious, in a century that adored good living —for abstinence. He mixed more water with his wine than was thought reasonable; he poured water in sauces. He hated beer and accordingly drank it; he was fond of pike—the delicious brochet of the Seine and Loire—and did not eat it for that reason. He also sacrificed what had evidently been a pleasure: the marriage bed. He slept alone on a wooden cot during Lent and Advent, for several days each week throughout the rest of the year, and on all vigils and holy days, which left precious few nights for Marguerite. He joined her, it appears, only when he felt his responsibility to add to the dynasty of Capets. "When he lay with the Queen, he did not have himself awakened at midnight for matins, but the next day, out of respect, he dared not kiss the shrines and relics of the saints."

Yet all this is but a side of a many-sided man. He knew he was called a priest-ridden "roi papelard" and "Friar Louis." Once an old woman mocked him, calling him king of the monks, and said he should be chased from the throne. He replied calmly: "You surely speak true—I am unworthy to be king, but if it had pleased Our Lord, another who knew better how to govern would be in my place." No one knew better how to govern, as he proved beyond doubt after the death of his mother. He sought and usually accepted the advice of his counselors, but once his mind was made up it could not be shaken. After all, he was the grandson of Philip Augustus. Once his old squire Poince was late in bringing up his palfrey, and he was forced to mount Joinville's:

And when his own palfrey arrived, he turned furiously on Poince the squire; and when he had given him a severe talking-to, I told him: "Sire, you should forgive much to Poince the squire, for he has served your grandfather, your father, and you."

"Seneschal," said he, "he has not served us, but we have served him, inasmuch as we have suffered him to be around us, considering his bad qualities. For my grandfather King Philip told me that our household servants should be rewarded, more or less, according to how they serve; and he told me further that no one can be a good governor of a land unless he knows how to refuse as boldly and as vigorously as he knows how to give."

Like his grandfather Philip the Conqueror, Louis IX was a great king. He was surrounded by even greater worldly pomp, for, in spite of prodigious alms-giving, Joinville notes that he expended tremendous sums for the upkeep of his household. The royal court was more "courteously" served, and "more liberally and abundantly," than under any previous Capet. The splendor of this court, with its cloaks of samite and taffeta, has already been attested to by Joinville; and although the King personally preferred simple dress, he did not prescribe it for others. "You should clothe yourselves well and appropriately," he told his sons, "so that your wives will love you better, and your people will prize you the more."

Do not look for faultless symmetry in the man, any more than in Notre-Dame. It does not exist. Saint Louis was a poised equilibrium of forces, of Church and Crown, Ideal and Real, Irrational and Rational; he was an exchange of colored light. What blues and reds filtered within him may be appreciated on any page of Joinville, or any morning in the Sainte-Chapelle. He had weaknesses. A cathedral, remarked Le Corbusier, is a difficult problem ingeniously solved; made artificially difficult by the ambition of its premise, and therefore not truly beautiful, not truly successful; *Hamlet* has been called a failure because of identical shortcomings.

Reasonable men do not wish a church so tall and complex; they prefer the sun-invaded temple of Doric Greece. Nor do reasonable men desire a divine king. Yet men must act within the limits of their age; Leonardo da Vinci could not burst through the final boundaries of environment; and the grandeur of Saint Louis, like the grandeur of Dante, is that he did not wish to. The limits of the thirteenth century were extended far enough: a genius had trouble merely in approaching them. Saint Louis attained them. He was an ingenious solution to the problem of divine government: an artificial problem today in the sense that Gothic art is now artificial, like the Princeton campus. It was real in the Middle Age. To be simultaneously saint and sovereign, at the moment Thomas Aquinas was exploring Heaven by the scientific method, when Jehan de Chelles and Pierre de Montreuil were constructing their roses, when Rutebeuf and Thibaut of Champagne were composing their songs, was to add the final golden thread to the tapestry hanging in the nave of the Cathedral.

Both Saint Louis and Notre-Dame leave much to be desired as structure alone. The wooden shelter roof above the stone vault was obviously vulnerable. It menaced the entire balanced structure beneath. A bolt of lightning, ripping through its lead cover or catching the pointed spire, could set the fifty-foot timbers blazing. The masonry might crack and stagger downward in the heat, so that a century of labor would perish in a single night. The roof of Chartres burned in 1836, in a conflagration that consumed every piece of wood in the upper portions of the church, including the belfries of the towers. Hot lead streamed into the vessel; some stones fell; the vaults were charred black. But the cathedral held, and its fragile glass survived. The roof of Paris—the most magnificent forêt left in France—has twice caught fire. Each time the flames were extinguished, by luck, faith, what you will; and the Cathedral stands.

The Gothic Age was aware of its failings. The crusades of Saint Louis were fiascos, which many clear-sighted men and women tried to avoid and later regretted. In 1244 the King fell gravely ill. For a time he lost the power of speech, and at one moment was thought dead. As soon as he regained his speech he called for the Cross, which was given him by Bishop Guillaume d'Auvergne. When Blanche of Castile heard he had taken the Cross, in spite of her joy at his recovery, "she carried on with as great mourning as if she had seen him dead." She and Bishop Guillaume and all the Royal Council did their best to dissuade him from the holy war. They told him he had been temporarily out of his mind, that no one would hold him to such a resolution. Pope Innocent IV announced his willingness to release the King from his engagement; and for an instant Louis actually did return the Cross to Guillaume. As quickly he took it back, declaring he would really have lost his mind if he reneged on a promise to God.

Thus commenced the grand adventure, which would end in a disaster as tragic as the Second Crusade of his great-grandfather, Louis VII, which had been launched by Saint Bernard. Four years were necessary for the preparations. At the advance base of Cyprus, commissary officers heaped up mountains of wheat and barley and stacked wine barrels so high that they "seemed like barns." By 1248 all was ready. Queen Blanche was left in command of the kingdom, and King Louis and Queen Marguerite departed with the Oriflamme from Saint-Denis and Notre-Dame. At the same time barons set out with their troops from every part of the realm, Joinville among them. "I left on foot, unshod, and in my shirt . . . and never once did I turn my eyes back toward Joinville, for fear my heart would melt at the sight of the fair castle I was leaving, and my two children." The baggage was floated down the Saône and the Rhône, and beside the barges, on shore, were led the great war horses. In August 1248 the host had collected at Marseille and other Mediterranean ports:

When the horses were loaded in the hold, our master mariner called to his seamen, who were at the prow of the ship, and asked them: "Is all made ready?" And they answered: "Yes, sir. Let the clerks and priests come aboard!" As they stepped forward, he shouted to them: "Sing, for God's sake!" And they all sang out with one voice: *"Veni creator Spiritus."* And he called to the sailors: "Unfurl, for God's sake!" And they did so. And in a short time the wind filled the sails, and carried us out of sight of land, so that we saw only water and sky; and each day the wind took us further from the land where we were born.

II

The ideal had transported them to an unreal country, Saracen Egypt, through which the Nile flowed from the terrestrial Paradise. There was no direct passionate thrust at Jerusalem. Instead of scaling Heaven, the Crusaders were bent on destroying Hell; and they struck at the serpent's head—Cairo, which they called Babylon. Whatever led the royal board of strategy to attack Egypt, which had already been the objective of the Fifth Crusade of 1218, there can be no doubt of the motive of the King. He was God's soldier. As soon as he heard that the Oriflamme was ashore at Damietta, at dawn on June 5, 1249, he jumped fully armed from his flagship, the *Montjoie,* into the sea, his shield hanging from his neck, his helmet on his head, his sword in hand, and ran up on the beach. Confronting the French was a force of six thousand infidels. He would have charged them immediately if his knights had allowed him.

Damietta was abandoned to the French, who then advanced through the delta to Mansura, where hard fighting began in December 1249. Joinville's account of what followed is finer military description than Tolstoi's. The courage and determination of the French, and their rugged strength in arms, could not cope with Saracen intelligence and technical superiority. They were handicapped further by the strange terrain and the unfamiliar heat, as well as by their childishness and greed. They were battered pitilessly by Greek fire. Their elaborate fortifications were sapped. Bedouins slipped past their sentries at night and cut off their heads. Their battalions were outmaneuvered, trapped, and systematically cut to pieces. On Shrove Tuesday, February 8, 1250, Joinville saw Saint Louis about to go into action before Mansura, the town whose name means "victory" in Arabic, where the Fifth Crusade had foundered three decades earlier:

. . . the King came up with his whole battalion, accompanied by great shouting, and with a great sounding of trumpets and clashing of cymbals; and he paused on a raised way. Never have I seen so handsome a knight! For he seemed to tower head and shoulders above all his people, a gilded helm upon his head, in his hand a sword of German steel.

That day the French suffered losses which included the death of the King's brother, Robert of Artois. Some tried to escape across the Nile, swimming, "which they could not do, for their horses were exhausted, and the day was so hot, that we saw the stream covered with lances and shields, and horses and men drowning and perishing." Three days later, in an onslaught described by Steven Runciman as "one of the fiercest battles that the men of Outremer could remember," the Saracens took the offensive. They attacked "as men play chess," leading with their men on foot and following with cavalry and Greek fire. The French, again suffering heavy casualties, drove them back.

But they were beaten. To their astonishment, the enemy had blocked the Nile, so that vessels could not mount with supplies and reinforcements. Food grew so scarce that an ox sold for eighty livres, a pig or a sheep for thirty, and a measure of wine for ten. The starving troops fed on eels from the river, but the eels had fattened on corpses and started an epidemic in the camp. "The flesh of our legs shriveled, and the skin of our legs became spotted, black and earth-colored, like an old boot; . . . our gums began to rot. No one could escape the disease, except by dying. The sign of death was this, that when there was a hemorrhage from the nose, death was inevitable."

On April 5 a general retreat was ordered. The French struck camp and began descending the Nile toward Damietta, only thirty-five miles away. They did not make it. Louis himself might have escaped by the river, but he refused to quit the main body of troops. He too was ill, and suffered so from dysentery "that it was necessary to cut away the lower of his drawers." Before a week was out, he and his army were prisoners.

Downstream, Queen Marguerite waited at Damietta. She was in the last week of pregnancy:

> Three days before she was brought to bed came the news that the King was taken, which so terrified her that often, while she slept in her bed, it seemed to her that all her chamber was filled with Saracens, and she screamed: "Help! Help!" And in order that the child she carried would not perish, she had an ancient knight, eighty years old, lie before her bed, who held her by the hand. Each time the Queen cried out, he said: "Lady, have no fear, for I am here."
>
> Before she was brought to bed, she ordered her chamber emptied, except for this knight, and she knelt before him, and begged a favor; and the knight promised it on his oath. And she said to him: "I ask you by the faith you have sworn me, that if the Saracens take this city, you will cut off my head before they capture me." And the knight answered: "Be certain that I will do it willingly, for I had already fully intended to kill you before you could be taken."

The child was a boy, who was christened John but called Tristan, because of the sadness that accompanied his birth; he would die at twenty during his father's second crusade of 1270. The day he was born the Queen was told that the Pisans and Genoans intended to heave anchor and leave with their fleet. She summoned their chiefs and implored: "Lords, for God's mercy, do not quit this city, for you must see that my lord the King would be lost, together with all those captured with him. And if this does not move you, take pity on this helpless creature who lies here, and wait until I am recovered." They replied that they could not stay because of famine in the city. To which she said they need not worry on that account, and ordered all the food in the city purchased for three hundred and sixty thousand livres—ten million dollars. The Italians stayed.

In the meantime the Crusaders were threatened with death and torture, to extract territorial concessions from them. Louis was told he would be put in the *bernicles*—a device which crushed every inch of bone in the legs, and to which the victim was returned three days later to have his swollen limbs smashed again. "To these threats the King replied that he was their prisoner, and they could do with him what they would." What the Saracens truly wanted was money. They demanded a million besants in gold, or five hundred thousand livres—another enormous sum, amounting to some fifteen million dollars. Louis consented but stipulated that, since it was not proper to barter his royal person for money, the city of Damietta would be his payment. When the Sultan heard this he declared: "By my faith! this Frank is large not to have bargained over such a sum. Now go tell him that I give one hundred thousand livres toward the payment of the ransom."

Although most of the French nobility, including the royal princes, returned home immediately, and although Blanche of Castile urged Louis to come back as well, he and Queen Marguerite and Joinville remained in the East. There was not much fighting, although there was continual danger of full-scale hostilities; and Louis spent most of his time and energy—and, again, immense amounts of money—in strengthening the Palestinian coastal fortresses of Acre, Tyre, Jaffa, and Sidon. Then, in 1252, news came that Blanche of Castile was dead:

He went into such mourning that for two days no one could speak to him. After that, he sent a valet from his chamber to summon me. When I came before him in his chamber, where he was completely alone, and he saw me, he held out his arms and said to me: "Ah! Seneschal, I have lost my mother!"

Shortly afterward the good Seneschal was surprised to find himself called in turn by one of Queen Marguerite's ladies-in-waiting:

And when I came there, I found her weeping, and I told her that it was truly said that no one should believe a woman: "For she was the woman you hated most, who is dead, and you are putting on such mourning!" And she told me that it was not for her she wept, but for the King's sorrow. . . .

III

As they sailed home, in the spring of 1254, the Virgin watched over the little fleet of thirteen vessels—so few compared with the armada that had left six years earlier. A fire broke out in Marguerite's cabin, and the Queen awakened just in time to seize her burning garments and run out on deck with them, quite naked, to throw them over the side. A few days later a squire fell overboard from a vessel a full league in advance of the King's. He was sighted while still far off, and thought to be a bundle or a barrel because he made no effort to save himself. He simply floated in the sea. When they picked him up, Joinville asked why he had not tried to swim or signal. "He answered that there had been no need . . . for as soon as he began to sink, he commended himself to Our Lady of Vauvert, and she held him up by the shoulders . . . until the King's galley rescued him. In honor of this miracle, I have had it painted in my chapel at Joinville, and in glass at Blécourt."

The catastrophe in Egypt, if anything, had intensified their faith and confidence in Mary. On the unpredictable sea of medieval life, the Virgin alone offered a stable hold. She had not abandoned the Crusaders; they had temporarily forgotten her! After the easy victory at Damietta they had caroused and banqueted, consorted with lewd women, and outraged the Virgin in innumerable other ways. Fools, they did not realize to whom they owed success. Joinville found out after the fighting was over, when he made a pilgrimage to Tortosa in Syria, "a very great shrine," because its altar was the first ever consecrated to Mary. At Tortosa the Seneschal was told how, some time before, the Devil had spoken through the mouth of a madman who had been brought there to be cured: "Our Lady is not here. She is in Egypt aiding the King of France and the Christians who will land there today, on foot, against pagans on horseback." The date was written down, and it coincided exactly with that of the landing, when the dismounted French had battled Saracen cavalry. "And be certain that she aided us that day," adds Joinville, "and would have helped us more, had we not offended her and her Son."

Of course they had offended her. Stupid boors and arrogant barons were continually taking her name in vain. Saint Louis did his best to correct this, for he "so loved God and His sweet Mother that he grievously punished all those he could catch who mentioned them profanely." On one occasion he ordered "the nose and lower lip of a bourgeois of Paris to be branded." To justify this campaign against blasphemy, "the saintly King used to say: 'I would be willing to be seared with a hot iron, on condition that all foul oaths be removed from my kingdom.'"

What makes a saint? The Middle Age seemed to know because Louis was considered a holy creature long before his death. His reputation extended half across the world; and once, in the Holy Land, some Armenian pilgrims begged Joinville to present them to the "sainted" ruler. The Seneschal repeated this to the King, adding, "But I'm not yet ready to kiss your bones!" Louis laughed *"mout clement,"* and ordered the Armenians admitted.

But has there not been a second saint on this voyage? From the opening phrase, "In the name of God Almighty, I, John, Lord of Joinville, Seneschal of Champagne," a child of Heaven has been relating the story of the superb men and women who are inseparable from Notre-Dame. "Of what substance is God?" Louis asked him. "Sire, it is so good a thing that there cannot be a better!" The twenty-five quarto volumes of Saint Thomas Aquinas are consumed in the reply.

"Now I ask you," continued the King, "which you would like better, to be a leper or to be in mortal sin?"

And I, who never lied to him, responded that I would rather have committed thirty mortal sins than be a leper. And . . . he called me to him alone, and made me sit at his feet, and asked me: "Why did you say that to me yesterday?" And I told him I would say it again.

Would the Seneschal, the King went on, wash the feet of the poor on Maundy Thursday, as Louis did regularly in Notre-Dame? *"Sire, en maleur! les piez de ces vilains ne laverai-je jà!"*—"Sire, it would sicken me! never will I wash the feet of those villains!" Louis asked if the Seneschal wished "to be honored in this world and attain Paradise after death"—a question which Schoolmen still debate interminably. Joinville simply answered: "Yes."

They were friends, and also king and baron. Each complemented the other. Each had been reared by a pious and widowed mother. Each acted differently from a common idealism. When their ship struck a sand bank and seemed in danger of breaking up, Joinville rushed to the fo'c'sle to consult with the seamen; Louis prostrated himself, crosswise, before an image of the Savior and prepared to drown. Each responded differently to Marguerite of Provence. Joinville repeatedly performed courtesies that delighted the Queen, but Louis, in his later years at any rate, was notorious for his coldness to her. He did not trouble to meet her, for example, when she arrived at Sidon from Jaffa, where she had been confined by the birth of another child; Joinville welcomed her instead. "And it was not right," observed the Seneschal, "so to be a stranger to his wife and children."

There, it has been said. Courtesy has spoken out. But did Joinville know all the facts? Marguerite, as Langlois described her, was a *"femme redoutable,"* and energetic as a man. At home in France she was as capable and strong-minded as she had been at Damietta. She had bold political ambitions, motivated by her hereditary interest in Provence. She was openly pro-English, and with her sisters Eleanor and Sancia she intrigued to obtain a far better peace treaty from Saint Louis than Henry III had any right to expect. Once a British embassy reported to London that the Queen had ordered them not to appear at the French court until she had had time to use her influence. She had a taste for secret negotiation and sent private emissaries to the Roman Curia and to hostile courts such as Aragon. To her husband's anger, she persecuted political refugees in France from her mother's despotic country of Savoy.

But what Louis found unforgivable was Marguerite's intention to dominate the crown prince—the future Philippe le Hardi—exactly as Blanche of Castile had dominated him! In 1263, when Prince Philip was eighteen, it was discovered that his mother had received a sworn pledge from him, containing these clauses:

1. Until the age of thirty, he would obey her without reserve.
2. That he would have no confidential adviser except his mother.
3. That he never become allied with his uncle Charles of Anjou, whose claim to Provence she bitterly contested.
4. That he inform the queen of any evil rumors which might be circulated against her.
5. That he spend his money carefully.
6. That he reveal the present engagement to no one.

The boy had sworn to this with an oath so binding that his father was forced to request his release from the Pope.

Yet, at the very time that husband and wife were fiercely at odds, about 1265, they together endowed the Portail Rouge of Notre-Dame, and there are at peace for eternity, beside the Virgin and Christ. If all four figures rose to their feet, Louis and Marguerite would be as tall as the gods—Louis tallest of all. Yet they remain on their knees before the ravishing vision of divinity: Louis candid, handsome, brimming with faith and expectation, clad in the plain robes he affected after the Crusade; Marguerite too is dressed with surprising simplicity, and her face is illuminated by a quiet radiance —she seems about to smile. They kneel, with perfect loyalty, as vassals of a king and queen higher than themselves, and whom they would no more dare hold to rational account than their own barons would hold them. There was no need for the complex proofs of Aquinas:

[The King] said that faith and creed were things in which we should believe very firmly, even though we might not be certain of them, but had them only on hearsay. On this point, he asked me my father's name. And I told him that his name was Simon. And he asked me how I knew it. And I answered that I thought I was certain of it and believed it firmly because my mother had been my witness to it. Then he said: "In that way you should believe in all the articles of faith, which the apostles witnessed, and as you hear sung on Sunday in the *Credo*."

IV

After the Crusade, Louis and Joinville saw each other rarely. The King was busy at Paris, strengthening the national government, instituting important municipal reforms in Paris, erecting churches and abbeys, establishing peace wherever he could in the Occident. The Seneschal returned to his forested fief in Champagne, which, he remarks, had been exploited by the agents of Blanche of Castile while he was away and needed his attention urgently. Then, during Lent, 1267, Louis sent for him; and, as Joinville feared, the King took the Cross again. The Seneschal flatly refused to accompany him and declared that all who advised the expedition had committed a mortal sin. For the King, at fifty-two, was worn out, and suffered from chronic erysipelas and anemia. He was so weak that he could neither mount a horse nor ride in a carriage; Joinville had to carry him across Paris in his arms. "Yet, weak as he was, if he had stayed in France he might have lived longer, and done many good works." Three years later, after a great service at Notre-Dame on March 15, 1270, Louis again set out against the Infidel. On July 1 he sailed from the military port of Aigues-Mortes for Tunis, where he arrived eighteen days later. The African summer overwhelmed the Crusaders before they could engage the Mohammedan enemy. Thousands perished in a terrible epidemic. Soon the King was stricken with a stomach ailment before Carthage, and died, on a bed covered with ashes, on August 25, 1270. His body was returned to France, received at Notre-Dame, and buried with his ancestors at Saint-Denis.

The Seneschal lived on, until 1317, to the great medieval age of ninety-three, just long enough to see Notre-Dame completed. With a steady rhythm, as the thirteenth century ended and the fourteenth began, the tremendous flying buttresses of the choir were sprung, one after the other, from the transept to the apse, down the sides of the church and around its eastern perimeter, their lean spines arching fifty feet to the summit of the twelfth-century wall. The Master now was Pierre de Chelles, surely a relative of Jehan, and he had learned construction from incomparable teachers. His flying arches are perfectly wedded, in spirit and structure, to the work of the unknown First Master of 1163. The major lesson of the Paris School was respect for existing beauty; and Pierre de Chelles not only retained but increased the loveliness of the church of Maurice de Sully. Few pieces of architecture are as gracious as the apse of

Notre-Dame, with its slender lines fanning outward from the circular sanctuary, and then retreating, arch after arch, to the massive crossing form of the transept.

Although their maximum power declined after the construction of the western façade, the builders of Notre-Dame kept their grand manner to the end. The signs of the approaching disintegration of medieval art and society are perceptible, but only slightly so; they vanish before the strength and beauty of the total effect. Between the buttresses, the chapels of the choir are richer than those of the nave; they are surmounted by gables and pinnacles which suggest the delicate lacework of the end of the Middle Age. The ornate windows which Pierre de Chelles' successor, Jehan Ravi—John the Red-Head—added to the tribunes after 1318 are more elaborate still. Surface decoration can be seen coming into its own, losing monumental relation with the wall; but however eloquent it has become, it is not yet vain and rhetorical.

A world was changing, and from Joinville the old Seneschal recognized that it was not for the best. When he visited Paris it was for official business only, such as his testimony before the Church board that was inquiring into the saintly acts of the dead King. He did not linger at court, for what he found there did not please him. Commoners were being ennobled—not *prud'hommes,* which might have been understandable, but rapacious businessmen. Fashionable dress, which he prized, had become effete. Courtesy was a blague; his own manners and speech seemed curiously quaint and out-of-date in the capital. Politics had taken the worst turn of all. Philip the Bold (1270-1285) had not been bold but rash; he had embarked on an expansionist adventure in Spain, and was paid for it with death at Perpignan. Philip the Fair was totally unsympathetic. He seemed as greedy as the new-type men about him. Joinville did not like the type.

He had outlived every one of his friends of the great days. In 1295, after a stirring widowhood, Marguerite of Provence died at seventy-four, the last of their generation. Then, in 1298, Louis IX was elevated among the confessors of the Church, and the bones which he and Joinville had joked about were declared sacred; they were exhumed, kissed fervently, and placed in golden caskets. The Seneschal was proud. The Church, he felt, "had done right" to the

King. He must have been filled with pride, too, when the new central chapel of the apse of Notre-Dame of Paris, directly behind the high altar, was consecrated to Saint Louis.

It was Queen Jeanne of Navarre who had the happy idea that he should write a book about the King; and so he returned to Joinville, riding eastward out of Paris, along the Seine, with Notre-Dame behind him, the Cathedral immense against the sunset, the gay white arches flashing upward to the colored roof; and then, farther away, detail vanishing in the shadowy mass of the transept, the spire narrowing higher, and the forward towers coming in view. And as the old man rode onward, and turned again, Notre-Dame was suddenly a great distance off, black and colossal on its island, the towers lifting, lifting, lifting, as the distance increased, taking the last golden light of the sky as they emerged in their full power above the church. And Paris spread beneath the sunset, a city of roofs and low battlements, growing smaller and indistinct, and the river going golden and red, and in the western circle of gold, the Cathedral dominating all.

the passion of notre-dame

THE PASSION OF NOTRE-DAME

*t*HIRTY BISHOPS of Paris, their miters and crosiers golden, their white pontifical capes fringed with gold, looked down from the high windows of the choir at the fourteenth-century splendor of Notre-Dame. Eleven hundred years had passed since Saint Denis had arrived at pagan Lutetia, nearly a thousand since Saint Marcel had turned the water of the Seine to wine. Now they reigned overhead, eighteen feet tall, in the central window of the apse, each beneath a pointed arch, and surmounted, in a greater arch, by the rose of the Virgin.

By the second quarter of the fourteenth century, the Cathedral of Paris had been completed. The last chapel had been inserted between the buttresses. The last window had been enlarged, the last pillar strengthened. The last flying arch had been sprung to the upper wall. Vault mounted upon vault, arch upon arch, pillar upon pillar, maintaining the church in a counterpoint of Gothic music, a mathematics of twelve, and four, and three, and one, of Trinity and Singleness, the Marian nervure reaching to the keystone of God. Above the stone vessel, the oaken roof, cut from the forest by moonlight, extended its arms north, east, south, and west; from its center, the spire narrowed upward like a display of intellect, striving toward Christ, spearing the cynical air, until the crowing of a gilded cock broke the air in fragments at its tip.

Chanticleer looked over a horizon ringed with masterpieces. The Gothic stood triumphant in all Europe, and, like most aging victors, had begun to show a taste for flamboyance. The style born in France —the royal domain of the Ile de France—extended from Cyprus to Sweden; the Cathedrals of both Nicosia and Uppsala resembled

Notre-Dame, and both had been constructed by French masters. Churches everywhere had drawn inspiration from the Cathedral of Paris.

Although the dark interior elevation of Notre-Dame had exerted little influence, and indeed was itself rebuilt in the thirteenth century, the western wall, in M. Aubert's phrase, had become the *type* of the Gothic façade. The façades of Reims and Amiens, and of countless other churches, developed from it; and although many possessed richer decoration, none was more beautiful or strong. The portals of Paris, too, had been copied and recopied, often to minute detail, as at Meaux. The transept façades, together with their spectacular roses, were also imitated, at Tours, Sens, and elsewhere. At Strasbourg, Master Erwin of Steinbach combined the western and transept façades of Paris in a striking tour de force, which culminated in the unique open tower that still dominates the Rhine. Spires modeled on the central spire of Paris lifted from the transepts of Bourges and Amiens, probing higher and higher, until the spire of Beauvais, the tallest of all, pierced the floor of Heaven at a height of five hundred and three feet (153 meters), against three hundred and twenty-five feet at Notre-Dame.

At its close, the Middle Age committed the deadly sin of pride. The spire of Beauvais, like the structure at Babel, perhaps was too ambitious. It crashed in 1573, one of the first medieval flèches to go. The others tumbled after, one by one, until the spire of Paris, the earliest of the great transept flèches of France, alone remained. Then, while the French Revolution battered the monument below, it too commenced to incline. Had the Chapter not wished to sell its lead covering, or had so capable an architect as Viollet-le-Duc been on hand, it might have been saved.

Not time, remarked Victor Hugo, but men have done most harm to Notre-Dame. The Cathedral suffered indignities long before the end of the Middle Age. With stalwart honesty the Parisians of the twelfth and thirteenth centuries had built the church outward from the altar of the Virgin; the Parisians of the fourteenth could do no more than work backward to Mary's shrine, decorating the monumental art of their fathers. On the northern wall of the apse, for example, the legend of the Assumption of the Virgin was again repeated: Mary flies elegantly to Heaven, enveloped in a long aureole and escorted by gracious angels, but the religious force of the sculpture, already reduced in the transept portals and in the Red Door, has here lost all relation with the powerful carvings of the western façade. The result is charming. It is a painting in stone. Yet, like a painting, it could be detached from the wall without damage to the basic structure.

Since what had been left them was beyond value, the men of the later Middle Age for a time lived on inherited artistic capital, only to realize, when the Huguenots stormed into Notre-Dame in 1548, that they had squandered it and were bankrupt. The first signs of catastrophe were evident about 1300, when the Chapter and Bishop Simon Matiffas de Buci, who still reclines on his tomb in the apse, decided to enclose the sanctuary with a wall of stone. Where tapestries had formerly provided sufficient privacy for the services, the priests installed a barrier they wished to be permanent. History proved that it was not. The carven screen, depicting the earthly lives of the Virgin and Christ, was broken through by the Protestants. It was further mutilated by the Catholic clergy and Bourbon kings of the seventeenth and eighteenth centuries. What remained, in the first three bays north and south of the choir, could not withhold the Revolutionaries in 1789. Today the sanctuary is again locked from the public, but with an open grill that will vanish at a gesture. And with it will disappear the present furnishings of Romantic bric-à-brac and Neo-Classic pomp. In their place, one must visualize the golden altars of the Middle Age and the jeweled treasures which surmounted them.

At the heart of the sanctuary was the master altar, covered with oriental cloths. The golden frontal offered by Maurice de Sully had been replaced, in 1335, by an altarpiece in gilded silver, of more elaborate design, depicting the Annunciation and Coronation of the Virgin, and also Saint Stephen and Saint Marcel. Among the vessels on the altar was a chalice of pure gold, trimmed with gems, which was purchased from the Cathedral of Cologne in 1216 for the equivalent of ten thousand dollars; the Paris Chapter outbid a score of French churches to obtain it. There was also a curious *Vierge ouvrante,* in ivory, whose white breast parted to reveal the Passion of the Redeemer. A glittering crucifix supported an angel who held the pyxis of the Host. Higher than the angel was a Virgin in golden vermeil, from whose hand hung the Holy Sash, the one which Mary had flung to doubting Thomas.

On pedestals to every side were gold and silver statues, encrusted with ruby and emerald cabochons, filled with souvenirs of Denis, Geneviève, Stephen, and other Patrons of the Cathedral. A golden bust of John the Baptist held the teeth of the Precursor; in its hands was a golden cylinder, which enveloped one of his long, meaningful fingers. A golden arm contained the arm of Saint Andrew. Within a crucifix studded with pearls and diamonds, sent to the Cathedral from Jerusalem in 1108, was a sizable portion of the True Cross. Nearby was the Nail of the Cross presented by Charlemagne. Other instruments of the Passion, donated by Saint Louis from the collection at the Sainte-Chapelle, were enclosed in a golden crown.

Any of these relics would have glorified a lesser church, but none compared with the shrine of Saint Marcel, directly behind the master altar. It rested on a platform fifteen feet high, held aloft by copper pillars, and sheltered by a gilded roof. Four angels, enameled wings outspread, were its guardians. The reliquary itself was a miniature church of beaten gold, complete with aisles, flying buttresses, and spire, which had been fashioned in the thirteenth century by the goldsmiths of Paris, who afterward were privileged to carry it in processions. Its tiny golden statuary related the life of the saint, and through the jeweled doors and crystal windows could be seen the remains of the patron who had rescued his city from the dragon. When this reliquary was transported to the Mint in 1792, its precious metal amounted to 436 marks, about three hundred pounds, Troy weight.

At the rear of the sanctuary, on a dais placed between the two central pillars of the apse, was the high altar of the Virgin. The Mother of God shared this shrine with no other saint, as she did the master altar. It was hers alone, jealously, femininely hers, and it could be shut off from the rest of the church by its blue curtains and canopy, adorned with golden fleurs-de-lis. When the heavy cloths were drawn, the shrine became, for Jean de Jaudan in 1323, "a room of Paradise." Close to the altar was another small golden cathedral, like Marcel's, which was the Virgin's major reliquary and contained, among other physical evidence of her beauty, tresses of blond hair, and a vial of her milk.

It was before the master altar, belonging to all the saints as well as the Virgin, that Count Raymond of Toulouse had surrendered to the French Church and the French Crown; but it was before Mary's high personal altar that the Capets had prayed for victory. Therefore this shrine, in the deepest recess of Notre-Dame, was guarded not only by angels but by Kings of France. On either side, their backs to the great pillars, Philip Augustus and Louis the Lion stood larger in stone than in life. They had been placed there by Saint Louis and Blanche of Castile, who had also strung their robes with colored pearls.

In this penumbra of blue and golden tapestries, before the burning candelabra of the Virgin's altar, a young Spaniard, Domingo de Guzmán—Saint Dominic—prayed passionately to Mary shortly after 1200, at the time Saint Francis was preaching to the birds at Assisi. In "a blinding flood of light," the image upon the altar came to life, as it did in the play for Théophile. The Virgin opened a Bible and gave Dominic the text of his sermon. Whereupon the founder of the Order which would cause an upheaval in the Church made his way back through the sanctuary, past the tombs of prelates and princes, including the gilded copper sarcophagus of Eudes de Sully, at the entrance of the choir, to address the people in the nave.

Turn, as Dominic did, from the eastern light of Jerusalem to the sunset of the western rose, at the end of the perspective of pointed arches; and imagine medieval Paris hurrying into the aisles, marching into the nave behind the banners of guilds, climbing to the tribunes, taking possession of its Cathedral.

Notre-Dame has been decked for a feast. For days carts have been arriving from the Cathedral fiefs on the south of Paris, such as l'Hay-les-Roses, which are still famous for their gardens, so that the church has been filled with blossoms and green plants. The pavements are strewn with sweet-smelling branches of evergreen. Vines cling to the pillars; and the carven flowers of the capitals have been hung with living flowers—for this is the Sunday of Pentecost.

Through the Portail Rouge on the north of the choir, beneath the kneeling figures of Saint Louis and Marguerite of Provence, marches the Chapter, preceded by the singing boys, then clerks and priests, canons and deacons, in hierarchal order, the dignitaries coming last: the dean, the precentor and the chancellor, and the lordly arch-deacons of the Brie, the Josas, and Paris, one of whom will be the celebrant. He is gowned in a chasuble of crimson velvet, embroidered with golden animals, the oldest vestment of the Cathedral, dating from the ninth century.

On the south, attended by his train in his personal portal, the bishop waits in golden cloak and miter. And as the crowd of ten thousand, filling every inch of available space, cramming the nave and the aisles and the transept, and the galleries overhead, falls to its knees and is silent, the Mass begins. Emile Mâle is the com-mentator:

The grave and sorrowful chant of the *Introit* opens the ceremony: it expresses the waiting of the patriarchs and prophets. The choir of clerks is the choir of saints of the Old Testament, who yearn for the coming of the Messiah they are never to see. Then the bishop enters, and he appears as the living figure of Jesus Christ . . . before him are carried seven torches to signify that, according to the Prophet, the seven blessings of the Holy Ghost have descended on the head of the Son of God. He ad-vances beneath a triumphal dais whose four bearers [symbolize] the Evangelists. Two acolytes walk to his right and left, representing Moses and Elias who appeared beside Jesus Christ on Mount Tabor. . . .

Throughout the first portion of the service the bishop sits silent on his throne, as a reminder that the first years of Christ were passed in meditation and obscurity. But the subdeacon who faces the blue northern rose of the Old Testament, and reads the Epistle in a strong voice, is John the Baptist crying in the wilderness. After he has spoken he bows before the bishop as John humbled himself before the Savior. The chanting of the Gradual follows, and then the cele-brant at last approaches the eagle-lectern, turns to the reddish fire of the southern rose, and reads the Evangel:

This is a solemn moment, for here begins the active life of the Messiah: his voice is heard for the first time in the world. . . .

The *Credo* follows the Evangel as faith follows the revelation of truth. . . . When the *Credo* is ended, the bishop rises and speaks to the people. In choosing this moment, the Church has wished to remind them of the miracle of its establishment. It desires to show them how truth, at first given only to the apostles, spread through the entire earth in an instant.

And the fiery Spirit descends in the nave! Flaming pieces of tow have been tossed through openings in the vaults by clerks in the roof, the brands burning themselves out in the long drop to the floor of the church. Then, in the fire and smoke, hundreds of white doves are released from above to soar over the chanting multitude.

Gloria! The bells of the towers are tolling through the Cathedral. The miracle of the sacrifice, of the bread and the wine, is only part of the larger mystery of the Church itself. The true miracle, exclaimed Saint Augustine, was that so many believed the miracle. It was the validity of the ideal, rather than its mystical foundation, which mattered in the end. Thousands of mysteries were loose in the world when the Asian Savior walked on the tawny earth of Palestine. There was only one Church. The Church was the Cathedral, which was Mary. It was a persuasion of colored light, converging on the snowy figure of the Virgin in the transept.

Notre-Dame is her Cathedral. It is suffused with her vitality and love. It is her personal shrine as the Parthenon was Athena's. Its restless confidence is the Virgin's restless confidence for humanity. In the great moment of the Middle Age, Mary lifted and civilized the entire Western world. In an era of continual male brutality, her emblem, the rose, became the sign of the less brutal woman; and as long as the West responded fervently to her, she made it lovely. A new stage of beauty, she proved in the Romanesque, the Transition, and the Gothic, lies always beyond the stage of beauty just achieved, idealism beyond idealism, god beyond goddess; a strange proof, perhaps, for life beyond life. And so the Cathedral is never in repose but is perfectly equilibrated. When most calm, it lifts, and lifts again, in a further serenity. Balance equals tension. Beauty equals power. The Virgin is at work.

The goddess was every goddess: Artemis and Aphrodite, Pallas and Demeter; as Cybele, she governed the Fête des Fous. Assisting here were all the ancient immortals. In the end, one hundred and fifty saints were given altars in Notre-Dame. Choose the patron you wish—their Christian names are beautiful: Catherine, Patron of Intelligence; Valentine, Patron of Lovers; Nicholas, Patron of Children; Vincent, whom a *jeu de mot* made Patron of Wine, as another pun made Claire the Patron of Stained Glass; those funny old shoemakers, Crispin and Crispianus, Patrons of Humble Toil; Thaïs,

Patron of Courtesans; Eustache, Patron of the Hunt; George and Theodore, Patrons of Chivalry; Barbara, Patron of Fire; Anthony, Patron of Madmen; and Julian, the Hospitable.

With these universal protectors of mankind were the Patrons of France. Notre-Dame is the true French Panthéon. Here the national divinities loomed above their lighted altars: the Apostle Philip, who preached Christ among the Gauls, and Denis, who brought the Church to them; Martin, who drove the Enemy to the depths of the forest; Marcel, who compelled the Fiend to wag his tail; Geneviève, whose prayers sent the Huns veering to the Alps; Rémi, the confessor of Clovis; Germain, teacher of faith; Landry, the founder of a public hospital in Paris; Bernard, who exhorted the nation to be worthy of itself; Becket, the Anglo-Norman who threw down the Plantagenets in their pride and saved the Capets; and finally, the king who, contrary to the tradition promulgated by Augustine, was not descended from Cain but from Abel: Saint Louis.

In the Church calendar the saints were responsible for each day of the year. If barley was planted on April 23, Saint George looked after the crop; by the 25th it was too late—Saint Mark was indifferent:

> A la Saint-Georges
> Sème ton orge;
> A la Saint-Marc
> Il est trop tard.

The jingle was as reliable as an almanac, and much more practical if one could not read. As a reminder it was easy to cut a sign on the bark of a tree: an arrow for Sebastian, a key for Peter, a sword for Paul. Overhead, at night, the Milky Way was the Way of Saint James. Phosphorescent light at sea, the experienced mariner knew, was Saint Elmo's fire.

The natural world was ordered and explicable; all depended on an empiric arithmetic. There were risks, as there were risks in building a tall church or assaulting Jerusalem. Frequently there were disasters. But usually the saints could be relied upon. If one of them was remiss, the people felt free to punish him, as the citizens of suburban Villeneuve-Saint-Georges dunked their patron in the Seine when he allowed frost to harm their vines.

In most cases, however, the saints acted quickly and effectively.

They emerged from their temples whenever they were needed, which was often. Because of heavy rains and flooding of the Seine in 1206, 1236, 1240, 1290, and 1303, and because of the plague in 1230, the shrine of Saint Geneviève was carried from the Left Bank abbey to the Cathedral, round and round the parvis, the populace marching with the priests, since, as Lewis Mumford noted, there were more participants than spectators in medieval demonstrations. When exceptional danger threatened, all the saints issued from the churches. In 1191, when the crown prince, later Louis VIII, lay ill, the monks of Saint-Denis came from the north with the skeleton of the Patron of France, the arm of Saint Sylvester, and other treasured relics; from the south, the monks of Saint-Germain-des-Prés and Sainte-Geneviève with their sacred shrines; and from the Cathedral, Maurice de Sully, followed by his clerks and canons, and an infinite multitude of students and ordinary people—*"infinita scholarium et populi concurrente multitudine"*—bearing the reliquaries of the Virgin, Saint Marcel, and the other divinities of Notre-Dame. The three processions met at the Palace, where Maurice led the way to the chamber of the prince, upon whom the Capet succession depended, and who was only four years old. Philip Augustus was away on Crusade; the child's mother, Isabelle de Hainault, had been buried the year before at the altar of Notre-Dame. The peril was extreme, but the aged Bishop calmly made the Sign of the Cross above the inflamed abdomen with each of the relics. Louis was cured that day.

Although the miracle resounded through Christendom, Maurice was never canonized. His contemporaries seemed almost wistfully to regret the Church's oversight. Many documents refer to "the blessed Maurice" as if he had joined the confessors. The Middle Age remained grateful to the Bishop long after his death. He was venerated as long as the beauty of the Cathedral was venerated, until about 1500; and his sermons, which might be thought old-fashioned for the age of Erasmus, were collected in one of the first editions issued by the printing house at Mainz. Today the sermons are unknown except to antiquarians, and the name of the Bishop himself is scarcely famous, even in France.

The nation has forgotten what once caused it to build: a willingness of the heart. The bright mosaic has shattered. Collective medieval art is claimed by priests as their achievement, by royalists as theirs, by populists in the name of the people en masse, each tugging at a limb of Ozymandias. The Middle Age did not see its art thus fragmented and isolated. It knew—and both its sacred and profane literature are suffused with the knowledge—that the cathedrals were the result of a common idealism, catalyzed by a small group of superior men, who were drawn from an infinite variety of backgrounds. They were not Plato's oligarchs, for their society was virtually as open as it was closed. It was flexible, and the medieval Church, concentrated about the Virgin, was the major source of flexibility. Luck played a part in the arrangement, granted; but it was more than luck which built Notre-Dame, and which has enabled it to survive. It was a planned organization of the community's potential to create. The plan was not perfect; nor was it, so far as art was concerned, dogmatic. It was human.

The proof is that its people were not much different from the human raw material of any society. They could not meet the present moral standards of Topeka—still less, perhaps, of Kiev. As for the conduct of the clergy, the Church prefers silence; Maurice de Sully, with the help of the Roman Curia, had trouble disciplining his concubinary priests. No medieval man—neither Maurice nor Saint Louis nor Suger nor Abélard—was perfect. The Virgin was.

Yet too often, as Joinville took care to inform posterity, the medieval man forgot his stake in Mary. The enchanted multitude, as it emerged from the unifying Cathedral, broke quickly into a multiplicity of emotions and talents and interests, into unequal capabilities and social rank, into refinement and brutality. The Church might follow the people into the violent streets, as it did with the dragon of Saint Marcel, which coiled through the Cité during Rogation and gobbled coins in its paper jaws; but in the very shadow of the façade the medieval man had fun according to his taste, which, as in modern France, often ran to lust and gluttony. On the last day of Lent the gastronomic *Foire aux Jambons*—the Ham Fair—was staged by the pork shops on the parvis. Those who could pay ate hoggishly and drank. By evening the party was sure to grow rough; the next day there would be a waiting list for the justice ladder or the oubliettes of the episcopal prison. The proletarian drunk, like the drunken peasant and the drunken river bargeman, has never been known for delicacy. At worst he was boorish and cruel. Sometimes, like illiterates on the American frontier, he fought savagely, gouged his opponent's eyes, tore off his ears, or killed him.

Nor was the medieval man above stealing from his Church. On the eve of the Feast of the Assumption in 1218, fire broke out in the choir. A thief of British origin (*"Anglicus natione"*) had concealed himself for several days in the roofing of the tribunes; and when the Cathedral's treasure was put on display for the fête of the Virgin, he tried to hook a valuable chandelier. The burning candles ignited a tapestry, and soon Notre-Dame was blazing.

The fire caused no permanent damage, but the thief's conscience may have been heavy a day or two later when he received his punishment before the sculptures of the façade, with their monumental theme of Vice and Virtue, their justification of honest toil in the laboring Months of the year, their promise of everlasting torment for evil, and eternal blessedness for good. From the naked figures of Adam and Eve far overhead, to the story of their fall, beneath the feet of the Virgin on the pier of the northern portal, the Church repeated the lesson: in this world man must live by the sweat of his brow. In a noteworthy sermon Maurice de Sully added that this included loyalty and obedience to one's lord, from the bottom of the feudal order—the serf—to the top, which was not the Capet king but God. *"Tu es mon serf, e jo ton sire,"* the Father admonished disobedient Adam in a mystery play—"thou art my serf, and I thy Lord." A man placed his hands between his lord's hands and hoped for the best.

With the sculpture dramatized in this way, with Adam or Théophile on the stage before him, the common spectator must have grasped some of the Cathedral's refinements. He had the advantage, which the modern tourist does not, of living from birth among the stone symbols of his religion: the Church Victorious and the Synagogue Defeated were queens he had seen more often than Blanche of Castile. Environment taught him much, but it could trick him as well—into such gross errors as his mistaking the Kings of Judah for the royal line of France. For the villein was a creature of his imperfect society. A "baboon," a satirist called him in 1284—*"li vilains babuins"*—a monkey-faced yokel standing before Notre-Dame, who "looks at the kings and says: 'See Pepin! See Charlemagne!' while his purse is cut from behind."

No one thought the mistake serious, although earnest clerks did their best to correct it. Church and State, villein and lord, priest and soldier, merchant and thief, architect and poet, were too meshed in the vivid fabric of society to be troubled by naïve inconsistencies in detail. But in the next hundred years the tapestry began to unravel. In three hundred years it was torn by wars of religion, ripped to shreds on Saint Bartholomew's Day. After five hundred years the last threads had separated forever. The Schoolman was replaced by the Encyclopedist; the King, rather than Saint Louis, was Louis XVI; the foremost French architect was Soufflot, the mutilator of Notre-Dame. All had changed, but nothing more than the common multitude. It had become a mob—simple, childish, boorish, cruel, yet no more cruel than the regime which starved and whipped and kept it illiterate; no more barbarous than the clerical vandals who had destroyed the stained glass of Notre-Dame, whitewashed the walls, replaced the medieval pavements, and, to crown the indignities, dismantled the medieval sanctuary, melted down the medieval altarpiece for money, and substituted a mass of marble and a Virgin who wailed like an actress at the Comédie above the corpse of her Son.

In 1793 the mob put ladders to the church. Nooses were attached to the necks of the twenty-eight kings; and then the crowd pulled them down, one by one, sixty feet to the parvis below, roaring as each statue fell. And with another cry the people rushed to decapitate each crowned image, and cut off its hands and feet, and throw the broken torso in the Seine.

What happened in the time of Louis XVI began five centuries earlier, in the reigns of Philip III and Philip IV, a strange son and stranger grandson for a king who had mounted to Heaven. Philip III—the Bold—Dante assigned to Purgatory; for Philip IV—the Fair—he contemptuously reserved a place in Hell, together with Pope Boniface VIII. Although Dante saw Philip IV lucidly, as "a second Pilate" and also as a sadistic political giant caressing a harlot Church, the King's outlines are vague. "He is neither man nor beast," was one description of his handsomeness, "but a statue." Perhaps his wicked chancellors, Flotte and Nogaret, truly dominated him; perhaps he insidiously used them as a front. They had several qualities in common: ruthlessness, cruelty, ill breeding, avarice.

For the first time financial transactions moved to the forefront of history. Capitalism was not created overnight in France; a bourgeois ethic had long been forming beneath the feudal economy—bills of exchange, for example, issued by Italian bankers, were current in France in 1200. But the triumph of the capitalist class was as sudden as the triumph of nationalism, and followed it by only three generations. It also coincided with the end of monumental art, and the transformation of builders into decorators.

Money tells the story best. No sovereign had been more honorable in financial dealings than Saint Louis; his currency was the best trusted in Europe. His silver mark yielded 2 livres 15 sous 6 deniers. His grandson, in 1306, debased the mark to 8 livres 10 sous—a devaluation of three hundred per cent. France immediately felt its effect. The speculators made a killing; the King filled his treasury for his economic war with the Flemish merchant cities; the proletariat saw its purchasing power vanish. The hardship of the working people was such that, in spite of Philip's methods of repression, they rose up armed in the streets of Paris and destroyed the house of the master of the mint. For a moment the King and his parvenu court were afraid to venture from the donjon of the Temple.

Midas had been trapped in his bank. If there was any building in Paris more cordially detested than the Louvre, it was the Temple. The Knights Templar, the warrior monks whose Order was founded in the twelfth century to protect pilgrims in the East, and to garrison the Crusader castles, had undergone a singular change in two hundred years. They still wore scarlet crosses on their white surcoats, but they were scarcely the mystical corps of chivalry which had suffered twenty thousand casualties in Asia Minor. They had been driven out by the Saracens, and now their headquarters was Paris, where the Temple was a walled city of sixty thousand square meters on the Right Bank, exclusively given to finance. In the fourteenth century, when the city was a fraction of its present size, the value of this real estate may be imagined. In addition to their banking operations and land speculation, the Templars were businessmen; they were rumored to have caused a famine by manipulation of the grain market; they traded in textiles; their castle in Paris was more sumptuous than the Palace of the King, and stocked with delicacies and wines. To drink like a Templar is a common saying in France.

The Temple was too rich a prize for Philip to resist; and with the aid of the Inquisition it soon was his. The Templars were notorious skeptics; years of sharp dealing and contact with a Mohammedan civilization had affected them strongly. In 1307 they were declared heretics. They were ambushed, surrounded, herded into dungeons, and put to the question. An unknown number did not survive the interrogations; the others were starved for months in solitary confinement. In the end almost all confessed to heresy, idolatry, blasphemy, sodomy, and a variety of unnatural practices.

Once removed from prison and placed before a Church court they believed impartial, the Templars denied everything. They cried out their innocence in tears and described their tortures. They commended themselves to the Virgin, to whom the altars of their circular chapels were consecrated. The chief judge, the Archbishop of Sens, was one of Philip's men: the King obtained his appointment precisely for this trial. He immediately condemned as relapsed heretics the fifty-nine knights who were under his jurisdiction in the Ile de France. In an enclosure of the faubourg Saint-Antoine, outside the walls on the Right Bank, they were burned at the stake. All died protesting their innocence and shouting devotion to Mary.

This was in 1310; in the next three years the lands and moneys of the Temple were gradually confiscated. But the Grand Master of the Order, Jacques de Molay, and the Preceptor of the Temple in Normandy, Geoffroy de Charnai, who had made full confessions, were still alive. On March 18, 1314, they were led to a high scaffolding in front of Notre-Dame, and there, before the populace, were sentenced "to know the wall"—life imprisonment. The Templars, who had been confined for seven years and had been promised liberty for their cooperation, shouted out: "We are innocent of the crimes of which we are accused, but we are guilty of basely betraying the Order to save our lives. The Order is pure, it is holy. The accusations are absurd, the confessions are lies!"

The crowd stirred. The cardinals present instantly turned the prisoners over to the Provost of Paris. King Philip was informed, and that evening, on a little island which has since been consolidated with the Ile-de-la-Cité, the garden below the statue of Henri IV, the Templars were burned to death. They died "with hearts so resolute and staunch . . . that they left the witnesses in admiration."

Few periods in history are more sad, more cruel, than the breakup of medieval civilization. As the years advance, the decline is revealed pitilessly in later medieval portraits of the Virgin. In the Portal of Saint Anne, the Visitation of the year 1165 was a tall embrace of goddesses; the Visitation of the choir screen, after 1300, shows a wealthy Parisian housewife paying a social call to another, who places a hand on her swollen breast to determine if she is pregnant. The scene is nearer to the Ecole de Fontainebleau, and the painting of Gabrielle d'Estrées and her sister in the Louvre, than to the Virgin in Majesty.

The Virgin aged visibly as the Hundred Years' War swept over France and the Capet Dynasty disintegrated. Her thigh curved in a baroque gesture, as in the fourteenth-century statue called "Notre Dame de Paris" which stands in the transept. From 1300 on Mary grew stylishly thin and, to compensate for loss of youthful freshness, resorted to elegance. Her gown was arranged to enhance her figure and trimmed with Flemish lace. Her hair was combed by the most expensive coiffeur of the Rive Droite. There were lines at her eyes and mouth, and she began to regard her Child with a trace of misgiving, as if to hold a baby were odd, so late in life.

Money, as the fifteenth century began, could buy anything, except beauty, strength, and happiness. The Virgin was desperately striving to give an impression of youth, without success. Her jongléors and trouvères had died—Rutebeuf had been one of the last—and in their place, before the portals of Notre-Dame, blind men sang plaintively for alms. A race of palace poets had developed, long-winded and pretentious; and palace painters, such as Pol de Limbourg, who worked for the Duc de Berri, Jacques Coeur, and other plutocràtic patrons, producing miniatures in the latest taste.

"Mais où sont les neiges d'antan?" cried François Villon after 1450. Where, where were the lovely ladies, the fresh young roses, the snows of yesteryear? Villon, the first of modern poets, was also the last great poet of the Middle Age. And for all the boisterous life that surges through his songs, he is a poet of death. *"Quiconques meurt, meurt à douleur"*—incessantly the theme recurs in his work—"Whoever dies, dies in pain." François himself had taken life in the brutal Paris of the fifteenth century. He had killed a libidinous priest in self-defense, fighting over a girl. He had also committed

a notable theft, stealing from the hoard of the Faculty of Theology. He was hounded by the police, jailed regularly, almost hanged, exiled from Paris.

Only rarely, in moments of remorse, did François come to church. He preferred the tavern of the Pomme de Pin, in the old Jewry, just off the parvis of the Cathedral. Yet his aged mother, weeping like Rachel for her lost child, knew that one hope remained in a Paris which had ceased to hope or to build. She made her way through the dangerous streets to Notre-Dame, shivering in her ragged clothes, *"povrette et ancienne, qui riens ne sçay"*—old and poor, knowing nothing—indistinguishable from a charwoman of the Fourth Republic. In the Cathedral she fell to her knees before the figure of Mary and repeated a prayer which her son had composed for her alone. "Lady of Heaven," she implored, "Regent of the Earth, Empress of Valleys Infernal, receive me, your humble Christian. . . . To your Son say that I am His, that by Him my sins may be ended; pardon me as Mary the Egyptian; or as He did for the clerk Théophile, who through you was forgiven and absolved":

> Dame du ciel, regent terrienne,
> Emperiere des infernaux palus,
> Recevez moy, vostre humble chrestienne. . . .
>
> A vostre Filz dictes que je suis sienne;
> De luy soyent mes pechiez abolus;
> Pardonne moy comme a l'Egipcienne,
> Ou comme il feist au clerc Theophilus,
> Lequel par vous fut quitte et absolus. . . .

One prayed to the "haulte Déesse," as one erected a Saint Christopher thirty feet high at the entrance of the nave, in 1413, near the great basket for abandoned babies, to ward against violent death and suffering. In the lifetime of the Villons, mother and son, Paris had been besieged, sacked, overrun by English and Burgundians, and, thanks to Saint Joan, retaken by the French. Famine was usual. At one point wolves entered the city and carried off infants. The year before François was born, on December 16, 1430, Henry VI of England was anointed and crowned King of France in Notre-Dame. The only other coronation in the Cathedral was Bonaparte's, who seized the crown from the Pope and himself placed it on his head (as he does in the David picture), December 2, 1804. Between these bizarre ceremonies the story of Notre-Dame is one of survival. During four full centuries of neglect, vaults cracked and roses split open; but the church held.

Step by step, in its *danse macabre,* the Middle Age perished. Beware of the dance—it is hypnotic as a Dürer. In the end, like Shakespeare's Richard, Europe became infatuated with graves and epitaphs. The ogive contorted in a Gothic baroque as at Saint-Séverin. Sculpture writhed as painfully as Bernini's ever would. Funerary projects enjoyed greater vogue than under the Merovingians. In a chapel of the nave of Notre-Dame, the stone of the Canon Yver, dead in 1468, shows with what glee the fifteenth century looked to the tomb: the body is shown in decomposition, nibbled by worms. This is the death-crazed Paris that Gargantua pished away.

In the arts, the invention of the printing press achieved mercifully what the discovery of gunpowder effected with violence in a new-style warfare. One by one the artistic strongholds of the Middle Age—the storied portal and the *Golden Legend* among them—surrendered to the books of the humanists. In architecture, the ogive lingered for a time in the Renaissance, after 1517 at Saint-Etienne-du-Mont; but soon domes began to rise among the Gothic spires: the chapel of the new Sorbonne in 1635, the Val-de-Grâce a decade later, the Invalides in 1670. The interior of Notre-Dame, at the turn of the eighteenth century, was itself made to look like a Neo-Classic structure. Louis XIII and Louis XIV supplanted Philip Augustus and Louis the Lion as guardians of the altar of the Virgin; and although these absolute monarchs were temporarily removed during the Revolution, they are back in the sanctuary today, beside an altar of their taste, still asserting privilege. The Cathedral bears the wound calmly, as it bears all its others. With time, most of the scars have healed over.

On occasion the Cathedral's misfortunes took surprisingly cheerful turns. On the 20th Brumaire of the year II of the Republic—November 10, 1793—after the last statues had been removed from the portals and the church stood edentate and profaned, although the bas-reliefs were spared because of supposed astronomical significance, a new goddess was enthroned in what was now the "Temple of Reason." A Rousseauistic stage set, transported from the Opéra, was erected at the croisée of the transept. Its centerpiece was a mountain at whose crest was perched a classical fane of Philosophy. From this sanctuary emerged a young actress, Mademoiselle Aubry, clad in a long white robe and blue mantle, wearing the red Phrygian bonnet and armed with the spear of Knowledge. Attending her was the corps de ballet, robed in white. Incense burned on a rose-covered altar. *"Toi, Sainte Liberté, viens habiter ce temple, sois la déesse des Français,"* chanted the multitude in the nave—"Thou, Holy Liberty, come dwell in this temple, be the goddess of the French."

The ceremony aroused such enthusiasm that, almost immediately, 2,345 other churches were transformed into Temples of Reason. In May 1794, however, only five months later, the inscription on the façade of Notre-Dame was changed to read: "The French people recognize the Supreme Being and the immortality of the Soul"; the Temple de la Raison had become the Temple de l'Etre Suprême. By the next year the "constitutional clergy" were conducting services very like the Mass at an altar in the northern transept, while other cults, such as that of the Theophilanthropes, were practiced elsewhere in the church. On July 15, 1801, Bonaparte concluded a concordat with Pius VII, and Notre-Dame was again Roman Catholic.

Periodically, throughout the nineteenth century, the priests were chased out and readmitted to the sanctuary, the last expulsion taking place under the Commune. On May 26, 1871, chairs—a modern convenience medieval worshipers had done without—were stacked in the choir and set aflame. The fire was extinguished by the interns of the Hôtel-Dieu, who broke in the doors which the communards had locked, and saved the monument.

Notre-Dame has resisted all, including the German bomb that pierced its roof during the First World War. It withstood the Nazis, who marched onto the parvis in 1940. It merely rose upward before them, a serene and massive lesson in history, unconquerable and silent, profiling the soul of its city.

In medieval documents Notre-Dame was properly called the *"sacrosancta ecclesia Parisiensis,"* the most holy church of the people of Paris. Its voice is the ponderous note of the bell Emmanuel, dispatching its music far downriver, as in August 1944, when the tanks of Leclerc drove straight to the parvis, and his victorious troops rushed up the turning stair of the tower, to set the enormous clapper in motion. And as Emmanuel rang out, the lost bells of the Cathedral added their bronze and silver music, joking with Gargantua, shaking the brawny shoulders of Quasimodo. Guillaume began to ring, and Gabriel, and Pugnese and Pasquier, and Chambellan and Thibaut. And Nicholas, the little sparrow, joined the chimes, and Jean, his heavy brother, and the ladies Marie and Jacqueline, Catherine and Anne, and Barbara, the bell of lightning. And beneath them all, at the base of the scale, sounded the great bell Emmanuel, which has endured.

And among the bells, on the high open terrace between the towers, where the sky is alive with birds, and sunlight revels on golden stone, and the gargoyles stretch their long necks outward, could be heard the laughter of the Virgin, singing to her city and her nation, to all the world, that mankind is again in a Romanesque, approaching a Gothic phase, and that of all the gods emerging from the Dark Age sleep, the Goddess of Idealism will command the most lovely cathedrals. For the gods are again on earth, claiming collective imagination and achievement: in the hydroelectric dam spanning the Tennessee Valley, or the valley in India; in the hospital in Sweden, and the university in Brazil. And the laughter of the Virgin sings through the vaults and arches of Notre-Dame, saying that the Cathedral itself is become a god and needs no others; and Notre-Dame rules its ancient city proudly, looking downward on towers and domes, as Paris is silent to the limits of the smoky industrial horizon; and the Virgin sings from beneath the Cathedral, church beneath church, temple below temple, to the first fragile shrine of wood, whose Builder meant it to please.

illustrations

NOTRE-DAME AND THE ILE-DE-LA-CITÉ, seen from above the Left Bank. At nearer end of island, the Sainte-Chapelle rises above the Palais de Justice, on site of Capetian palace. Medieval Paris occupied most of the area visible. Saint-Germain-des-Prés (*lower right*) stood beyond a wall which met the river near dome of the Institut (*lower left*). (*Greff*)

THE WESTERN FAÇADE: The classic Gothic of first half of the 13 c. Portal of the Virgin is at left; Portal of the Last Judgment, center; Portal of Saint Anne, right. (*Joly*)

THE CENTRAL VESSEL, seen from the height of the western rose. (*Sougez-Tel*)

IV

DRUID GAUL: Esus, woodsman god (*below*): altar found beneath choir of Notre-Dame, now at Cluny Museum. (*Arch. Phot.*)

ROMAN GAUL: The Maison Carrée at Nîmes (*above*); and Pont du Gard (*below*). (*Syn. d'Init.; Bellon*)

MEROVINGIAN GAUL: Baptistery of Saint-Jean at Poitiers, 7 c. (*top*); and its apsidal chapel. Marble pillars are Roman. (*Arch. Phot.*)

V

THE FIRST ROMANESQUE: Saint-Germain-des-Prés (*directly above*), oldest standing church of Paris, marks the close of the Dark Age. Its fortress-like tower, except for the belfry and spire added in the 12 c., dates from shortly after 1000. This impressive monument soon was overshadowed by experimental Norman churches, such as the Trinité of Caen (*at top*), begun in 1064. The groin vaults of its choir are among the earliest to cover a vessel this size, before 1100. Norman precocity shows also in the ogival vaults of the nave, which replaced a wooden roof early in the 12 c. (*Marcel; Roubier*)

MAURICE DE SULLY'S HOMELAND: The Romanesque in full development at Saint-Benoît-sur-Loire. Although its flanking spires have been lost, the apse (*right*) appears much as in the 12 c.; the interior (*above*) is typical of an abbey church: the vessel rising in stages to the sanctuary, consecrated in 1108. (*Sauvageot; Bandy*)

THE FORTRESS AT SULLY: The Loire passing the present château, built in the 14 c. (*Sauvageot*)

THE TRANSITION: The new architecture of the Ile de France in second quarter of the 12 c. is displayed by the spire of Etampes (*left*) and by Suger's façade at Saint-Denis (*top right*). Suger's own portrait (*bottom right*) appears in the stained glass of his Chapel of the Virgin. (*Arch. Phot.; Bulloz; Giraudon*)

TRANSITIONAL INTERIORS: Sens (*upper left*), a 3-level church, rests on massive arcades. Noyon (*upper right*) and Laon (*below, two views*) have 4 levels, including the intermediate tribune. Although the same height, Laon seems taller than Sens, and terminates in a great 13-c. rose. (*Bulloz; Roubier*)

CHARTRES: The Cathedral, largely 13 c., dominates the city (*above*). The façade (*top right*),
with its superb old tower at right, is middle 12 c.;
the rose was added in 1200, the northern spire
in 1507. The portals date from 1145, and their
sculptures, such as the Shepherds (*top left*) and
the statue-columns (*lower left*) influenced similar
carvings in the Portal of Saint Anne at Paris two
decades later. (*Roubier; Arch. Phot.; Dreux*)

LATE ROMANESQUE: Well after 1100, the Romanesque could still produce Vézelay (*left*), and at the end of the 12 c., the sculptures of Arles (*below*). (*Bulloz; Yan*)

THE SCHOOLMEN: From the *Miroir de l'Humilité*, MS. from the workshop of Guillaume Vrelant d'Utrecht, c. 1450, now in the Bibliothèque Municipale, Valenciennes. (*Joly*)

THE FOUNDERS OF NOTRE-DAME: The Virgin in Majesty rules the Portal of Saint Anne. At left, beyond the angel, are Maurice de Sully and Barbedor; at right kneels Louis VII. (*Joly*)

THE CATHEDRAL AND EPISCOPAL PALACE, at end of the 17 c., by Israel Sylvestre. The fortified residence of Maurice de Sully, surmounted by its donjon, is at center; beyond is the Hôtel-Dieu. (*Joly*)

THE NAVE: The great pilasters at far right introduce the work of the Second Master, after 1180. The first bay shows 12-c. fenestration, replaced in the 13 c. by the clerestory seen in other bays. (*Giraudon*)

THE AISLES OF THE NAVE: The alternating colonnade. The tribune which it supports is shown in Plate XVI. (*Arch. Phot.*)

THE SEARCH FOR LIGHT: The open structure of the tribune of the nave. (*Arch. Phot.*)

THE NORMAN FAÇADE: Saint-Etienne of Caen, begun in 1064, and completed by 1100 up to the birth of the spires, which were added at the end of the 12 c. (*Arch. Phot.*)

THE FRENCH-NORMAN BORDER: Mantes (*right and below*), begun before 1200. The upper gallery and towers are totally restored, and the decoration of the southern portal dates from the early 14 c. Ruins of Château-Gaillard (*lower right*) recall the French-Norman Wars. (*Arch. Phot.; Goursat; Petit*)

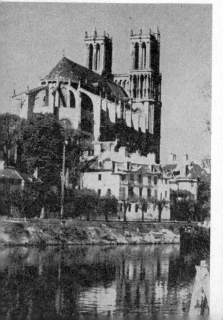

FRANCE AND NORMANDY: The same spare, militant Norman temper unites the Trinité of Caen (*upper left*), built in the last third of the 11 c., and Coutances (*upper right*), which dates from the first third of the 13 c. Contemporary with Coutances is the French eloquence of Laon (*lower left*). The later French façade of Amiens (*lower right*) shows the influence of Laon and Paris. (*Roubier; Arch. Phot.*)

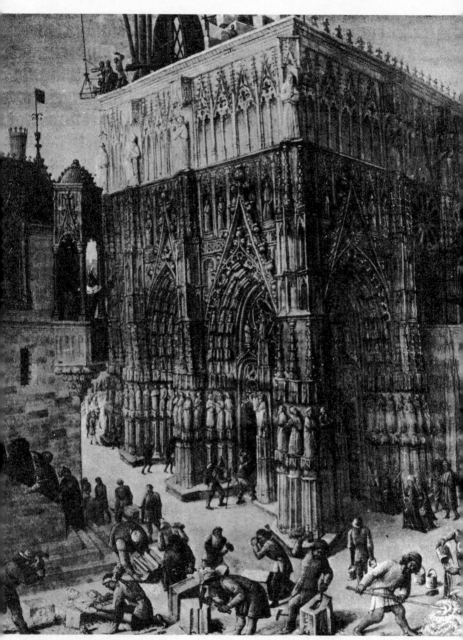

A LATE GOTHIC FAÇADE UNDER CONSTRUCTION: "The Building of the Temple of Jerusalem," miniature by Jean Fouquet, d. 1480. In the foreground are sculptors, stonecutters, masons, and other workmen. A medieval derrick, powered by a wheel, is visible at top. From a balcony of his palace a French king, representing Solomon, supervises the work with the master builder. (*Giraudon*)

THE VIRGIN IN MAJESTY: The central figure of the tympanum in the Portal of Saint Anne, c. 1165. (*Joly*)

THE PORTAL OF SAINT ANNE: The Virgin in Majesty presides over the drama of her mother's life. (*Joly*)

THE PORTAL OF THE VIRGIN: The full monumentality of 13-c. Gothic sculpture. (*Sougez-Tel*)

THE CORONATION OF MARY dominates the tympanum of the Portal of the Virgin. The frieze in the center depicts her resurrection during the vigil of the Apostles; Saint Peter (*see page facing*) is second from left. Below, three Old Testament Prophets and three Kings flank the Ark of the Covenant. (*Sougez-Tel*)

SAINT PETER (*detail from page facing*). From a cast taken before restoration. (*Giraudon*)

THE JUDGING CHRIST (*at top*) with details of Heaven and Hell from the voussoirs, Portal of the Last Judgment. (*Sougez-Tel*)

THE WESTERN ROSE: The Kings guard the immense halo of the Virgin. (*Ali-Giraudon*)

THE SOUTHERN TRANSEPT: The glass wall of the second half of the 13 c. (*Arch. Phot.*)

THE NORTHERN ROSE: The masterpiece of Jehan de Chelles. (*Joly*)

THE MIRACLE OF THÉOPHILE: Tympanum of north portal. The clerk kneels to Devil at left, and an imp gives him money. But later he repents, and Mary wrests from Satan the deed displayed by the bishop at top. (*Sougez-Tel*)

THE GIFT OF SAINT LOUIS: The Portail Rouge. The pious King and his Queen, Marguerite of Provence, kneel beside the Coronation of the Virgin. (*Joly*)

NOTRE-DAME COMPLETED: The apse, terminated in the first quarter of the 14 c. (*Arch. Phot.*)

Acknowledgment is made to the following photographers or suppliers of photographs, all in Paris unless otherwise indicated, for permission to reproduce the plates listed after their names.

Alinari–Giraudon: XIIIc, XXVIII; Archives Photographiques: Va, Vd, Ve, VIIIa, Xc, XV, XVI, XVII, XVIIIa, XIXb, XIXc, XXIX, XXXII; Ina Bandy: VIIb; Photo Denise Bellon: Vc; J. E. Bulloz, Editeur: VIIIb, IXa, XIa; Dreux–Tourisme: Xb, Xd; Giraudon: VIIIc, XIIIb, XIV, XX, XXV; Photo Goursat: XVIIIb; Editions Greff: II; Photographies "JM," Pierre Joly: III, XIc, XIIa, XIIb, XIIId, XXI, XXII, XXX, XXXIb; Photo Jean Marie Marcel: VIa; A. Petit–Tourisme: XVIIIc; Photo Jean Roubier: VIb, IXb, IXc, IXd, Xa, XIXa, XIXd; Sauvageot: VIIa, VIIc; Sougez–Editions "Tel": I, IV, XIIIa, XXIII, XXIV, XXVI, XXVII, XXXIa; Syndicat d'Initiative: Vb; Yan–J. Dieuzaide (Toulouse): XIb

Chronology

	CONSTRUCTION OF NOTRE-DAME	HISTORY OF THE CHURCH OF PARIS	HISTORY OF FRANCE	ARTISTIC AND ARCHITECTURAL DEVELOPMENTS	
1160	Decision taken to rebuild the Cathedral of Paris	Maurice de Sully succeeds Peter Lombard as Bishop of Paris	Louis VII weds his third queen, Alix of Champagne	Cathedrals of Laon, Noyon, Sens, and Senlis under construction, as well as western front of Chartres	1160
1163	Work begins on choir and apse. Cornerstone thought to have been laid by Pope Alexander III			New choir of Saint-Germain-des-Prés terminated. Chrétien writing at Troyes (latter half 12th century)	1163
1165	Portraits of Founders carved for Portal of Saint Anne		Birth of Philip II Augustus		1165
1168		Barbedor named Dean of Notre-Dame			1168
1179			Philip associated with the throne		1179
1180		Pierre le Chantre attacks magnificence of Notre-Dame	Death of Louis VII	Mantes begun (c. 1180–1190)	1180
1182	Master altar consecrated; choir completed. Nave and primitive transept begun				1182

Year	Notre-Dame construction	Church of Paris	General history
1185			Heraclius, Patriarch of Jerusalem, preaches Third Crusade in Notre-Dame
1187			Birth of Louis the Lion
1190			Philip Augustus and Richard Coeur-de-Lion on Third Crusade
1194			After fire destroys all but crypt and west front, reconstruction of Chartres begins
1196	Nave completed except for roofing	Death of Maurice de Sully	War between France and England until death of Richard in 1199
1197		Eudes de Sully 74th Bishop of Paris	
1200	Western façade undertaken	Episcopal palace sacked by royal sergeants during excommunication of Philip Augustus	Marriage of Blanche of Castile and Louis the Lion; Bourges begun c. 1200
1204		Fall of Château-Gaillard; taking of Constantinople	Mont-Saint-Michel burned; the Merveille endowed by Philip Augustus
1208	Sculptors surely working on portals	Death of Eudes de Sully. He is succeeded by Pierre de Nemours	

	CONSTRUCTION OF NOTRE-DAME	HISTORY OF THE CHURCH OF PARIS	HISTORY OF FRANCE	ARTISTIC AND ARCHITECTURAL DEVELOPMENTS	
1210				Reims begun	1210
1214			Battle of Bouvines		1214
1215		Inquisition founded	Birth of Saint Louis		1215
1219		Guillaume de Seignélai named Bishop of Paris			1219
1220	Façade completed to level of Gallery of Kings			Amiens begun	1220
1223			Death of Philip Augustus		1223
1224	Western rose completed, c. 1225	Bartholomew, Bishop of Paris		*Aucassin and Nicolette* (13th century)	1224
1226			Death of Louis the Lion; Queen Blanche assumes Regency; revolt of the nobility; Thibaut of Champagne aids Crown		1226
1228		Guillaume d'Auvergne, Bishop of Paris			1228
1230	Reconstruction of the nave and installation of present flying buttresses begun; Chapels inserted between exterior buttresses of nave			Pierre de Montreuil begins reconstruction of Saint-Denis	1230

1234		Marriage of Saint Louis and Marguerite of Provence			1234
1236	Guillaume de Lorris composes first part of the *Roman de la Rose*; songs of Thibaut de Champagne	Majority of Saint Louis		Work in progress on southern tower of façade	1236
1240				Southern tower finished; work continues on upper gallery and northern tower	1240
1243	Construction of Sainte Chapelle and of Beauvais begun				1243
1244		Saint Louis takes the Cross			1244
1245			Albertus Magnus and Thomas Aquinas at Paris	Northern tower probably finished	1245
1248	Sainte-Chapelle completed		Death of Guillaume d'Auvergne	First bell, "Guillaume," is cast	1248
1250	Rutebeuf writing in Paris	Disaster of Saint Louis' Crusade in Egypt	Renaud de Corbeil, Bishop of Paris	Reconstruction of nave finished; new transept façades undertaken by Master Jehan de Chelles: northern, c. 1250; southern, 1258	1250
1252		Death of Blanche of Castile			1252
1265	Saint-Denis reconstructed			Pierre de Montreuil replaces Jehan de Chelles as Master of Notre-Dame; builds Portail Rouge before his death	1265

Year	CONSTRUCTION OF NOTRE-DAME	HISTORY OF THE CHURCH OF PARIS	HISTORY OF FRANCE	ARTISTIC AND ARCHITECTURAL DEVELOPMENTS	Year
1267	Death of Pierre de Montreuil	Stephen, Bishop of Paris			1267
1270	Transept façades terminated. Chapels and flying buttresses added to choir		Death of Saint Louis at Tunis; Philip III the Bold, King of France	Central vessel of Amiens completed	1270
1284				Disaster at Beauvais	1284
1285			Philip IV the Fair, King of France		1285
1289		Simon Matiffas de Buçi, Bishop of Paris			1289
1292	Master Pierre de Chelles living in the Cité, near parvis; he directs the work as the reconstruction of the chancel makes the turn of the apse			Second half of the *Roman de la Rose* by Jean de Meun	1292
1295			Death of Marguerite of Provence		1295
1298		Saint Louis canonized. Central chapel of the apse of Notre-Dame consecrated to him			1298
1300	Start of the enclosure of the sanctuary with a carved screen. Bas-reliefs of northern side of the apse carved			Dante writing and Giotto painting	1300

1306	Philip IV debases French currency
1307	Philip IV suppresses the Temple
1307	Joinville begins his Life of Saint Louis, which he finishes in 1309
1314	Death of Philip IV
1317	Death of Joinville
1318	Jehan Ravi replaces Pierre de Chelles as Master of Notre-Dame; he decorates the exterior of the apse and continues the work on the choir screen
1351	Ravi's nephew, Jehan le Bouteiller, completes the screen

MAJOR RELATIONSHIPS AMONG THE CAPETS AND PLANTAGENETS

Only those names have been included that have some bearing on the text

ENGLAND, NORMANDY, ANJOU, and AQUITAINE   FRANCE

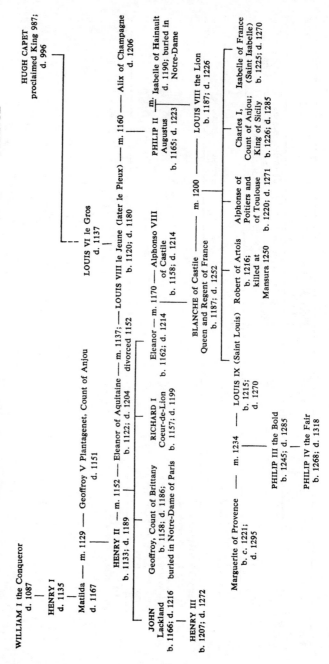

Books which may be consulted

The following does not pretend to be a complete bibliography of the literature which has concerned itself with the Cathedral of Paris. Comprehensive bibliographic references will be found, however, in the two books of M. Marcel Aubert which are basic to any study of the monument:

Notre-Dame de Paris, Notice Historique et Archéologique, new revised edition, Paris, 1950.

Notre-Dame de Paris, Sa Place dans l'Architecture du XIIe au XIVe Siècle, second edition, Paris, 1928.

A third work by M. Aubert, *Notre-Dame de Paris, Architecture et Sculpture*, Paris, 1928, provides a magnificent photographic documentation of the Cathedral.

I. HISTORICAL AND LITERARY

Abbo [Abbon]. *Le Siège de Paris par les Normands*. Original Latin text edited and translated into French by Henri Waquet, Paris, 1942.

Auzas, Pierre-Marie. *Les Grandes Heures de Notre-Dame de Paris*. Paris, 1951. A handsome book, illustrated with photographs by Pierre Joly, which presents the history of the Cathedral from the time of Maurice de Sully to the present.

Batiffol, (l'Abbé) Pierre. "L'Eglise Cathédral de Paris au VIe Siècle," in *The Journal of Theological Studies*, 1916, pp. 354-70. An excellent article on the Merovingian basilica.

Berger, Elie. *Histoire de Blanche de Castille, Reine de France*. Paris, 1895.

Boutaric, E. "Marguerite de Provence," in *La Revue des Questions Historiques*, Tome III, 1867.

Cartulaire de Notre-Dame de Paris, 4 vols. Paris, 1850. Published, with a valuable introduction, by Benjamin Guérard.

Corrozet, Gilles. *Les Antiquitez, Histoires et Singularitez de Paris*. Paris, 1550. An absolute delight.

Coulton, G. G. *The Medieval Village*. Cambridge, 1925. An impressive reply to Romantic theorizing on the Middle Age.

————. *Art and Reformation*. New York, 1928. See p. 338 ff. on the "Cult of the Carts."

Du Breul, Jacques. *Le Théâtre des Antiquités de Paris*. Paris, 1639.

Dupuis. *Origine de Tous les Cultes ou Religion Universelle*. Paris, 1792. Reveals the misunderstanding of the Cathedral and its sculptures which existed at the time of the Revolution.

Favre, E. *Eudes, Comte de Paris et Roi de France, 882-898*. Fundamental for the period of the Norman invasions.

Gilbert, A.-P.-M. *Description Historique de la Basilique Métropolitaine de Paris.* Paris, 1821. Useful for the condition of the monument before the restoration.

Gregory of Tours. *The History of the Franks.* English translation by O. M. Dalton. Oxford, 1927.

Guilhermy, F. de and Viollet-le-Duc. *Description de Notre-Dame, Cathédrale de Paris.* Paris, 1856. Contains many interesting details for the period of the restoration.

Halphen, Louis. *Paris sous les Premiers Capétiens.* Paris, 1909. A study of the city in the twelfth century. Maps.

Haskins, Charles Homer. *The Renaissance of the Twelfth Century.* Cambridge, Mass., 1927.

Hugo, Victor. *Notre-Dame de Paris.* Many inexpensive translations exist. This great Romantic appreciation of the Cathedral remains the best evocation of the medieval city that built it.

James of Voragio. *La Légende Dorée.* Translated into French by Téodore de Wyzema, Paris, 1929. An English translation of the *Golden Legend* exists in the Temple Classics.

Joinville, John, Lord of. *Histoire de Saint Louis.* The original text, accompanied by a translation into modern French by Natalis de Wailly, Paris, 1874. An inexpensive English translation by Sir Frank Marzials is published by Everyman's Library. See also H.-François Delaborde, *Jean de Joinville*, Paris, 1894.

Langlois, Ch.-V. *Saint Louis, Philippe le Bel, les Derniers Capétiens Directs (1226-1328).* Tome III, Part Two, of the monumental *Histoire de France* edited by Ernest Lavisse, Paris, 1911.

———. *La Vie en France au Moyen-Age,* 3 vols. Paris, 1927. The best book on the subject.

Lea, H. C. *A History of the Inquisition of the Middle Ages,* 3 vols. Philadelphia, 1888.

Lebeuf (l'Abbé). *Histoire de la Ville et de Tout le Diocèse de Paris,* 3 vols. Paris, 1863-1867.

Le Roux de Lincy (editor). *Paris et Ses Historiens.* Paris, 1867. Contains many fascinating texts, including Jean de Jaudan's fourteenth-century appreciation of Notre-Dame.

Luchaire, A. *Louis VII, Philippe Auguste, Louis VIII (1137-1226).* Tome III, Part One, of Lavisse's *Histoire de France.*

———. *Social France at the Time of Philip Augustus.* Translated by E. B. Krehbiel, London, 1912.

Maurice de Sully. *Sermons.* Avranches, 1858. See also the biography by Victor Mortet, *Maurice de Sully, Evêque de Paris (1160-1196),* Paris, 1890. This is an extract from the *Memoires de la Société de l'Histoire de Paris et de l'Ile de France,* Tome XVI, 1889, pp. 105-318.

Mumford, Lewis. *The Culture of Cities.* New York, 1938. Invaluable for an understanding of the medieval city and of what has happened to Paris since the Middle Age.

Pachtère, F.-G. de. *Paris à l'Époque Gallo-Romaine.* Paris, 1912. Although rather dated, this study contains much information concerning the foundation of the Church in Lutetia.

Petit-Dutaillis, Charles. *The Feudal Monarchy in France and England.* Translated by E. D. Hunt, London, 1936.

Pirenne, H., in collaboration with G. Cohen and H. Focillon. *La Civilisation en Occident du XIe au Milieu du XVe Siècle.* Paris, 1933.

Poëte, Marcel. *Une Vie de Cité: Paris de Sa Naissance à Nos Jours,* 4 vols. Paris, 1924-1931. See especially Vol. I, "La Jeunesse." A remarkable work of erudition and intelligence. Many maps.

Rohault de Fleury. *La Sainte Vierge,* Paris, 1878. The best anthology of the literature of the Cult of the Virgin.

Runciman, Steven. *A History of the Crusades,* 3 vols. Cambridge, 1951-1954.

Rutebeuf. *Le Miracle de Théophile.* Edited by Grace Frank. Second revised edition, Paris, 1949. See also the transposition in modern French by Gustave Cohen, Paris, 1948.

Suger. *Abbot Suger on the Abbey Church of St.-Denis and Its Art Treasures.* Edited, translated, and annotated by Erwin Panofsky, Princeton, 1946. A brilliant translation preceded by an equally admirable introduction.

Tawney, R. H. *Religion and the Rise of Capitalism.* Penguin Books. See especially Chapter I, "The Medieval Background."

Taylor, H. O. *The Medieval Mind,* 2 vols. Third edition, New York, 1920.

Thibaut of Champagne. *Les Chansons de Thibaut de Champagne, Roi de Navarre.* Edited by A. Wallensköld, Paris, 1925.

Vacanard, E. *La Vie de Saint Bernard.* Paris, 1910.

Valois, Noël. *Guillaume d'Auvergne, Evêque de Paris, 1228-1249.* Paris, 1880.

Villon, François. *Oeuvres.* Edited by A. Longon. Third edition, revised by L. Foulet, Paris, 1923. See also the study of Gaston Paris, *François Villon,* Paris, 1901.

Wallon, H. *Saint Louis et Son Temps.* Paris, 1875.

II. ARCHAEOLOGICAL

The fundamental work concerning the construction of Notre-Dame remains Viollet-le-Duc's *Dictionnaire Raisonné de l'Architecture Française du XIe au XVIe Siècle,* 10 vols. Paris, 1867-1873.

Indispensable to an understanding of the iconography of the Cathedral are the following works by Emile Mâle:

L'Art Religieux du XIIe Siècle en France. Fifth edition, revised and corrected, Paris, 1947.

L'Art Religieux du XIIIe Siècle en France. Eighth edition, revised and corrected, Paris, 1947. An English translation of the first edition was made by Dora Nussey, London and New York, 1913.

L'Art Religieux de la Fin du Moyen Age en France. Fourth edition, revised and augmented, Paris, 1931.

Art et Artistes du Moyen Age. Fifth edition, Paris, 1947.

The best general introduction to medieval architecture is Henri Focillon's sensitive and erudite *Art d'Occident. Le Moyen Age Roman et Gothique.* Second edition, Paris, 1947.

Excellent guides to virtually all the French monuments discussed in this book will be found in the collection of the *Petites Monographies des Grands Edifices de France* published under the direction of Marcel Aubert (Paris, Laurens). All contain bibliographies and architectural plans.

Those who do not read French will wish to consult Arthur Kingsley Porter's *Medieval Architecture, Its Origin and Development,* 2 vols., New Haven, 1912. Henry Adams' *Mont-Saint-Michel and Chartres,* Boston and New York, 1933, is also valuable.

Congrès Archéologique de France, Paris, 1919 (published 1920). Contains articles on all the leading churches of Paris, as well as Mantes and Etampes.

Crosby, Sumner McK. *The Abbey of St.-Denis, I.* New Haven, 1942. Only the first volume of this impressive monograph has yet appeared.

Czarnowski, Stéphane. "Les Autels des Nautes," in the *Revue Celtique,* XLII, 1925, pp. 1-57. On the Gallo-Roman altars.

Hubert, Jean. *L'Art Pré-Roman.* Paris, 1939. Excellent on the Merovingian and Carolingian periods.

Launay, l'Abbé de. *Bourgeois de Paris, Maçons au Moyen Age.* Paris, 1908. See also his article on Pierre de Montreuil in the *Nouvelle Revue,* May, 1920.

Lefrançois-Pillion, Louise. *Maîtres d'Oeuvre et Tailleurs de Pierre des Cathédrales,* Paris, 1949; and *Les Sculpteurs Français du XIIIe Siècle,* second edition, Paris, 1931. Both these books are good on the conditions and techniques of medieval workmanship.

Le Vieil, Pierre. *L'Art de la Peinture sur Verre et de la Vitrerie.* Paris, 1774. The only detailed description of the medieval glass of Notre-Dame, by the man who destroyed most of it.

Lenoir, A. *Statistique Monumentale de Paris,* 2 vols. of plates and 1 volume of commentary. Excellent on excavations of the Cité.

Mortet, Victor. *Etude Historique et Archéologique sur la Cathédrale et le Palais Episcopale de Paris du VIe au XIIe Siècle.* Paris, 1888. But see also Marcel Aubert, "Les Anciennes Églises Épiscopales de Paris, Saint-Etienne et Notre-Dame," in *Comptes-Rendus des Séances de l'Académie des Inscriptions et Belles-Lettres,* 1939, pp. 319-27.

Stein, Henri. *Les Architectes des Cathédrales Gothiques.* Paris, 1929.

Vloberg, M. *Notre-Dame de Paris et le Vœu de Louis XIII.* Paris, 1926. On the transformation of the medieval choir at the end of the seventeenth century.

Index

A NOTE ABOUT THIS BOOK

This book is set in Times Roman, a typeface designed by
Stanley Morison in 1931 for the London *Times*.
The cover was printed by Livermore and Knight Co.,
Providence, Rhode Island.
The binding is by J. W. Clement Co., Buffalo, New York.
The paper, TIME Reading Text, was supplied by
the Mead Corporation, Dayton, Ohio,
and the cover stock by
the Plastic Coating Corp., Holyoke, Massachusetts.

I